Educat... 21st Century

# Educating Disabled People for the 21st Century

By
## Edward J. Cain, Jr.
Private Special Education Technology Consultant
Lakehurst, New Jersey

and

## Florence M. Taber, Ed.D.
Director, Northern Indiana Computer Education Lab
Indiana University at South Bend

**A College Hill Publication**
*Little, Brown and Company*
Boston/Toronto/San Diego

College-Hill Press
A Division of Little, Brown and Company (Inc.)
34 Beacon Street
Boston, Massachusetts 02108

**Library of Congress Cataloging-in-Publication Data**
Main entry under title:

Cain, Edward J., 1944–
    Educating disabled people for the 21st century.

    Bibliography: p. 222.
    Includes index.
    1. Handicapped children — Education — United States.
2. Educational technology — United States.    3. Twenty-first century — Forecasts.    I. Taber, Florence M.    II. Title.
LC4031.C18    1987        371.9′0973        87-13776

**ISBN 0-316-12381-1**

Printed in the United States of America

We would like to dedicate this book to all of our children, who have given us so much joy and happiness. Therefore, we make this dedication with all of our love to:

Charlie
Katie
Kristen
Kym
Terri
Tricia

# Contents

# Preface

*Educating Disabled People for the 21st Century* provides a comprehensive analysis of the impact of current and future electronic technologies upon special education programs, and thus on students who have handicaps.

The primary emphasis of the book is based upon the reality that handicapped students currently enrolled in special education programs will live, work, and enjoy leisure activities for most of their lives in the 21st century. In order for them to maximize their potentials, they must be prepared to live in a new kind of world, one that involves access, manipulation, and control of information, not industrial-age assembly-line thought and products. The book considers projections about life in this new "Information Age" and the potential impact of advanced technologies upon populations with handicaps in that ever-changing society. Curriculum suggestions are offered which will assist in preparing these various populations to live in this new age; and each chapter contains a brief summary, which succinctly covers the most important concepts discussed in that chapter. Students will find this information especially helpful. The book is a useful tool for special education teachers; special education administrators; support service personnel such as speech, physical, and occupational therapists; and parents.

*Educating Disabled People for the 21st Century* can be used as a college and/or "in-service" textbook and as a resource guide. The book is divided into three major sections. The first part presents an overview of futurist projections about life in the 21st century, the Information Age. It begins with a summary of the current uses of technology with handicapped persons today. It then looks at projections about life in the 21st century and analyzes the potential impact of four advanced technologies upon individuals with handicaps. The second part of the book concentrates upon the curricular implications of the futurist projections and upon advanced technologies and their relationship to special education programs of today. The areas of communication, electronic problem solving, compensation, vocational preparation, and electronic recreation are discussed. Specific curricular suggestions are provided in each area. The book's conclusion considers some perspectives about the future, so that the concepts and curriculum suggestions that have been presented can be assimmilated by the reader so as to remain current in a rapidly changing world.

This book takes the reader through three stages: (1) an understanding of the possible technologies and life in the 21st century and their implications for use with handicapped people; (2) a discussion of various types of programs and curricula that should be integrated into today's special education programs in order to prepare the handicapped to live in the Information Age; and (3) insight about integrating electronic technologies into curricula in a constantly changing world.

# PART I

# Educational Technology Today and Tomorrow

**W**e live in a rapidly changing society, one that is experiencing the transition from an industrial world to a new world that has been termed the "Information Age." The major factor spurring this passage has been the rapid development of electronic technologies. As one looks back over the past decade and views all of the developments we now take for granted — microcomputers, videodisc players, computerized games, electronic mail, and so forth — one must ask, What will the world of the 21st century be like? The 21st century: It sounds far away, but it is only around the corner.

The importance of considering what the society of the 21st century will be like lies in the fact that the handicapped students currently enrolled in our special education programs will live most of their lives in this new era. Students who entered special education programs in 1984 at age five and who remain in these programs through their twenty-first year (their full entitlement under federal law) will exit these programs in the year 2001. If the true purpose of special education is to help students realize their maximum potential and prepare them to enter society, then all individuals concerned with the education of handicapped people must begin to consider the world in which these students will live, the Information Age.

Chapter 1 presents an overview of the ways in which the computer and other electronic technologies are being used today with handicapped people. Primary emphasis is placed on applications in special education; however, the areas of rehabilitation and rehabilitation medicine are also presented since they are closely related fields. This chapter is the touchstone against which all future applications will be measured.

Chapter 2 focuses on the projections of futurists about life and learning in the 21st century. Although futurists maintain many divergent views, this chapter will provide a summary of those ideas on which they do agree. The purpose of Chapter 2 is not to provide an extensive analysis of these predictions, but rather to summarize them and to indicate briefly their potential impact on the handicapped.

Chapter 3 looks at the possible effects on the handicapped of four technologies — artificial intelligence, robotics, interactive simulation, and interactive multisensory communication systems — that we believe will be basic daily living tools in the near future. Their significance to the instruction of the handicapped will also be discussed.

CHAPTER 1

# How Technology is Used with Handicapped Students Today

The impact of electronic technologies upon the education of students of all exceptionalities, including the gifted, is not going to *become* dramatic — it already is. Electronic technologies are not only tools of the future but have become important instructional and compensatory implements of today. Increasing numbers of special educators are turning to these technologies and integrating them into their students' daily programs. Two of the most common technologies currently being used in special education are the computer, in particular the microcomputer, and electronic assistive communication devices (Reinhold, 1986; Taber, 1982).

The dynamic characteristics of the computer make it a natural extension of the more traditional instructional methods employed in the field of special education. This technology permits the individualization of instruction, allowing the user to proceed at his or her natural learning pace and style. It should be noted that individualization of instruction does not necessarily mean that the student to computer ratio is one-to-one. Two or three students at a time can interact cooperatively with the computer, provided that those students' Individualized Educational Plans (IEPs) indicate the need for that particular program or exercise. The computer is an infinitely patient machine, permitting needed repetition in drill and practice. It never passes judgment on the skills of the user; it is a neutral tutor, one that provides consistent feedback to the user. It can, through its software, present the content in a logical sequence of developmental skills. The computer's ability to retain information makes it an ideal medium to record and maintain student information and assist teachers in analyzing student performance. Thus, it can form the basis of a diagnostic and prescriptive learning system. It can also present an environment of electronic exploration through the use of special languages such as LOGO (Judd, 1983).

The computer's most important distinction for handicapped children in all categories is as an electronic instrument that can enhance abilities and compensate for deficits, both in the classroom and beyond; particularly when the child has intellectual or neurological problems. This quality permits both the student and the teacher to focus attention on what a student can do, rather than on what cannot be accomplished due to physical, mental, or emotional reasons. For example, the computer can communicate for the linguistically impaired and the nonverbal, it can write for the sensory impaired, and it can translate from braille into the written word or vice versa. Also, the memory and sequencing capabilities of this technology permit the handicapped user to enhance skills in various areas where there is a functional deficit. In other cases, the technology is applied as a prosthetic device, one which will be used to replace a physical dysfunction such as speech or physical movement. Regardless of how the computer and related technologies are applied, they represent important instructional and functional applications for all disabled people.

One of the more important dynamic characteristics of the computer is its role as an interactive medium. It is the only truly interactive instructional machine available to special education today. A computer will do nothing unless the student initiates the action. Other media, such as television, film, filmstrip, and radio, are passive in their nature and mode of presentation. It is only the computer that permits the personal involvement of the user during the instructional process. Further, the computer allows the matching of the student's preferential learning modality with the method of receiving and expressing information. A handicapped student can receive information visually, aurally, in a multisensory or multisequential method, or through the use of an output device such as a braille printer. In a similar manner, the method for inputting information can be matched to the student's sensory learning modality preference: touch typing, voice, visual focusing, picture selection, joystick, and so forth. The computer is therefore a communication device, one which can leave the user in complete control of a number of processes: communication, environmental control, and mobility.

Electronic assistive communication devices have been increasingly used with handicapped children. The devices are often connected to microcomputers so that the dynamic capabilities of the computer can be used most effectively. In other instances, microchip-based electronic communication designs can function independently of the microcomputer; for example, the electronic communication board.

In special education today, there are three primary ways in which computers are used: Computer Assisted Instruction (CAI), Computer Managed Instruction (CMI), and Computer Assisted Management (CAM). CAI utilizes the computer as an instructional tool, one which can enhance the learning process. CMI utilizes the computer to control and monitor the student learning process. Finally, CAM utilizes the computer as an information manager.

People in the fields of rehabilitation and rehabilitation medicine are also using electronic technologies extensively in a manner similar to that found in special education. Electronic devices in these fields are used for both education and reeducation, for communication, and to assist with client functioning in areas such as mobility, self care, working, environmental control, and leisure activities. The people served by these fields include not only the handicapped but also the disabled, or those who have become disabled due to accident, disease, or age.

## COMPUTER ASSISTED INSTRUCTION

The most common classroom use of computers with handicapped students (and that with which the majority of teachers and support service personnel are most familiar) is Computer Assisted Instruction (CAI). The computer is used to assist in teaching the students; it helps develop and reinforce knowledge, concepts, and skills. The instruction generally involves a varying degree of dialogue between the student and the computer.

A second aspect of CAI is the use of computer technology as a compensatory or prosthetic tool. The computer enhances the mastery of knowledge or the performance of a task by modifying the input process or the output of information according to the needs of the individual. The technology is used to adjust instruction rather than to direct instruction. The computer, therefore, can enhance student abilities and compensate for deficits. One of the more common instructional uses of CAI in this application is word processing; a computer procedure that includes information management, interactive information recall, text editing, translation, and text formating. This software allows and encourages students to develop print materials. Word processing, therefore, permits handicapped students to focus attention on the content of what they wish to communicate while letting the computer perform the physical process of writing. The word processing system enhances their conceptual and expressive linguistic skills while compensating for their

their sensory or motor deficits. It can overcome the paper and pencil blockade that inhibits the performance of many handicapped students. (Madin, 1986).

## Types of Computer Assisted Instruction Applications

There are five basic types of CAI software currently in use in special education programs: tutorial, drill and practice, educational games, discovery learning, and simulation. Each of these applications has a different general instructional objective. The special educator chooses software in the same manner that other instructional materials are selected, by assessing the needs of the student and then evaluating the instructional material to determine if it will effectively meet those needs.

Tutorial software is designed to assist a student in acquiring new knowledge and skills through the direct presentation of information. Once new information and concepts are introduced, the student is provided an opportunity to recall and integrate the newly learned material by means of the computer program. The new skill is usually related to prior learning so that it can be further developed, refined, or transferred to new situations. Tutorial systems provide feedback to the user concerning whether the response is correct or incorrect. Cues are often furnished in order to help the user find the right answer, and when incorrect responses are given, remedial material is presented, which allows the student to better understand the new information. Many tutorial programs contain a pretest component. This is designed to provide information about whether the student has mastered the prerequisite skills to begin a new area of study, and it may determine where in the teaching sequence the user should enter the program. Finally, tutorial systems often include a record keeping element, that provides information about the student's progress in the program, including the number and types of errors that were made by the user, which instructional objectives have been met, and where more instruction is needed.

Drill and practice software tends to be the most common form of instructional computer software used in special education programs and, indeed, in all education. These systems are designed to transmit and retain information. Their primary purpose is to assist a student in mastering newly presented concepts and in internalizing this knowledge so that it can be used in daily performance. The software generally presents a question or some stimulus to which the user responds. Immediate feedback is provided as to whether the answer was correct or incorrect. The feedback to incorrect responses is not judgmental and usually directs the student to try the problem again. The immediate feedback encourages repetition so that overlearning is achieved in a nonthreatening electronic environment. In some drill and practice programs, a tutorial is provided after a problem has been tried two or three times. The combination of tutorial assistance with drill and practice is seen in more and more programs and is more effective than either type in isolation. In addition, some drill and practice software furnish a management component that provides error tracking and error analysis data to the instructor. This component is an important instructional element and should be a major consideration in selecting drill and practice software.

Educational games provide the student with entertaining and motivating activities that help the user practice a newly introduced skill or reinforce newly acquired knowledge. These electronic games provide excellent motivation and often make the tedium of repetition and overlearning both enjoyable and challenging. Most game software is designed to be used by one student, so the user is competing against the machine. Motivation is enhanced because, other than the user, only the nonthreatening machine is aware of errors. Other systems allow two or more students to compete against each other on the computer. Many electronic educational games contain variable levels of difficulty so that students with different skill levels can use the same software. Also, this component permits a student to concretely experience growth and progress, further enhancing motivation and a positive self-concept. The computer stimuli and responses are frequently random. This element of the game format contributes to student willingness to practice a new skill multiple times. On the other hand, some programs can use a nonrandom presentation of stimuli, a presentation in which a new stimulus is added only after the student has learned a particular fact. This nonrandom approach can be changed to a random presentation after a number of facts have been mastered. Many educational computer games are shell programs, or are designed to provide only the game structure. The teacher then enters the specific material to be presented to the student. Such software permits great flexibility and multiple applications, and it enhances the individualization. Examples of this type of open-ended game software are hangman, tic-tac-toe, and baseball math.

Discovery learning allows the computer to be used as a problem-solving tool. The most common form of this type of software provides the user with structural rules that apply to the solution of a specific type of problem. The student enters the information that applies to the presented problem, and the software uses the embedded structural rules to assist in the solution. This type of problem-solving software not only provides assistance in finding a solution to a specific dilemma but also teaches the user proven problem-solving techniques. Another aspect of discovery learning is the concept of learning by doing. The student uses the computer to explore and manipulate an electronic environment in order to investigate and express ideas. LOGO, a computer language developed to assist children in discovery learning, is the software most commonly used to achieve this type of self-expression. There is no right or wrong in LOGO. It is a system, or philosophy, that allows children to interact with a computer as a learning tool. There are no constraints upon the creativity of the user. The student is in complete control of the computer and uses it to solve problems in a self-directed manner rather than reacting to preprogrammed tasks (the case with much of today's commerical software). Students use their personal method of reasoning to reach a solution to a problem. There is no right or wrong answer; there is only the student's personal solution. Another type of discovery learning involves a problem-solving process whereby principles or concepts are uncovered as a result of analysis or synthesis of facts. Software that has the user solve mysteries is an example of this kind of program.

A related type of software, which may or may not involve discovery learning, is simulation software, that is, learning by doing or through decision making. Situations are similar to real life circumstances and present general guidelines to the solution of the problem. These systems permit students to apply previously mastered knowledge or values to new situations, ones that simulate real life predicaments or environments. In simulation software, the users suffer the consequences of their decisions. However, there is no personal risk involved in simulation as there is in the real world. The user can change responses to the situation in order to achieve a desired result. Simulation software bridges the gap between the real world and the world of the classroom. It allows students to gain experience in applying knowledge and skills to real life situations so that they will be able to use these skills in actual daily experiences. For example, this type of software could place a student in an on-the-job situation involving a problem with a fellow employee. Based on probable consequences, alternative solutions can be tried, explored, and analyzed, thus providing instruction in the affective domain.

## Authoring Language Systems

Authoring language systems are software tools that permit instructors to design individual computer learning experiences for students without having to learn a programming language. These systems provide a skeleton, or shell, to which the teacher adds specific instructional sequences or stimuli. These skeleton programs, usually presented in a menu format, simply require the addition of the tutorial sequence to turn it into an individualized electronic lesson. For the teacher, the greatest advantage of authoring systems is that the individual creating a personalized lesson for a student does not have to know a programming language; the instructor writes the electronic lesson using the English language, often working from a menu that specifies the alternatives and specific directions. For the student, the greatest advantage is being able to interact with programs specifically designed to meet individual learning needs. The major disadvantage of authoring systems is that the design of the program constrains the space that can be used for actual instruction and responses. In the future, however, authoring systems will permit more flexibility in design, instructional modes, and program length (Taber, 1982).

The simplest form of authoring system software permits the instructor to create drill and practice lessons. Such software is usually in the format of question and answer, true or false, multiple choice, or games. The structure is provided, and the teacher simply adds specific and very limited instructional content. This type of program is basically a mini-authoring application. Examples of this type of software are word finds and hangman.

Major authoring systems allow the instructor to create considerably more interaction in the educational software. They permit the teacher to create individualized electronic lessons that include graphic, sound, and print stimuli. Reinforcements for correct responses can also be personalized by using the modalities of sound, graphics, or print. Further, it is possible to personalize the statements which tell the student that he or she has given a correct or an incorrect response and why the response is right or wrong.

The Multisensory Authoring Language System (MACS), developed by The Johns Hopkins University, is an authoring system designed specifically for use by special educators (Schiffman & Tobin, 1987). It is a multisensory program that permits the use of sound, voice, graphics, and print. The program is menu driven so that the instructor simply makes choices as to the specific stimuli and reinforcements to be employed in the lesson. The teacher can also choose the frequency of the reinforcement, that is, after each response, after a specific number of responses, or at a specific time. Material can be designed to be presented in only one modality, in a multisequential manner, or in a multisensory format depending upon the individual needs of the handicapped student for whom the lesson was created.

Authoring systems can be important and powerful instructional tools for the special educator. They permit the instructor to create individualized electronic lessons rather than force students to adapt to a predetermined courseware (the case with most commerically produced

CAI). The modality of presentation and response can be matched to the preferred style of the pupil in order to maximize comprehension. Most important, authoring systems allow the instructor to create these lessons in "normal English" using a menu format; they do not require the teacher to know a programming language in order to design individualized electronic lessons for handicapped students. Further, there appears to be a direct negative correlation between the amount of software available and the severity of the handicap. Authoring systems, then, provide one answer to the special educator's need for appropriate software.

## COMPUTER MANAGED INSTRUCTION

Computer Managed Instruction (CMI) systematically controls instruction by developing and monitoring individualized education programs for handicapped students. CMI permits the special educator to keep records, score tests, monitor pupil progress, prescribe what each student should learn, and decide how to approach instruction. Computer managed instructional systems provide the educator with information that assists in the decision making process about the individual learning strengths and weaknesses of students. It is a computerized inventory that maintains records about instructional objectives, methods and materials employed, and pupil mastery. There are three basic types of computer managed instructional systems: cluster or mastery learning, computerized test scoring, and computerized IEPs.

Cluster or mastery learing CMI systems are criterion-referenced data bases composed of personalized goal statements and instructional objectives. The goal statements are often organized into clusters of skills that must be mastered in order to learn a concept. The clusters are arranged into strands that represent the major elements of the curriculum sequence. Finally, the strands are organized into major curricular domains. This use of CMI software permits the instructor to monitor individual students' mastery of the skills and objectives contained in the data base of behavioral goals. The system provides the teacher with a variety of student reports, which indicate the specific achievement of each pupil. Most CMI systems provide the following types of reports: student progress, enrollment or class lists, current assignment, correlation reports, and survey statistic reports. Often, charts and graphs are also provided.

Computerized test scoring is another aspect of CMI that is of particular help to the special education practitioner. Test scoring systems are designed to provide the educator with criterion-referenced test analysis of individual student performance. This information assists in the diagnosis, prescription, and placement recommendations for handicapped children. Computerized test scoring services come in two formats: test scoring computer programs and outside test scoring where test protocols are sent for analysis. All of the major publishers of achievement tests offer criterion-referenced analysis of student performance. The reports that these services generate identify the skill mastery levels of students in the subject areas that have been tested. The individual pupil profile also indicates the specific areas of academic strength and weaknesses. Most test publishers also provide composite reports for classes, grades, and individual schools.

In recent years, there has been an increase in the number of microcomputer test scoring programs available to special educators. These systems furnish diagnostic information for tests such as WISC-R, Woodcock-Johnson, and the Peabody Individual Achievement Test. Other systems permit the teacher to obtain criterion-referenced information regarding pupil performance on informal reading inventories (IRIs), instructor designed tests, or textbook chapter summary tests.

There has also been an increase in the number of available individual educational plan (IEP) programs available for use by special educators. Basically, these programs are available for one of two systems: micorcomputer programs designed for use by an individual teacher or an individual school, or large minicomputer systems designed for use by a school system. These computer programs are intended to comply with Public Law 94-142 regulations, as well as subsequent federal legislation, state requirements, and local criteria. Although they are all designed to create, monitor, and evaluate student progress in compliance with federal, state, and local regulations or objectives, all of these programs provide a variety of report formats. The goal of these programs is to decrease paper record keeping while using the diagnostic and prescriptive capabilities of the computer to more effectively monitor student progress.

## COMPUTER ASSISTED MANAGEMENT

Computer Assisted Management (CAM) software has been designed for administrative and management purposes. These systems provide the special education administrator with a variety of information including the appropriate combination of data and algorithmic solutions, which can then be analyzed and used to assist in the decision-making process. CAM software programs were originally developed for use in the private sector, business and industry, but are equally applicable for use in school systems because, in reality, schools are small to moderate sized commerces.

There are three types of CAM software of particular use to special educators: word processing, data base management systems, and electronic spreadsheets. Many of these programs can be used on a microcomputer with a printer either directly attached or attached through a network system. Other programs are designed for mini or mainframe computers used by school districts or entire states. State special education departments are now beginning to use systems that will electronically link data from the classroom to management systems for federal reporting requirements. Also, many of the systems that have been developed were created for the individual who has little or no computing experience, though training in the use of the specific program may be required.

Word processing via computer software permits the writing, editing, and formatting of letters and reports. These programs allow the user to type, edit, revise, and print documents with minimum effort. Letters, reports, and documents can be reused totally or in part without having to retype the entire manuscript. Formatting permits the user to change the appearance of the text by altering items such as line spacing, column width, and justification (the lining up of print on the left, the right, or both sides of the paper). Once the information has been retained, or saved on a disc, it can later be called back for revision or updating. Word processing is the most commonly used CAM system in special education, as it is in other areas of education and business. Some of the most common word processing systems used in education are: *The Bank Street Writer, Quick Brown Fox, Fred Writer* and *Easy Writer* in the classroom for instructional purposes, and *Word Star, Apple Works,* and *Lotus I, II, III* for management purposes.

Data based management systems permit the user to store, update, and retrieve information stored as data items. These items are generally stored in the form of records in a specific file. The files consist of a series of inscriptions that are made up of a number of fields. Each field consists of one type of recorded information. The information contained in the data based management files can be manipulated upon request in a variety of ways to provide the specific data required. The files can be quickly and easily updated by changing only those facts that require alteration. Some of the most popular data based management systems are *PFS* (Personal Filing System), *Db III, INFOPRO,* and *Quick File.*

Electronic spreadsheet software provide the user with the ability to explore "what if" alternatives. They can process hundreds of numbers at once, find patterns, explore alternatives, and draw conclusions. Electronic spreadsheets replace manipulating and calculating numbers with paper, pencils, and calculators. They permit the user to organize numerical information into categories and define how they are to interrelate. Budget projections, service fee analysis, and inventory control are just some of the tasks that can be performed on these systems. These programs, therefore, allow the user to solve problems for any set of unknowns. Some of the most popular versions of the electronic spreadsheets are *VisiCalc, Multiplan, SuperCalc, TK!Solver,k* and *Lotus I, II, III.*

## THE PHYSICALLY CHALLENGED

There are two primary applications of the computer to the needs of the physically handicapped: as a prosthetic device, a tool that performs tasks which the body cannot otherwise accomplish, and as a compensatory device, especially for specific learning problems and communication deficits.

One of the most dramatic uses of the computer with these people is as an environmental control and leisure activities artifice. The principle concern in the use of technology by these people is access to the computer, which requires modification in order to permit the physically challenged to control the system. In most instances, management of the electronic mechanism is achieved through the application of a single or multiple switch or of a voice activated routine, though any movement under relative control of the individual can be used. These applications provide the physically handicapped access to the computer for activities such as basic communication, mobility, education, and environmental control.

The most common modifications made to the computer for the physically handicapped are the one switch or multiple switch scanning devices. These systems allow the handicapped to pick from a menu by means of utilizing a switch. Many educational and recreational software programs have been adapted for use with these single or multiple switch interactions. Most of these systems also permit the user to modify the speed with which the menus are presented. Some communication devices have been developed that utilize Blissymbols or pictorial programs instead of the more typical word menus. These systems allow the handicapped individual to control the program and access the microcomputer software.

When using the simple switch for input, the program is surveyed or scanned by means of the cursor. Almost any small muscle, even an eye blink, can then be utilized to control the switch either to enter data or to retrieve information from the program. Switches should be reliable and maintain a maximum of comfort; they should be simple, sturdy, and easy to maintain and clean.

Another type of adaptive system for the physically challenged includes pointing devices. These include joysticks, light pens, mice, digitized tablets, touch pads, and touch screens, which permit the user to move the cursor around the screen and select the desired information from the computer.

Many physically challenged students encounter, to varying degrees, difficulties with expressive language and most often with speech. Electronic language boards provide one compensatory alternative for many individuals with these disabilities. These systems, which can be personally adapted, allow the disabled user to "speak" with others. Most of these units are portable and can be attached to wheelchairs. Their use in the classroom allows the physically disabled to communicate orally with the other students and with the instructor. Further, these systems have proven to be effective communication tools for physically challenged students in a regular classroom setting. They permit the student to express questions, thoughts, ideas, and emotions to others in a discernable manner. The only major limitation of these elecronic tools at the present time is their rather limited word and phrase capacity, however, there are systems that allow the user to spell out their communication using the language board. Once the communication is completed, the board will "speak" what the user denoted. Further, they are as effective in the home and the general community as they are in the school setting. These systems are particularly useful in helping the physically challenged student to express statements of personal needs and desires. Although the electronic communication boards of today have rather limited memories, which makes spontaneous communications rather difficult and laborious, the boards of tomorrow will have the capability of virtually unlimited vocabularies through touch speech technology and "limitless" menu capabilities. Even today they are important compensatory electronic communication tools for these people, and in the future, they will be even more portable, making them extremely versatile instruments.

### Voice

Another input and output alternative for the physically handicapped is voice. Although voice input or recognition is in its primitive stages, voice output is relatively more advanced. Except on expensive systems, voice input usually requires the user to train the computer to understand each word individually. Then, in order to operate the computer, only one word commands can be said at a time, thus making input slow and unnatural with hesitations between each word. For example, if the program read, "on: turn the television on; [z]," when the user gave the one word command of "on," the words "turn the television on" would appear on the screen and the control key would actually turn on the television. With very expensive systems, no training of the computer to recognize the voice is necessary and there need be no hesitation between word commands. One advantage of a voice recognition system that requires training, however, is that the user is not required to have intelligible speech since a consistent sound can be designated as the word command.

The computer, therefore, can be equipped with adaptive devices for voice output. The computer's memory capability is vastly larger than that of the electronic language or communication board thereby expanding its capability to be used as a compensatory oral language tool for the physically challenged student. However, it should be remembered that many computers are not yet truly portable, as are electronic language boards. Therefore, the use of the computer as a compensatory oral language tool is primarily limited to a single location, such as the classroom. In certain instances, the computer that is connected by means of a telecommunication system can in fact transcend great distances. This is particularly the situation with homebound and hospitalized people because an interactive computer system enables them to participate in classroom instruction from their homes or hospitals.

The computer as a stand-alone interactive electronic medium allows the physically challenged student to communicate via a voice output system with others in the immediate vicinity in an oral language format. Large vocabularies of both words and phrases can be stored in the computer's memory, which these students can access in order to compose communications to other individuals. Adaptive hardware and software devices provide students of almost any physical disability with access to these communication alternatives. The addition of interactive telecommunication capabilities to such systems enables these people to communicate with other individuals over great distances in print or in voice, although the print medium is the most expedient.

The memory capabilities of the computer allow the physically challenged individual to compose entire original statements for communication. The computer will store the message until the user gives the command to communicate. The machine will then "say" the complete thought or statement that has been composed. This ability of the computer makes this compensatory electronic tool far more lifelike than the electronic communication board, which is now primarily limited to predetermined single words or phrases. As computers become smaller, the microcomputer as we know it today can be combined with the electronic communication board, thus eliminating the limitations of the communication board. Even today, a recently released computer has the entire capability of its predecessor on one small chip.

Speech output is available in two formats: analog or digital speech. Analog speech uses voice chips that store phonemic rules. The nature of the speech is a major disadvantage, since the quality of expression tends to sound as if it were produced by a robot. Digital speech, on the other hand, is human sounding. The difficulty with this method is in storage, since each word must be retained. It is, of course, possible to combine voice recognition with voice output so that, as in the earlier example, if "ugh" was said consistantly for "on," the voice output would say, "Turn the television on." The use of the video disc, however, with its extensive memory capacity, offers the potential for using digital speech for both educational and daily living applications.

Word processing is an important compensatory application of computer technology for the physically challenged student. The addition of this capability to a voice output system permits these students to compose more complex statements and to edit them before the machine "says" the idea that has been composed. Students using these systems will no longer have to devote a great deal of attention to the actual process of speech and to the formation of sounds, a process which often distracts their attention from the content of the message. The use of a word-processing voice output computer system allows them to devote most of their attention to the content of the message they are composing while leaving the actual process of oral communication to the computer.

Word processing, then, when used for written expression, is an essential compensatory tool for physically challenged students, particularly in the classroom setting. Written expression has traditionally been an area of difficulty for most if not all pupils with these disabilities. Many of these students, in fact, are not able to master this skill at all. Prior to the introduction of the computer and word processing, the severely physically disabled students were limited to using some form of communication board. Given the variety and types of both hardware and software adaptive devices that exist today, almost all memebers of this group can use some form of word processing.

Word processing is also an important instructional compensatory alternative for all physically challenged students, even those with some ability to express themselves in written form. These systems allow students to compose and to "write" their classroom assignments. Since the computer performs the actual process of writing, they only have to be concerned with the content of their composition. Adaptive input devices modify the computer and the software to the individual's functioning needs so that all segments of this population can compose written messages. Word processing has not only been an effective method of written communication in the special education classroom but has also proven to be an important element for physically limited students who attend regular classes, since this ability allows them to compete better with other students in the class. If the school classroom has some form of networking system or an electronic bulletin board, the physically challenged student can use word processing to complete regular classroom assignments from anywhere — home, hospital, self-contained classroom, or resource room. Finally, these interactive systems also permit the physically challenged student to communicate with other students at some remote site through the use of the computer and word processing, thus transcending the walls of their confinement.

The education of physically or other health handicapped pupils who are homebound has likewise been positively affected by the application of electronic technologies. Interactive communication for the purpose of instruction can be accomplished through the use of a microcomputer in the student's home. The computer is connected to the child's classroom or to the teacher's office by a modem and a telephone in order to permit interactive instruction. A modem is an electronic device that converts data from a form compatible with a computer to a form compatible with telephone transmission and then converts it back to a form compatible with the computer. In order for this system to operate, the special education classroom with which the home bound pupil is communicating must also contain a microcomputer, a modem, and a telephone. This electronic system of home instruction can also be used in a hospital setting or in any other kind of remote location. All of the previously mentioned adaptive devices for both input and output can also be used by the handicapped student at home or in the hospital, depending on the specific needs of the individual.

Electronic technologies have also been applied to instruction in environmental control, preparation for the world of work, and general communication. Software programs have been developed for microcomputers that allow these individuals to control most appliances, including lights. They can be voice activated or controlled by screen or keyboard. Other software programs will answer the telephone and permit the handicapped user to communicate through the appropriate adaptive device.

Mircocomputer technology also allows individuals with physical disabilities to work from their homes. In a manner similar to that employed with the homebound, direct communication with the office can be achieved with the user of a microcomputer, modem, and a telephone. Software such as word processing, data base management systems, and electronic spreadsheets can, therefore, be used for work at home in the same manner as they would in the office. Interactive communication between the office and the physically handicapped person at home can thus be accomplished. Finally, the physically handicapped can use these same systems and software to communicate with other members of the household or with friends via a telephone connection.

More and more special education programs for the physically handicapped are including instruction in these applications of electronic technologies both as supportive systems and as a part of the core curriculum (Lindsey, 1987; Taber, 1982).

## BLIND AND VISUALLY IMPAIRED

The blind and visually impaired were among the first handicapped people for whom electronic technologies were adapted. As is so often the case, these developments were initially designed for adults with disabilities. However, special educators soon recognized the importance of these technologies and began to employ them in the instruction of visually handicapped children. In most instances these students do not manifest significant intellectual or neurological difficulties. Their primary problems are physical, and therefore they require prosthetic technology interventions, rather than compensatory ones. As a result, a greater number of specialized adaptive devices have been developed for these people, and there tends to be a growing use in special education programs. Further, special software has been designed for use by these people. The microcomputer and other electronic technologies are, therefore, important instructional and daily living tools for the blind and visually impaired with either primary or secondary handicaps.

Some of the most significant developments in adaptations of electronic technologies for these people have been in the area of hardware or machine modifications. Perhaps the best known development in this field employs the concept of print to voice, a device termed the Kurzweil Reading Machine. This machine can read printed text and translate the information into voice by utilizing a speech synthesizer. Although the quality of the voice is rather robotic in tone, it does permit the blind and visually handicapped to access books, magazines, and journals that previously would have had to be converted into braille. The Kurzweil Reader allows these people to receive information that had formerly been denied to them. Thus, they have the freedom to select their reading materials without being dependent upon another sighted individual to establish what they should read. An increasing number of public libraries have acquired the Kurzweil Reader and some have even connected these machines to telecommunication devices so that the blind and visually impaired can access library materials from home.

The primary adaptations that have been made to electronic technologies for the blind and visually impaired have dealt with modifications to both input and output devices. The most common forms of adaptive input and output modifications made for these special populations are in the form of braille keyboards and braille printers. These hardware and software systems allow them to enter or receive information in their own language system, braille. Students can take notes in class using a computer with either a braille keyboard or voice input capabilities. These notes can be reviewed later using the voice output braille printer capabilities of the computer. The braille output, incidently, can be either a hard copy or a temporary form, a system which allows the braille print to be erased once the material has been reviewed. Using any appropriate input capabilities, a teacher can create a lesson, give a classroom assignment, or assign homework to a blind or visually impaired student on the computer. The student can prepare lessons in braille or voice input and can obtain the output in more than one way, one for the student in a braille output form and another in printed form for the teacher. Thus, the teacher will not have to be familiar with braille, an important factor for regular classroom teachers responsible for providing instruction to students with these disabilities.

A far more applicable input device for the blind and visually impaired is voice recognition. Although still in the developmental stages, these systems allow the computer to recognize and interpret human voice and sound. Current applications of this approach require that the computer be trained to recognize the user's voice or sound commands. Each word or phrase to be used in the voice recognition system must be individually entered into the computer's memory, a process that amounts to developing a dictionary of words and phrases for each user. Therefore, it requires an extensive amount of time to create a practical vocabulary of reasonable size. Further, current forms of voice input systems require the user to be consistant in producing a word or sound in order for the computer to recognize the input.

The first modifications made to computer output for the blind and visually impaired were in the form of braille print. Although this approach provided these populations with computer data in a format they could interpret, it also required that the user be fluent in braille. Recent developments in voice output have negated this requirement and permit the handicapped user to hear what is written on the screen. There are two basic types of voice output systems: analog and digital speech. As was mentioned earlier, analog speech is the most common form of voice output. However, it produces a robotic sound, using phonemes to create words. Digital speech, on the other hand, stores human speech word for word and, as a result, yields a highly intelligible communication. The greatest disadvantage of digital speech output is the large memory required to store an entire dictionary of words and phrases as well as the time required to search this depository in order for the user to create sentences and paragraphs. The interactive video disc appears to offer a solution to the current limitations to digital speech by permitting the storage of large amounts of data. Further, the speed with which the data files can be accessed allow the production of human-sounding speech at normal conversational speeds.

## DEAF AND HEARING IMPAIRED INDIVIDUALS

Deaf and hearing impaired individuals have trouble translating oral communication into their inner language systems. As a result, a great deal of information conveyed to them by the hearing world, either in the form of print or oral communication, is often lost or misinterpreted by them. They have not had the variety of auditory stimulants to which the hearing person is exposed (Hagen, 1984).

Sign language is the communication system of most deaf and significantly hearing impaired people, even though many develop speech reading skills. As a matter of fact, sign is the fourth most common language used in advanced societies (Gannon, 1981). Despite this fact, most hearing individuals cannot communicate in this language system. Electronic technologies have provided a vehicle that permits hearing-impaired people to communicate with hearing people in a conversational manner and to gain access to a variety of informational sources previously denied to them. These machines and word processing software are the translation tools that allow this handicapped population to learn to "speak" with the rest of the world either in a print or a speech format or via telecommunications. Word processing assists the deaf and hard of hearing by empowering them to manipulate and practice the rules of written English. The message to be communicated is not transmitted until the handicapped user is satisfied with the content. Interactive communication via a microcomputer connected to a telephone and modem provides immediate feedback and, therefore, helps the disabled child to modify the quality of written communication through personal experience with a nonhandicapped individual. The hearing person actually serves as a role model and, through the communication process, provides the hearing impaired user with instruction in the process of written English.

The deaf and hard of hearing do not generally require special hardware modifications to the microcomputer in order to use this technology as a daily communication and learning tool. The primary modality for receiving information from the computer is visual, either in the form of screen graphics or print or in the form of visual information created on an attached printer. The principal method of entering data into a computer is motoric, via a keyboard. The visual and motor systems are generally areas of strength for the deaf and hearing impaired, the primary reason they do not require hardware modifications to use the microcomputer.

A number of specialized software programs have been developed for these people. These include programs that provide training and retraining in speech reading, sign language, and finger spelling. Most are in the format of drill and practice instructional programs. Since these programs use a visual presentation, they can be employed effectively by hearing individuals who desire to learn how to communicate with hearing impaired people though sign communication systems.

A number of unique software programs using biofeedback techniques have been developed to assist the deaf and impaired hearing in improving their oral language skills. These systems allow handicapped users to compare their voice patterns with a visual model represented on the screen. The objective is for the users to match the sounds they create while speaking into an attached microphone with the displayed model. International Business Machines-France (IBM-France) has recently developed a series of games designed to assist the deaf and hearing impaired in producing and maintaining vocal pitch and tone. The objective of these games is to move a target through an obstacle course. The movement of the target is controlled by the sound produced by the user. A change in pitch controls the target in a vertical manner and the maintance of a tone moves it across the screen horizontally.

CAI software has proven to be a very effective educational tool for the deaf and hearing impaired. Since CAI software utilizes a visual presentation, these handicapped students can avail themselves of the variety of instructional materials designed for use by the general population. Other CAI programs have been designed to assist these special students in developing problem-solving and critical thinking skills.

Printed materials used in classroom instruction are based on oral language, not sign language. As a result, many deaf and hearing impaired students have great difficulty in obtaining the same meaning from oral and print communication as do their hearing classmates. The dynamic qualities of the computer can provide compensatory assistance to these students by interpreting the correct meaning from printed material. The graphic and video potentials controlled by the computer allow this medium to be used to support the printed word. Thus, the deaf or hearing impaired student can use pictorial material to assist them in gaining the correct meaning from the printed word. Further, syntax checkers can translate inappropriate expressive language into a more acceptable form.

One of the most important compensatory applications of the computer with deaf and hearing impaired students is word processing. Since these students often have inner language systems that are significantly different from those of their hearing peers, they must continually translate into their personal language system an oral and written language that is based on the language of the hearing world. This process often results in miscommunication. Further, the rules of grammar pose difficulties for these pupils since they too are based on the hearing world's language. Word processing provides the deaf and hearing impaired student with a translation tool that allows them to compensate for these difficulties. Word processing programs allow students to manipulate and to practice the rules of grammar and of written language. They can express their thoughts on the computer using their inner language systems of grammar and structure and then go back at a later date and reorder their message so that it is in proper written form. Therefore, they can concentrate on the content of the communication rather than on the grammar and style. Grammar and other "checker" types of software further this compensatory application of the computer. These programs will do the actual reordering of the student's original composition and will apply the appropriate grammar and syntax to the communication. In this instance, the area of student strength that the computer is supporting is the student's inner language system.

The interactive videodisc provides important compensatory learning tools for the deaf and hearing impaired student. Many of these students have difficulty in developing social relationships, in "reading" the implicit meaning in the behavior of hearing peers, and in interacting appropriately in group social settings with hearing peers. Again, this is primarily due to the fact that they do not always get the same meaning from oral speech as do their hearing peers. An extension of this difficulty is the fact that many individuals with these disabilities have difficulty in making appropriate decisions in the world of the hearing. The interactive videodisc provides an electronic medium that allows these students to practice both social and other daily living functional skills in simulation so that they can learn appropriate behaviors, thus compensating for possible inaccurate perceptions. Therefore, they can practice social skills and decision-making skills in the nonthreatening environment of the classroom. Since the interactive videodisc system provides cause-and-effect learning, they can gradually modify their responses until they are personally satisfied with the results. Although this may at first seem to be a learning experience for these people, it is in fact compensatory.

Computers and word processing can also serve as a compensatory tool for the deaf and hearing impaired student in communicating with other individuals. The communication process in this instance is through electronic communication systems such as electronic bulletin boards. The disabled user can "speak" with other individuals at his or her own pace, organizing their message on the computer using a word-processing program. Messages are transmitted to another individual over the electronic bulletin board only when the user is satisfied with both the content and structure of the message. The deaf and hearing impaired, therefore, can communicate with the hearing world at their own pace and not at the pace of the hearing world, as is the case with face-to-face interpersonal oral communication. Further, this type of communication process provides disabled users with valuable instruction and experience in the use of language and grammar. They can learn from the language system and grammatical patterns used by the hearing individuals with whom they are communicating. One other factor often important for some deaf and hearing impaired individuals who use such a system for communication is that no one on the bulletin board will know that they are disabled unless they choose to divulge that information. For those individuals who are self-conscious and uncomfortable in interpersonal social settings because of their disability and linguistic difficulties, the use of the computer and electronic communication systems removes these pressures. Such systems can be used withing the classroom for these students if there is a telecommunication capabilty or if there is an internal network system.

Other software programs have also proven to be effective instructional tools with the deaf and the hearing impaired in daily living skills and in prevocational and vocational preparation. Many of the daily living skills programs have focused on functional proficiencies, such as banking and shopping. These programs allow the handicapped student to develop and practice these activities in a visually simulated environment. The user can modify responses to the presentation until an acceptable solution is reached. The purpose of these programs is to assist the student in making the transition from the classroom into the world at large. Borrowing from the success business and industry have experienced in using electronic systems to train their workers, special educators have begun to use microcomputer and interactive video systems, either in isolation or in conjunction with simulators, to provide prevocational and vocational training for the deaf and hard of hearing. These approaches provide a structured, simulated work task and permit the handicapped student to develop proficiency in an individualized manner. For example, students who might drive a fork lift truck could learn how to do so in a simulator that moves on its axis while providing visual representations of what would be seen and what would happen in an actual situation. Thus the student learns in an environment that is safe from actual harmful consequences. Other programs stress the development of the interpersonal and work habit skills required to be an effective employee.

## THE MENTALLY CHALLENGED

Mentally challenged students are those with moderate severe developmental disabilities. They can and do benefit from interaction with electronic technologies in areas such as environmental control, communication, and instructional systems; however, the use of these technologies have tended to be employed with this handicapped group less frequently than with other special education populations. The types of electronic applications currently applied vary greatly. The primary factor determining this variation is the degree of developmental delay manifested. Most mentally challenged people need to use some form of adaptive or prosthetic device to use computer technology, because of their limited mental and physical abilities. This is particularly the case with young and very low functioning individuals since they usually do not have the cognitive nor the motor skills necessary to use these systems in the traditional manner. Other functioning within what is often termed the trainable range tend to require few hardware alterations, although they often need special software that is designed to meet their special linguistic and conceptual requirements.

Young and severely mentally challenged students require modifications to both input and output devices in order for them to successfully interact with electronic technologies and, in particular, with the microcomputer. The types of alterations are similar to those used with the physically challenged and are primarily compensations for motor and sensory deficiencies. Among the types of input modifications that are used with the young and low functioning developmentally disabled are single switches, video printing devices, joysticks, and touch tablets, such as the Koala Pad from Koala Technologies Corporation. In addition to these hardware modifications, special software programs are often employed in order to facilitate the use of the single switch or touch pad. These programs adapt the instructional or the simulation software to accept the modified input commands. Examples of these special software programs are the Adaptive Firmware Card produced by Adaptive Peripherals, Inc., and the Handi-Routine disc from ComputAbility Corporation. Output modifications for these people often include the use of voice, sound, or magnified graphic or print video displays.

The dynamic qualities of the microcomputer lend themselves to use with young and low functioning mentally challenged. Response to input commands is immediate and can be provided either in a single auditory or visual mode, in a multisequential manner, or in a multisensory fashion. This capability makes the microcomputer an ideal tool to provide sensory stimulation and perceptual motor development and to teach the concept of cause and effect. The latter is an important prerequisite to the use of this technology for environmental control and for communication. Further, developing the concept of cause and effect is an essential first step in the mastery of an electronic communication board. The graphic potential of this technology permits semi-abstract pictures to be employed in cognitive and language development, especially when the picture is accompanied by voice output. In combination with video disc technology, it provides even more realistic images and animation of these images. In teaching a skill or a concept, the task can be broken into a minutely controlled sequence in which success is constantly monitored. Finally, this technology is a patient tutor. The machine will wait for a response for an indefinite period of time unless commanded by the teacher to alter the stimulus presentation to a predetermined, timed sequence.

Communication is a basic need. Computers can serve as a compensatory tool for the mentally challenged. The microcomputer and electronic language board have proven to be effective language devices for the nonverbal and for individuals with limited verbal ability. Pictures and symbols with words and phrases attached to them can be shown on the computer screen. When the user selects the appropriate graphic representation, the microcomputer or the electronic language board, through the use of a voice synthesizer, communicates verbally what has been selected. After single word and concept communication has been developed, sentences and phrases can be constructed and communicated verbally through the use of software programs using scanning procedures. All of these communication alternatives can be controlled by means of the input modifications previously mentioned. Some of the recently developed multisensory authoring language systems permit the special education teacher to design individual language development programs for students, and they allow the total language approach to be incorporated into microcomputer instructional software. The computer is compensating for the disabled user's inability to use oral expressive language and is serving as a translation device. This approach has been very effective in total language programs used with many mentally challenged people.

Word processing can also be used with the more severely mentally challenged, but in such instances the use is more prosthetic than compensatory or remedial. For example, by using a single switch device and scanning icons, the individual could input his or her needs, which could then be turned into print or voice output using syntactically correct sentences. An alternative to single switch input, or any other movement-sensing adaptive device, could be voice input. Whatever the individual says is turned into appropriate speech output because the computer has worked with the individual enough to "know" what is meant by only a few words — whether comprehensible to other people or not. Eventually, the advanced computer systems and artificial intelligence of the future will indeed by able to read thoughts and respond appropriately.

Electronic technologies have proven to be effective devices in providing environmental control and self-help assistance to the mentally challenged. Many of these applications have been developed by people in the fields of bioengineering, rehabilitation, and rehabilitation medicine. Some of the applications currently being used with these people include: special software that permits the control of electric appliances such as lights, radio, and television by means of a microcomputer that can itself be controlled by an adaptive input device; automated electronic memory machines that will verbalize a sequence of instruction or cues for completing a specific task; and biomedical systems such as the Bladder/Bowel Sensation Exaggerator, which is employed during toilet training. It can be anticipated that the number and variety of electronic self-help and environmental control systems will significantly increase as more research and development is devoted to the rehabilitation of the permanently disabled and the aged. These devices will, of course, have applications to special education groups such as the developmentally disabled and the physically handicapped.

Although the total number of appropriate programs for the mentally challenged is severely limited, a number of special software programs have been developed that use the graphic potential of the computer coupled with speech synthesis to teach oral language concepts, as well as basic grammar and other specific skills. In addition, many of the developmental language and reading programs developed for younger nonhandicapped children and designed for use with the deaf and hearing impaired have been employed successfully with this group because they rely on graphic support.

Drill and practice software has been used successfully with these people to teach concepts in the basic preacademic and academic areas. Often the software employed was originally developed for younger nonhandicapped students or for other handicapped groups. It is the dynamic qualities of the computer that have made the microcomputer a viable academic teaching tool, one which is highly motivational for this audience of special students. Each student can progress at his or her own pace. The modalities of input and output can be selected so that they enhance the areas of learning strength for each pupil. Finally, these microcomputer systems are nonjudgmental and, therefore, the student's self-concept and feeling of self-worth are increased.

The development of self-help and environmental control are essential if the mentally challenged individual is to achieve semi-independent or independent functioning as an adult. Several special survival skills software have been developed for this group and provide microcomputer instruction in areas such as home safety, money management, banking, shopping, and interpersonal relations on the job. Recently, self-help and environmental control programs have been developed for this group using the interactive video disc. These systems allow the user to learn through cause and effect, and they assist in the translation of a learned concept from the classroom to the world at large. They have been particularly effective in developing appropriate job attitudes and in teaching appropriate interpersonal relationships.

The computer and related electronic technologies can also serve as a compensatory tool for the mentally challenged in the area of creative arts. Physical problems, poor eye-hand coordination or poor fine motor control often present particular problems for the mentally challenged when they attempt art using the more traditional mediums of paper, crayons, and paint. The computer, equipped with certain peripherals or adaptive devices, can permit these individuals to have meaningful and satisfying art experiences. This does not mean that art experiences in the more traditional mediums are not also satisfying; however, computer generated art is often physically easier and, at the same time, a creative experience for these individuals because the computer can compensate for some motor and physical problems. A Koala Pad, for example, allows the mentally challenged to create art on the screen or as a printout using limited muscular movement. Individuals using such a system do not have to be concerned with grip and fine motor control since they can create their art simply by moving their hand or finger along the pad. Further, the creation can be retained in memory and recalled at any time.

It should be noted that color is not appropriate for all students any more than extraneous stimuli would be. Some students require no extraneous stimuli to learn, whereas others require exceptional amounts and varieties of stimuli, as evidenced by children's television and music videos. Music synthesis has also been used successfully with this group both as an instrument to play as well as a tool to create music. The development of electronic creative arts can provide challenging and fun alternatives for this group and can become lifelong recreational options.

The computer and modified systems such as the interactive video disc are the only truly interactive recreational technologies. They obligate users to be actively involved in the exercise because they require interaction for the activity to take place. Other technologies, such as radio, television, and cinema, are all passive systems, ones in which the user is an inactive recipient of entertainment. All too often these people are limited to such passive leisure activities because they tend to recreate at home and not avail themselves of community alternatives. The use of the microcomputer for the creative arts, as previously discussed, is one type of interactive lifelong recreational alternative. Electronic games also offer interesting leisure activities. Since these systems have varied skill levels, since they are controlled by devices such as joysticks, and since they allow players to compete with the computer or against the last score, they offer challenging and fun recreational activities. The immediate feedback of these systems provide additional motivation for their continued use. Some of the recently developed fantasy interactive video systems provide another interactive alternative. The user creates individual graphic and sound stories by selecting responses to questions structured within a generic scenario. Every change in the response creates a different story. These leisure time technologies are being increasingly incorporated into special education programs for this group.

The areas of prevocational and vocational preparation for the less impaired mentally challenged have also been enhanced through the use of electronic technologies. As mentioned previously, special programs have been developed to teach appropriate interpersonal employment skills and job attitudes, area which have traditionally inhibited this group's ability to secure and retain employment. Other systems have been developed to teach specific job related skills in both drill and practice and problem-solving formats. Modifications to industry-developed interactive video disc and simulator training programs have proven to be very effective with these people as well as with previously mentioned groups because of the "realness" in the situations. Further, the voice descriptions and directions that accompany the visual and motion output reinforce the multisensory electronic instruction. Students are able to progress at their own pace and specific subskills can be experienced until they are mastered. The use of this approach has proven to be extremely effective and has facilitated the student's transition from the vocational training center into actual job placement. Increasing numbers of vocational training programs for the less impaired mentally challenged are turning to electronics to supplement their existing courses.

## MILD AND MODERATE IMPAIRMENTS

The largest population of identified handicapped students — mild to moderately impaired — include individuals categorized as mentally retarded, emotionally disturbed, and learning disabled. Children in the mild category tend to spend the majority of their day in regular class-room settings, receiving special educational services in a resource room or at support services stations. Moderately impaired pupils are often mainstreamed into regular classrooms in the areas of their academic strength or into situations where they have a high probability for success. Others are placed in self-contained classrooms because it is perceived that their needs can best be met in these settings.

Traditionally, some of the most effective instructional approaches used in special education with mild and moderately impaired students deal with identifying the areas of the student's sensory strength and weakness and using the areas of strength to support the areas of weakness. Thus, a strong visual system may be used to support a weak auditory system. Electronic technologies, and most particularly computers, provide diagnostic and prescriptive information to the special educator regarding the learning strengths and weaknesses of students and they allow the instructor to select the most appropriate modes of input and output for each student. Further, computer content can be presented in a unisensory or multisensory manner, depending on the needs of the pupil. The key the application of this technology is its graphic, sound, speech output, and individualization capabilities. Students can be presented with software material which, if presented in print, would be above their functional level. For example, auditory learners can hear phonemes that are blended into words. These learners can respond out loud and the computer will analyze their auditory attempts and will provide appropriate feedback. Visual learners can see the entire word supported with graphic representations to assist in comprehension, read silently, and then respond by typing, using single switch devices, touching screens, and so forth. "Streetwise" students with normal cognitive reasoning skills will not have to be held back simply because they have functional skill deficits. As an example, students with limited mathematical algorithm skills can learn mathematical problem solving on the computer. Graphics, sound, or voice can be used as cues to support the child in reading or mathematics mastery activities. This multisensory ability of the technology can assist the student in making the appropriate associations and, therefore, assist them in learning the skill. To meet the needs of the individual student, modifications in any of these approaches can be made by the educator through any number of teacher options in commercial programs or through "programming" within shell programs or authoring language systems. By considering each individual pupil's primary learning modes and modalities, the capabilities of the computer can be used to present advanced concepts to students without being limited by possible deficient functional skill levels.

Drill and practice software has proven very successful with the mildly and moderately handicapped. These systems are patient and motivating, permitting pupils to practice a skill in a randomly selected sequence at their own pace. Further, the use of microcomputer courseware allows students to achieve a level of independence. They can drill independently without ponderous reliance upon the teacher. The machine may simply record errors, or it may evaluate them in a manner that is not judgmental.

Tutorial programs allow the user to enter into a dialogue with the computerized lesson in order to support the concepts that have been presented in the regular classroom. Tutorial systems are, thus, interactive with the student. Often offered as an alternative, branching is an option that provides a choice between two or more possible courses of action. The student may select a topic, or the teacher may select a functioning level. Branching can also occur as a result of the program's evaluation of student responses. The use of authoring language systems to develop tutorial programs allows the instructor to design instructional programs that delineate educational materials unique to the needs of the individual handicapped child.

Word processing is particularly effective with mildly and moderately impaired individuals. A great many of these pupils have difficulty with written expression because of a number of factors, some of which are memory and sequencing difficulties, central language dysfunctions, perceptual difficulties, eye-hand coordination problems, and dysgraphia. Word processing allows these students to achieve success in activities of written expression because allows them to focus attention on the content of the message to be communicated rather than on the actual process of writing, forming the letters, and placing the words on paper. Problems compensated for by using word processing include visual-motor integration problems (handwriting); memory problems caused by visual integration difficulty, or changing eye contact from one place to another; and processing problems that involve such things as spelling, syntax, and grammar. Once these difficulties are compensated for, remediation in specific areas can begin, singling out one area at a time based on the individual's deficit areas. Further, students can enter their expressive thoughts at their own pace and in their own particular linguistic style. Once the complete thought or expression has been recorded, they can go back and correct the material and put it in the proper expressive format either on their own or by using the appropriate "checker" program. When the student is satisfied with his or her expression, the computer will perform the actual task of "writing." Thus, the first printed copy, the computer copy, may be the final and correct copy, or if corrections are needed, they can be made easily and a second copy printed out. The key to this important compensatory use of the computer for the mild and moderately impaired is that this application allows them to concentrate upon the content of their expression while allowing the computer to perform the actual process of expression. The machine is compensating for their specific expressive deficits, allowing them to use their strengths and to express their personal ideas; then, as indicated earlier, remediation in specific areas can be isolated and initiated.

Electronic simulation programs provide another learning alternative for the mild and moderately handicapped student. These systems allow them to discover concepts and abstractions through the proven method of trial and error. Since these systems simulate real life situations, the handicapped user can experiment with alternative solutions and subsequent consequences without personal risk. This type of software permits the pupil to develop problem-solving strategies that apply learned concepts to real situations. The simulation, when enacted multiple times, permits the student to explore alternative solutions and to experience the logical results of the choices until a satisfactory answer is achieved. This type of software is especially effective for teaching appropriate behaviors in social situations.

Because many students enter special education programs after they have failed in regular education classes, they often have a very poor opinion of themselves as learners and as individuals. The computer is a teaching device that can do much to change these self-perceptions. It is a patient and obedient tutor and learning tool. It passes no judgment about the ability of the user and simply accepts the person at his or her level, unlike the human teacher or tutor who may inadvertantly display impatience or displeasure with the student's performance through such unconscious behaviors as tone, pitch of voice or body language. The computer never shows any unprogrammed displeasure when students make a mistake or if they take an inordinate amount of time to process information or to memorize. Thus, this technology can both compensate for and assist in the remediation of the pupil's poor self-concept as well as help the student develop an appreciaton and fondness of learning.

## THE GIFTED

The gifted are the exceptional children with whom electronic technologies have been used most extensively. Today the technologies used in programs for these students often include microcomputers, interactive communications networks, robots, and interactive video disc systems whether the programs are conducted in special schools, in self-contained classrooms, or in resource centers. This is not meant to imply that all gifted students will desire or need to become technology experts, since many do not; however, most special educators in this field agree that this group must be exposed to these technologies, learn how to access and process information electronically, and learn how to make decisions based upon this information. Special educators feel, therefore, that these systems should be intergrated into the children's basic programs of study.

Computers can play an important role in the education of gifted students. Drill and practice and tutorial software provide these pupils with the opportunity to expand their basic curricula through independent study in areas that are of particular interest to them. These programs can also provide them with assistance in mastering subjects in which they may not be as proficient as their peers, since not all gifted students excell in all subjects. These programs allow them to study and investigate knowledge at their own pace and, as a result, to learn how to assume responsibility for their own programs of learning.

Electronic technologies are also being applied as tools to develop logic and problem solving. In addition to software specifically designed to teach these skills, the use of electronic exploration languages, such as LOGO, and authoring language systems have been increasingly employed as instructional tools to enhance and develop these areas. Prior to the advent of these systems, anyone desiring to create a computer program had to learn a programming language. However, not all gifted children are interested in learning how to program, a situation that is also true for the general population. Electronic exploration languages and authoring language systems now permit a user to create a program without having to learn a programming language. The use of these systems to create a program teaches the individual the skills of planning, logical sequencing, and problem solving. Further, it can be very rewarding to students to see their programs run on a computer screen. The use of this teaching approach can therefore be highly motivational.

Simulation software has proven to be particularly effective in programs for the gifted. They are designed to promote discovery learning, that is, learning by actually doing. They also promote decision making and the use of logic since each selected alternative changes the results or the direction of the entire program. Students can see the results of their choices and, by using the software again, experience the effects of employing alternate strategies. These programs encourage the pupils to explore and manipulate their physical, historical, current, and future worlds electronically within their classrooms. The recent development of educational interactive video systems has greatly expanded the simulation opportunities available to the gifted student.

Telecommunications, electronic data bases, and electronic bulletin boards have become important electronic vehicles in the education of gifted children. These systems permit the user to communicate and share information with people outside their individual schools or to access large data files for the purposes of research and information retrieval. Electronic bulletin boards permit the user to communicate with other individuals located over a large geographical area. These systems allow the gifted student to interact and share information with other individuals who have similar interests regardless of their physical location. Further, these systems have been employed to establish a "mentor" relationship between a gifted child interested in a specific topic and an individual with more expertise in that area. In this application, the "mentor" expert guides the student in learning, researching, and applying the newly mastered skills in the specific area that is of interest to both of them. Thus, telecommunications can expand upon the expertise of the child's local instructor.

The inclusion of these electronic communication and research systems is an important element in the program of study for gifted students. These pupils are frequently described as the future leaders of our society. Since our world is rapidly entering the Information Age, it is essential that these students learn how to access, control, and use information. One reality of the Information Age is that the amount of available information is expanding exponentially because of electronic data bases and communication systems (Cleveland, 1982; Molitor, 1981). As a result, the individual in this age must cope with the rapidly expanding source of information and must develop not only deductive but inductive reasoning skills. When information changes so rapidly, as it does today and will do in the future, one may never have all the facts necessary to deduce the solution to a problem. Therefore, it is important that these gifted pupils learn today the use of the electronic data bases and communication systems and apply the art of inductive reasoning.

Electronic technologies are also employed to teach gifted students recreational alternatives. Computer games are one alternative in this area. Adventure games, games of intellectual skill such as chess, and mind-teasers are often used in their instructional programs. In addition to being entertaining and fun, they prove to be highly motivational since a user pits his or her skill against a computer or against a past performance. Most of these software are designed with variable levels of difficulty and contain the element of randomness. Another area of recreational instruction involves the use of electronic technology to develop the creative arts. Computer drawing software permit the user to develop creative and imaginative art on a screen or in print. Often these systems employ light pens and touch pads as the input device, tools that enhance the drawing process. Music software systems permit the user to compose and play music via computer. Electronic keyboards can be interfaced with a microcomputer to permit storing a composition in memory. Most of these systems display graphically what is being composed. The use of electronic data bases and communication devices mentioned earlier offer other recreational alternatives. Independent research and study and long distance communication can be conducted from the home using a microcomputer connected to a telephone through a modem. All of these alternatives permit their users to avail themselves of the power of these electronic technologies as tools for recreation.

Finally electronic technologies are used in the instructional programs for gifted students to teach them to use these devices as tools for daily living, as implements which make their lives easier. The power of electronic communication and of access to computer data bases has already been discussed. These systems perform directed tasks at speeds far beyond human capacity and, therefore, are important instruments for learning and for future use in the world of work. They permit the user to access and control information and to communicate with others rapidly. Another important electronic daily living device in which gifted students usually receive instruction is word processing. These systems greatly enhance the written communication capabilities of the user. They allow the student to enter, store, edit, and format text considerably faster and more effectively than by using traditional methods, such as handwriting or typing. The final printed copy accurately reflects what was written and appears in a final draft form, thereby removing the need for laborious rewriting. Further, the written text can be transmitted electronically through a microcomputer connected to a telecommunication device via a modem. The use of the technology applications can and do make the users' lives easier. They are essential daily living tools for the worker and the potential leader in the Information Age.

## Summary

■ Electronic technologies have already made a dramatic impact on special education, particularly as instructional and prosthetic tools. Electronic tools have promoted improvements in instruction, planning and monitoring student activities, and independence for disabled users.

■ Electronic technologies are ideal for special education applications because they are dynamic, patient, consistent, and nonjudgmental. They permit individualization of instruction and pacing. They enhance strengths and compensate for deficits in the learner.

■ Computer Assisted Instruction (CAI) allows for hardware modifications to both computer input and output to permit special children (gifted and disabled) to interact with the technology.

■ Computer Managed Instruction (CMI) helps teachers and administrators to control and monitor students' progress, particularly in the areas of scoring tests, keeping records, and prescribing individualized programs.

■ Computer Assistant Management (CAM) is an electronic information manager, most commonly used for word processing, data bases, and spreadsheets.

# CHAPTER 2

# Projections About Life and Learning in the 21st Century

**O**ur nation stands on the threshold of a revolution, one that will transform our society dramatically and far more than the agricultural and industrial revolutions of the past. This new revolution has been given different names by futurists: the "Computer Revolution," the "Third Wave," the "Information Revolution," and so on. Although futurists differ significantly in their visions of the 21st century, they all agree that this revolution has already begun and that our future society is inescapably tied to rapid technological change.

One may ask, why should the special educators of today be concerned about futurists' projections? What does this topic have to do with the individualized educational programs for handicapped students? The answer is very simple. For handicapped students currently enrolled in special education programs, the future is now. These young people will live most of their lives in the 21st century. Since the basic objective of special education is to assist handicapped pupils in realizing their maximum potential and in preparing to achieve the greatest degree of independence possible, then special educators must look carefully at the world in which these students will live as adults — the world of the early 21st century, the Information Age.

Futurism is not science fiction. It is also not an exact science. The ranks of futurists are composed of scientists, researchers, medical professionals, economists, sociologists, educators, and other academicians. Futurism is an attempt to project the future based on an analysis of past history and current trends (O'Toole, 1983). It is a very serious field, as evidenced by the number of think tank projects located throughout the country that are sponsored by government or private sector funds. Making projections, particularly those that are short range, can be somewhat risky. It is like playing leapfrog with a unicorn — if one is shortsighted, one can become painfully impaled on the horns of a dilemma. Historically, projections of futurists have tended to happen sooner than predicted, an indication of the speed with which changes occur. Although futurists differ greatly in their projections and at times contradict each other, they all agree that the future is not constant and predictable. There are, however, three major elements that determine the future:

- *Continuity* — The future is always influenced by the past and the present.
- *Change* — The future is always influenced by unexpected events those developments that break the continuity of history.
- *Choice* — The future is always influenced by the choices that people make when confronted with a new development.

One of the best sources of information regarding projections of the future is the World Future Society, Bethesda, Maryland. It is a nonprofit scientific and educational organization whose membership is composed of individuals concerned with future scientific, social, and technological developments. The organization conducts meetings and publishes a monthly journal entitled *The Futurist*, as well as books, reports, films, and other specialized documents.

As mentioned earlier, our nation is in the midst of rapid change. We are moving from a society perceived as being resource-constrained to one that is information-rich (Hald, 1981). We are entering a new era in which economic growth is derived from the exchange of information and the creation of knowledge rather than from the accelerated consumption of natural resources. The introduction of microelectronic capabilities into the office, the classroom, and the home is initiating a period of explosive innovation and is dramatically changing the world around us. These technologies are increasing our ability to recall information, communicate, create knowledge, and understand complex relationships. Our nation's economic stability and vitality as a world power in an era of international corporate competition depends on creative technological invention and productivity. Not only is our future tied to accelerated technical development but our emergence into the information era is also profoundly influencing it. It would appear that the old expression "here today, gone tomorrow" is an accurate description of this rapid change. This is not meant to indicate that new technologies will always replace the old. They very often become intertwined with older technologies or are modified based on how the older technologies are utilized by the general public. Television did not replace radio. It did, however, cause a significant change in the type of programming that was broadcast on the radio; it modified the radio industry. On the other hand, another technology, the automobile, rapidly replaced the horse and buggy as the mode of transportation in American society. Although historically, nonelectronic technological advances have very often caused new developments to replace the old, these examples tend to demonstrate that electronic technologies, particularly those involved in communication, become intertwined with older technologies.

Technology has been developing exponentially, and this trend is projected to continue through the early 21st century and beyond. The information bases with which we must deal are currently doubling every twenty to twenty-four months. It is projected that these information bases will double every twelve months in the early 21st century. An example of this explosion of information is television. A few year ago, most individuals could receive no more than ten to thirteen stations on their home television sets. The advent of cable televsion has expanded the number of stations available to the home user in some areas to more than fifty stations. The projected nationwide introduction of videotex in the very near future will again dramatically increase and probably double the number of stations or sources of information available to the home user (Dunn, 1980; Tyderman, 1982). In a speech a few year ago, William Schramm, a communications expert and futurist, dramatically pointed out the exponential growth of information and information industries (1985). To paraphrase some of Schramm's comments:

From spoken language to writing — at least *50 million years.*

From writing to printing — about *50 thousand years.*

From printing to the development of sight and sound media — about *500 years.*

From the first sight and sound media to the modern computer — fewer than *50 years.*

To understand the potential impact of the futurists' projections for the early 21st century, we must look at the primary factors that will effect the lives of individuals inhabiting the society. Again, it must be stated that futurists differ significantly in their visions of the future. These projections represent those factors about which most agree. Many of these predictions are based upon *anticipated* developments in electronic technologies (see Chapter 3).

■ ■ ■ ■ ■

As mentioned earlier, our society is moving rapidly into a new era, one which is information-rich. In this new age, one's ability to access, process, and communicate information will determine in good measure one's economic viability. Economic power in this society will be based on the control of data and the exchange of information rather than on the consumption of natural resource. Prior developments of new technology have always been concerned with the improvement of material production. The new age will be governed by a different type of technological development, innovations in the electronic computer communications area, and will have as its primary product the mass production of information, communication, electronic technology, and knowledge. The development of new electronic technologies will, in turn, cause the more rapid growth of new additional electronic technologies and result in even more rapid change in the nation's economy and in society as a whole.

In a communications age, it is not information itself but the *use* of information which is power. Interactive telecommunication-linked systems using advanced technologies will be the medium of communication in the Information Age. It is only with these computer-based interactive systems that the individual can hope to compete in a world of almost instantaneous information without becoming totally overwhelmed by the amount of information available and the speed with which it is presented.

A century ago fewer than 10% of the American workforce was engaged in information or communication employment. At the present time, more than 50% of the workforce is employed in information related jobs (Munro, 1981). This percentage is projected to increase as we move more deeply into the Information Age and is expected to reach 85% of the total American workforce in the foreseeable future. Thus, it is an inescapable reality that both our nation's pattern of employment and the general economy will be dramatically altered due to the consequences of electronic knowledge-processing technologies.

The impact of the Information Age and the electronic technologies on which it is based will affect all aspects of society. Our economy is already being dramatically changed by these new developments, and this pattern will continue at an increasing speed. The home is also being altered due to the increase in electronic communication and service devices, which are already considered daily living tools. As with the general economy, this alteration in the types of activities that occur in the home will continue to change as new technologies are developed and adopted by the general public. The values and concerns of our society are also undergoing rapid change due to the development of new electronic technologies. Issues, such as equal access to information and the confidentiality of personal records maintained in computer data bases, are increasingly becoming concerns of the general public. New medical, rehabilitation, and electronic biomedical developments are raising new questions regarding topics such as the quality of life, the right to die, genetic engineering, and the extension of the human life span.

Although the promise of the Information Age is great, one must keep in mind some of the potential problems that the concept of access to instantaneous and unlimited information might hold for the citizen of the early 21st century. The potential for easier communication also holds the potential for easier and greater miscommunication. More communication and information is not necessarily better. Simply having better systems to receive and transmitt information does not, in itself, imply better comprehension and use of the information. The system is not the solution. If some individuals are overwhelmed with the amount of information they have to process today, how will they fare in the world of the Information Age? Chronic "communication pollution" and "terminal information overload" may become real diseases in the future for these individuals. Those citizens of the Information Age who cannot master information processing or who lack the language and information processing skills to be technologically literate may, in fact, become the peasants of the 21st century's knowledge society (Cleveland, 1982).

## COMMUNICATION

The ability to communicate efficiently and effectively is one of the most important skills necessary for an individual to function in the Information Age. Communication can be described most simply as the interchange of thoughts and ideas in the form of body language, words, or written messages. The computer and interactive telecommunication systems are two of the most important electronic devices of the Information Age. Both of these technologies are basically related communication systems and are the vehicles that permit their users to access, manipulate, and transmit information. Computers store and manipulate information, whereas telecommunication systems transmit the information from one point to another.

Several dramatic changes in the manner in which individuals communicate have already occurred, and many more will undoubtedly occur as we move further into the Information Age. Prior to the advent of electronic communication and information technologies, the primary form of communication was direct human to human contact either in person, in written or graphic form, or via telegraph or telephone. Computers are changing television into an interactive medium, and closed circuit television-computer conferencing allows not only print and voice communication but the transmission of gestures and body language (Jennings, 1979). Information searches were limited to an individual's ability to ask questions of another person or to read documents. All of this is changing with the advent of electronic computer-based technologies.

Computer conferencing is a growing electronic technology that is expected to expand into one of the basic forms of information exchange in the early 21st century. The basic elements of these systems are microcomputers connected via telephone, fiber optic, or cable lines. Computer conferencing allows individuals in various locations to communicate or "attend a conference," at any time of day that participants desire. At its simplest, computer conferencing is a written electronic form of the telephone conference call. The user communicates with the other conference members by typing a message on the terminal and reading what the other individuals are saying on the computer screen or on a printout. The computer system automatically notifies all members of the group when someone enters or leaves the discussion. When an individual leaves the discussion, the computer system records the person's location in the discussion and resumes transmission at that point when the individual reenters the discussion. Other conferencing situations include a type of closed circuit television in which voices are electronically translated into print and saved in memory. It is projected that the use of computer conferencing will increase and that it will, in more advanced forms, become the basis of world-wide communications. Further, these communication networks will be used both at work and at home and will serve as the major method of information exchange (Vallee, Johansen, & Spangler, 1975).

Computer conferencing will dramatically change the manner in which people communicate in the Information Age, since it differs from direct traditional person-to-person communication in very important ways. In most present computer conferences where video is not included, there are no gestures, vocal cues, or facial expressions to assist in the comprehension of the message being communicated. In this type of computer conference, every participant can either send a message or listen at the same time since the computer system monitors, maintains, and posts all communications. When individuals in geographically different areas can communicate at any time of day or night, their concepts of time are often altered. This distortion of time is made more acute since the computer conference user enters or leaves the conference at any point without losing contact with the meeting. When this occurs, the computer will store all of the messages that are missed and display them when the user returns to the conference. Further, the user can work at his or her own pace and make a contribution to the discussion when ready. In the traditional face-to-face conference, the participant is expected to reply when the other members of the group indicate that such participation is required. Also, the reality that participation is anonymous leads to more open discussions. Obviously, many of these differences are eliminated or minimized when video or interactive closed circuit television is involved. It is projected that computer conferencing will replace items such as journal articles, memos, reports, conferences, and meetings for special interest groups whose members may reside in widely separated geographic areas.

Computer conferencing appears to hold some specific benefits for handicapped users. For example, current electronic communication systems designed to assist deaf people in communicating with hearing individuals are limited to one-to-one dialogues. Computer conferencing would permit a deaf person to participate in large group conversations. Computer conferencing also provides handicapped people the opportunity to dialogue and interact with nonhandicapped individuals without fearing bias because of their disability. There is often no way to determine whether or not someone is handicapped in a computer conferencing communication system (Turoff, 1975).

As can be seen from the example of computer conferencing, the communication process of the early 21st century's Information Age will be significantly different from that employed in the late 20th century. There will be more communication among individuals using electronic telecommunication networks and less direct interpersonal dialogue. Users of these advanced technology systems will have to learn how to send and receive information through a computer and adapt their mode of communication to reflect the dynamics of this new medium. Although these new systems will provide a more flexible vehicle for dialogue, many of the nonverbal clues which now support the verbal communication process will be lost, except when video is used; also there will be greater emphasis on the written communication model.

## THE NET CONSOLE

Networking, as it is used today, is a computer-controlled method of sending information to diverse locations by means of a telecommunication system. These systems allow the user to communicate with others through electronic bulletin boards and information sharing systems and to access information data bases. The electronic bulletin board permits a user to leave messages for an individual or group and to receive individual, group, or general information through a microcomputer connected to a telecommunication system via a modem. These systems are not group interactive, as in the case with computer conferencing. Networking also allows a user to enter a data base as a subscriber in order to research and receive information by means of a microcomputer connected in the same manner as the bulletin board. These information networks, which include large data bases such as encyclopedias, the Library of Congress, newspaper archives, and the New York Stock Exchange, permit a subscriber to research and receive information by means of a microcomputer connected in the same manner as the bulletin board. There are well over 500 commerical information data bases available today. Other forms of networks currently available allow the user to reach a data base through a cable television linked interactive system which is generally termed videotex. Again, the user can access information and can also enter transactions for activities such as banking, shopping from home, accessing information data bases, and booking travel arrangements. Although videotex is not currently available in all parts of the country, it is anticipated that it will become available to all homes having cable television connections in the near future and that it will offer an increasing variety of data base options for the user to access. In order to make the videotex profitable for the service provider, there is, of course, a service charge for each individual or group of data bases used by the subscriber.

The Net Console (Cain, 1985a) is one of the few electronic technology projections for the early 21st century about which most futurists agree (Baran, 1973; Jones, 1973; Vail, 1980). The Net Console is the home/work/education-based system projected for the control of information and of the home itself in the Information Age. It is an interactive system composed of advanced technologies and designed for the delivery of information and communication into and from the home.

The Net Console will be an interconnected system of communication delivered to the home computer terminal by means of cable television, direct satellite transmission, telephone line, or cellular radio. The home system will be linked into a world grid matrix of communication and data transmission called "The Net" (Cain, 1985b). The home/work/school station, the Net Console, will incorporate a variety of computer interface devices; including adaptive input devices, microphones, video cameras, video disc recorders, biofeedback units, and so forth.

Via the Net Console, the home electronic technology user of the early 21st century will have direct and instantaneous video and voice access to anyone, anywhere in the world. Since the home console will be linked to the world grid, it will be able to provide the home user immediate access to the sum total of all human art and knowledge. The Net Console will also serve as the central monitoring system for the home's environment and will control all appliances including the home's service robot(s). Not only will the system form the basis of home communication, education, and recreation, it can and will serve some individuals as the workplace, permitting access to the employer's head-quarters and to other workers situated in multiple locations.

The Net Console is not science fiction. The major components of such a system exist today and are used in a somewhat more primitive form by government, business and industry, and certain individuals in their homes. An increasing number of workers are using their interac-tively linked home computer station as their office workplace. One of the best examples of this phenomenon is the newspaper industry. An increas-ing number of reporters work primarily from their homes and transmit their stories to the newspaper through their microcomputer which, in turn, is linked to the telephone line via a modem (Skaraulis, 1982). Communication from the newspaper to the reporter can occur by means of electronic messages that are left on an electronic bulletin board.

SRI International Business Intelligence Project, a California-based think tank group, developed in 1986 a projection of the services that would probably be available to the home Net Console user in the early 21st century:

- Expert "parenting" systems that monitor children's activities, warn of possible problems, and advise appropriate responses
- Intelligent games that interact with several players and auto-matically adjust the parameters of play, introducing new con-tingencies based on levels of play
- Story generators and animation packages for creating person-alized forms of entertainment
- Expert systems for diagnosing problems in the home and pro-viding advice for do-it-yourself repairs
- Intelligent control of appliances in response to oral directions
- Advice on nutrition and interactive medical preventative health care networks
- Advice on tax computation, financial planning, budgeting, and legal questions
- Expert interactive home work stations
- Better systems to aid in identifying, overcoming, or compensat-ing for specific learning or physical disabilities
- Expert "librarian" systems capable of helping to develop strat-egies for information search and the retrieval of data

The Net Console, as it is envisioned by futurists, will serve as the electronic telecommunication center for interactive communication, the delivery of information, and the control of the home environment. It can also serve as an employee's or student's interactive work or learning station. Adaptive switches and other prosthetic devices for input and multisensory output options make it a system that has the potential to dramatically reduce the barriers to independent living for many handicapped and disabled individuals; it can permit them to take part as equal participants in the Information Age. This system portends the potential for the exceptional person to live, learn, work, and recreate in a "barrier free" technologial environment.

## DEMOGRAPHIC PROJECTIONS

One of the most significant demographic changes that will have impact on our society in the early 21st century is an anticipated shift in our population distribution. Americans and other citizens in industrial nations are living longer. Individuals over the age of 65 constituted approximately 11.5 percent of the total population in the mid-1980s. In fact, there were more individuals over the age of 65 in the mid-1980s than there were teenagers. This trend of extending the life span and of the increase in the number of older citizens will continue into the 21st century. It is projected that the percentage of the population over the age of 65 will increase to approximately 14 percent in the early 21st century. Federal estimates project that by the end of the first quarter of the 21st century there will be twice as many citizens over the age of 65 as there will be teenagers (Best, 1978; Cetron, 1985). The early part of the 21st century will see the post-World War II baby boom become the senior boom. America and other industrial nations will be aging societies in the Information Age.

Not only is the number of older Americans increasing, but the life expectancy rate is also increasing for both men and women (Best, 1978; Stunkel, 1979). Most of the improvement in life expectancy has occurred since the early 1970s, and this trend is anticipated to continue well into the 21st century. This increase in life expectancy has been directly attributed to biomedical, technological, and electronic rehabilitation advances. Future advances in these and related fields can be expected to continue this trend.

During the same period that the number of older citizens was increasing, the national birth rate and fertility rate among women of child bearing age was declining. This decline in fertility rate has been attributed to technical medical developments that permitted fertility planning. The other factor that has been indicated as a cause of the decrease in birth rate is the change in the marriage pattern. Nationally, couples have tended to marry later in life and have fewer children

(Coates, 1982). It should be noted, however, that minority groups have continued to have children at a relatively young age, which could increase the gap between those who are technologically literate and those who are technologically deprived.

One fact that can be interpreted from these demographic projections for the Information Age is that fewer younger individuals will be supporting significantly more older citizens in the early part of the 21st century, especially if the current mandatory retirement and social security age requirements remain in effect. This reality will have some dramatic effects on the work force and on the types of jobs that are available at that time. It would seem to portend a required increase in the number of service jobs. Another factor which may become important is that this dramatically increased number of older Americans would compete with schools and other educational and rehabilitation agencies for federal funds. Due to the increased percentage of older citizens in the population, they will definitely wield increased political power, which could slow the acceptance of technology and technological change, at least for this segment of the population, a group that would benefit greatly from its use.

Technical developments and change have been traditionally viewed in this country as the concern of the young. It has been seen as their future; however, our national demography is changing, and no longer will the nation enjoy the luxury of a large youthful population supporting a much smaller aging minority. The youth will be the minority in the early 21st century. If change and new technologies continue to be viewed as the primary concern of only the young, the nation's economy will suffer, and the potential benefits of the new technologies will accure to only a small segment of our society.

Another demographic factor which will have impact on life in the Information Age is that there will be a continuing increase in the percentage of women who work. Current projections estimate that about three-quarters of all women of employable age will be working by the early 21st century (Coats, 1982). This will occur at the same time that there will be an increase in the number of workers who will work at home because of the development of the net console and related electronic communication devices. As a result, it is projected that the mother and father will share more of the child-rearing and household duties since both may be working part or full-time in the home. It is also projected that there will be a continuing need for more day care and early childhood programs due to the projected increase in the percentage of working mothers.

A final demographic factor that should be considered concerns a projected change in the pattern of volunteers available to assist in school and rehabilitation settings. Traditionally, volunteers for these programs have been women and, in particular, women of child bearing age. However, with a significantly larger percentage of women becoming employed, they cannot form the core volunteer base in the Information Age. At the same time, however, there will be a much larger percentage of older and fully or partially retired citizens. It is anticipated that this group, whith their rich variety of life experiences, can and will form the volunteer base for educational and rehabilitation programs in the early part of the 21st century. This trend is already seen in a number of areas where senior citizens are sharing their talents and skills in educational institutions and other service-oriented organizations.

## EMPLOYMENT AND THE WORKPLACE

Rapid technological development, shifts in demographic patterns, and the impact of electronic technologies are having, and will continue to have, a dramatic effect on our economy. The world of work in the early 21st century, therefore, will be molded in good part by these and other factors. If one of the roles of special education is to prepare as many handicapped individuals as possible to be independent or semi-independent workers, then the variety of jobs that are projected for the world of tomorrow, the Information Age, must be explored now. The current individual educational programs of these students must reflect instruction that provides them with the attitudes, academic knowledge, and vocational skills required to prepare them to be workers in the early part of the 21st century.

Our economy has been shifting from manufacturing or industrial employment to a service economy. More than half of the workers of today are engaged in service or information-processing jobs. Employment in the tertiary sector of the economy (finance, insurance, government services, and so forth) has been expanding rapidly. Ninety-two percent of all new jobs created since the mid-1960s have been in the tertiary sector (Cetron & O'Toole, 1982; Cleveland, 1982). Increases in the manufacturing industry's productivity have themselves created the economic growth which in turn led to the increased demand for services in the tertiary sector. Futher, the increase of jobs related to information processing and to the delivery of such information has also increased at an equally dramatic rate. The difference between manufacturing and service employment is often hard to distinguish. For example, is a secretary employed in an automobile manufacturing plant engaged in an industrial or service job? Most economists would say that the individual is employed in a service since the individual is not directly occupied with goods production. Manufacturing or industrial employment can be defined most simply as jobs that create or change physical objects. Direct support of production activities are, therefore, service jobs; the inescapable fact is that service related jobs will constitute the primary form of employment in the Information Age.

One of the most dramatic implications of new technological developments and of rapid technological change has been better manufacturing productivity with fewer individuals engaged in the production of goods. One piece of microelectronic circuitry can substitute for hundreds of moving parts. Although these technologies hold the potential to significantly improve the lives of citizens, many manufacturing workers view technological change as a dark and threatening force rather than as a bright promise. Communities throughout this nation and thoughout the industrial world have become depressingly familiar with the impact of technological or structural unemployment; that is, joblessness that occurs because workers are suddenly obsolete due to industrial technical innovation. Current projections show this trend will continue into the early part of the 21st century due to the anticipated impact of advanced technologies such as robots and other technical changes in the manufacturing industries. It is estimated that, by the turn of the century, only about 5% of the total work force will be employed in manufacturing, food production, or industrial goods production. The remaining 95% will be employed in service and information-processing jobs.

The impact of robotics in manufacturing industries is projected to be significant by the early part of the 21st century (Albus, 1983; Cetron & O'Toole, 1982; Coates, 1983; Cornish, 1983). Robotics has already had some impact on our factories and the jobs available within them, although its use has been more pronounced in Japan. The number of robots and other members of the electronic work force will continue to grow in the next decades as will the variety of their applications. The factory of the Information Age will include robots, computer-controlled manufacturing, and computer-aided design systems. The reason for the use of these new electronic technologies in the manufacturing industries is very simple; it can be stated in one word — productivity. The use of these devices increases the productivity of the firm using them. Robots and their related electronic manufacturing technologies are a manager's and stockholder's dream. They never take lunch or coffee breaks. They do not complain about doing unpleasant or hazardous tasks. They work around the clock for the typical three factory shifts. Robots can perform many tasks faster, cheaper, and better than human beings. Although robots and related electronic manufacturing technologies may replace many factory workers, their development has created a host of new jobs. Someone must monitor and run the robot at the workplace, since these devices are not intelligent and can only perform the task(s) for which they have been programmed. Further, someone must install, maintain, and repair the robot factory worker. In fact, the development of robots and all other current and future electronic technology developments have created a whole new range of jobs that never existed before the development of the new technology. The continued growth of new advanced technology manufacturing devices will cause the displacement of certain factory workers; however, they will also cause the creation of a variety of new support, modification, and design jobs related to the new development. For instance, artifical intelligence will play an important role in the use of robots because the robots will be able to process information and make decisions based on previously stored data. This, in turn, will cause changes in human job needs and functions. (Robotics is discussed in detail in Chapter 3.)

It must be remembered that while the industrial revolution made available and employed vast amounts of mechanical energy, the information revolution is and will continue to be extremely sparing of energy and materials. The primary economic products of the Information Age are, of course, data and knowledge. Our society passed the 50% point for information-connected employment in the mid-1980s. At that time, the number of computers produced in the United States alone exceeded the total number of individuals born in the country. It is projected that the trend of continued growth in the development of electronic information-processing technologies and their commensurate increase in the number of information-connected jobs will continue into the early 21st century and will probably reach about 85% of the total work force by the turn of the century.

Although the vast majority of workers will be engaged in some form of service or information-processing employment in the early part of the 21st century, this does not imply that their jobs will remain static. These workers are as prone to the impact of technological unemployment as are those engaged in good production. In fact, individuals employed in information processing, a subcategory of service employment, are particularly vulnerable to new electronic technology developments. It has been repeated many times that our society and its economy is in the midst of rapid change, a trend that will continue into the 21st century. Electronic technologies have been growing and are anticipated to continue developing exponentially. As a result, those individuals employed in the use of or delivery of information services can anticipate dramatic and continual changes in job requirements and in the specific types of jobs available in these fields. These changes will affect the service workers of the Information Age as dramatically as it did those employed in manufacturing and food production in the Industrial Age.

Nearly 4% of the entire workforce received some form of job training or retraining annually in the mid-1980s. The average workers of today will be retrained from five to seven times during the course of their work lives. Business and industry represent the largest providers of educational services today. Their instructional services are related to new employee training programs, career ladder training programs, and worker retraining. An implication of this trend for both public and private vocational and rehabilitation programs is that specific job-related skill instruction is often not an appropriate component of instructional programs because of the impact of rapid technological growth. Further, educational institutions cannot keep up with these new developments. Therefore, their vocational equipment, upon which students receive instruction, is usually obsolete by the time they get it — or shortly thereafter. Also, more employers are seeking high school graduates who have a general knowledge of the field and who have developed the appropriate academic, problem solving, and interpersonal skills to be successful and productive workers. The employer would prefer to provide the specific job skill training at the workplace, that is, on the job. Students participating in these programs receive their academic and interpersonal skill training in the school and their specific employment skill training in a real work situation. Therefore, those vocational, educational, and rehabilitation programs that are run in concert with the potential employer have proven to be most successful. For example, there are indications of a higher employment and retention rate among students trained in joint vocational training programs between education and business or industry.

The training and retraining trend will continue, and the frequency of required retrainings will increase for the employee of the 21st century. This is primarily due to the anticipated exponential growth of current and anticipated new advanced technologies. The flexible worker is the employee who is most receptive to retraining and, therefore, of more value to the employer. The individual unwilling to learn a new way of performing a task or a new skill represents the potentially unemployed person. Therefore, flexibility and a willingness to learn constitute crucial employment characteristics for the successful worker of the Information Age (Barnes, 1982). Today's students must be provided with these types of attitudes in their basic instructional programs and must learn skills which will prepare them to find and hold employment in the decades ahead. This is not meant to imply that all students must become proficient in the use of advanced technologies as a basic employment skill. It suggests that they must be prepared for the sociological, educational, and demographic realities that will effect their employability in the early part of the 21st century. Therefore, educational and training institutions must be willing to form active, flexible partnerships with business and industry, they must be willing to change their attitudes toward priorities in education, and they must be willing to change the curriculum and teaching approaches to meet the constantly changing educational needs of students at any age. If educators do not meet these changes, they will find themselves unemployed, and the task of education will transfer from educational institutions as we know them today to other sectors of society willing to make appropriate changes as needed.

Although many individuals think jobs in the fields related to the development and use of advanced electronic and information technologies, biomedical technology, and biomedical engineering as the areas of job growth in the 21st century, this is a very limited view of the employment picture projected for this era. As mentioned earlier, some rather significant changes in our society's demography are forecast for the Information Age. The projected increase in the number of older individuals and the anticipated increase in the average length of life will create a whole new range of service jobs. A large and growing older population will cause an expansion in the demand for medical support related services. This is particularly true for the population considered to be aged or elderly. As the life expectancy continues to rise into the 21st century, diseases whose incidence rises with age will become more prevalent, and new and unexpected medical problems will also appear. This factor will increase the demand for an increased number of health care and medical support workers.

The projected increase in the percentage of the total population that is older will also create the demand for other types of human services. It is forecast that the demand for recreational and leisure-related services will increase in direct proportion to the increase in the older population (Strom, 1982). As a result, the demand for workers in these fields will also rise. For example, many retirement communities hire social directors who plan and initiate a variety of activities from aquasizes to electronic games. Related to this topic is the anticipated increased demand for information. The older individual in the latter part of the 20th century and the early part of the 21st century is the person who will most likely require electronic technology systems for not only recreation, but also for communication and work. As new advanced technology systems become available for use by the general population, it is predicted that this population will become the prime consumer of these new information systems. The number of older people enrolled in colleges reinforces this perceived need for knowledge growth (Abbott, 1982). Further, this demand for information will create an increase in the number and variety of jobs in the electronic communication industries. The majority of these jobs will not be in the areas of designing systems or maintaining data bases; rather, the greatest demand will be in related communication fields such as knowledge and entertainment systems and program production support, clerical office support, sales, installation, and repair.

Another predicted change in the demography of the early 21st century, the dramatic increase in the percentage of women who work, will create a demand for other types of service occupations. There will be an increased need for day care centers and workers as more women embark on full or part-time careers. Further, it is projected that an increased number of working women will create a commensurate increase in the demand for home care; related support laborers; service workers; and electronic shopping, banking, and other errand-running or timesaving services (Coates, 1982).

Economic forecasts also indicate that there will be a rise in the number and variety of cottage industries in the Information Age (Turoff, 1975). Many of these will take the form of "electronic cottage industries" and will employ the interactive home computer as the primary work tool. This projected increase in cottage industries is primarily attributed to the increase in the number of older citizens, women in the work force, and all other workers who find working at home timesaving and cost-effective. The use of electronic communication technologies will permit these individuals to work on a part-time or a flex-time basis from their homes. Another group for whom a growth in the electronic cottage industry type of employment is projected is the handicapped, particularly the physically disabled. Adaptive communication devices, interactive electronic communication systems and robots will allow them to compensate for their weaknesses and permit them to enter the labor force by means of working at home in an employee or contractual capacity (Turoff, 1975).

The areas of environmental and hazardous waste collection and disposal plus energy provision are fields in which occupations are predicted to increase in the early part of the 21st century. Waste technologies are primarily concerned with the collection, transportation, and disposal of industrial and human waste materials. They are also involved with the reprocessing of certain of these materials so that they can be reused in an age of dwindling natural resources. The disposal of radiological, chemical, and biological hazardous wastes is another area of concern for this rather new occupation field. Current projections indicate that is would take almost one and a half million workers to clean up our nation's air, water, and land in the next decades. Dwindling natural energy resources in the 21st century are expected to generate a large demand for workers who produce and deliver synthetic fuels and solar energy to homes, government, and business and industry. Economic forecasts estimate that approximately one and a half million workers may be engaged in this type of employment by the turn of the century. (Cetron & O'Toole, 1982).

The structure as well as the location of jobs is projected to change over the next few decades. Business complexes are predicted to become decentralized, doing away with the large corporate or business headquarters (Baran, 1973). The primary reasons for this change are cost savings, better productivity, and the impact of electronic communication technologies. Large business complexes are costly to heat, light, maintain, and insure. They were originally conveived of as a location where the company's management and support clerical staff work and interact. The prime reasons for their development was to collect and maintain a central information storage and retrieval facility and to facilitate communication among workers. In this type of design, workers are required to commute to the central location. Traffic congestion and distance often add hours to the employee's day and, thus, waste the human resources of time and energy. Reliance upon mass transportation and traffic patterns cost thousands of hours of work time because of unavoidable communiting delays. Further, workers often arrive at their place of employment already tense and tired due to the rigors of traveling to work. All of these factors reduce productivity and increase corporate costs.

An increasing number of companies, particularly the large multinational corporations and the banking industry, are decentralizing their corporate headquarters operations; this trend is projected to become the most common form of business organization in the Information Age. In addition to the issues described above, the increasing availability of interactive electronic communication systems has contributed to this pattern of decentralization and will continue to do so. Workers do not need to be housed in one complex with close proximity to their colleagues and corporate records when computer based interactive communication networks are used by the employer. Business records and transactions are stored in electronic data bases and can be accessed by any employee with the appropriate security clearance at a linked computer terminal. Communication among workers is also conducted through teleconferencing rather than in personally attended meetings. Messages and memorandums are transmitted by electronic mail. As a result, the corporate headquarters is decentralized into strategically placed remote sites which are electronically interconnected. Not only does such a management and support staff distribution system reduce costs in terms of overhead expenses, it also causes savings in terms of human resources and a commensurate increase in productivity. Workers can live closer to their jobs and, therefore, spend less time commuting to work. Further, the decentralized sites will tend to be placed away from large urban areas, decreasing the commuting worker's loss of time due to mass transit or traffic delays. Less worker time is spent during the work day traveling to and from meetings, record files, and the work stations of other employees, which increases the amount of productive work time available.

Current forecasts indicate that decentralization will become the most common form of corporate organization in the Information Age. Knowledge and information will travel electronically rather than people traveling within a larger complex or to smaller remote corporate support sites. Worker productivity will increase with the use of computer linked communication and data retreival systems. Teleconferencing will replace the great majority of personal meetings. Workers will live closer to their work site and will spend less time commuting to their place of employment. Further, an increased number of workers will spend part of their time working from their home computer work station, which will be electronically linked to the company's communication network.

Interactively linked microcomputer-based information-processing and communication systems will form the basis of the office of the future (Mankin, Biksom, & Gutek, 1982; Michels, 1982). All clerical and management workers will be required to be able to use these systems as a condition of employment. Business records will be maintained on electronic data base systems. Computer-based artifically intelligent expert systems will assist the corporate decision maker with evaluating an ever-increasing amount of information, weighing alternatives, and inferring a solution to a problem. As stated earlier, the control and use of information is economic power in an Information Economy. Therefore, advanced electronic technologies will form the backbone of the structure of business and industry in the 21st century, the Information Age.

The concept of employees in the Information Age working from home computer work stations has been mentioned several times. This home-work station is linked to the business headquarters and to fellow employees by means of an electronic communication network. Although this type of work arrangement is projected for many workers in the 21st century, it does have a number of limitations. Current research by several large companies into the use of such a system indicates that the average employee cannot work exclusively from the home and that direct contact with fellow employees and with management must be maintained on a periodic basis in order to forestall feelings of isolation on the part of the home worker. These findings indicate that one day per week should be spent at the business work place in order for the worker to continue to be motivated to produce, to maintain the needed interpersonal contact, and to retain the concept of teamwork.

There are other problems that might affect the home-work station employee. When the office is moved into the home, the more traditional routine of going to the work place will have to be replaced by self-imposed discipline. There will be no one around the electronically connected home-work station to give the employee direction and to bring the individual back to the task at hand. There are no time clocks to tell the home worker when to begin the day, when the coffee break is over, or when to return from lunch. At home, there is no interpersonal incentive or tactile reinforcement for making that extra effort in doing an exceptionally good job. In the home-work environment, the worker has to make that commitment to return to the task at hand after each little distraction that occurs in the home. Further, when the office moves into the home, the sense of being "at home" will also change. No longer will the worker be able to leave the frustrations, angers, and headaches of work at the office. It will become more difficult for the worker to draw clear distinctions between work and recreation, between effort and relaxation.

Although these factors are important to the success of the home-work computer-linked station, most futurists project that more and more workers will be employed in this capacity on a full or part-time basis in the 21st century. Implicit in this forecast is the fact that management styles will have to change in order to accommodate the dynamics of the home worker. Business and industry are already exploring ways to compensate for some of the inherent problems mentioned (Mankin, Biksom, & Gutek, 1982; Michels, 1982). The incentive for them to find solutions to these problems and to make these new home-work situations successful is great: increased productivity, less overhead, and, therefore, greater corporate profits. An increasing number of workers who will use their home as their primary office is going to be, therefore, a reality of the Information Age.

Students currently enrolled in special education programs will also be the workers of the 21st century. They must receive instruction now that will prepare them to find and hold a job in the Information Age, and they must receive the basic foundations for learning specific skills. They need to understand the concept that careers and jobs will change rapidly because of constant technological advances. They must learn how to communicate and cooperate effectively with others both directly and through nonhuman electronic systems. They must understand that learning and retraining are necessary throughout one's life, and of necessity, they must become lifelong learners. Finally, they must understand that increased numbers of workers will use technical equipment to perform nontechnical jobs. If today's students master these employment concepts now, they will be better prepared to become productive and valued employees in the 21st century, the Information Age.

## MEDICINE AND HEALTH

The post–World War II era has experienced spectacular growth in the delivery of medical and health services (Lesse, 1978; Medicine in the post-physician era, 1978). These industries have merged brainpower, imagination, and technology to produce dramatic breakthorughs in the prevention, treatment, and care of the individual afflicted by disease or disability. During this period, the percentage of older citizens has continued to increase and the average length of life has expanded. Further, reductions in the infant and neonatal mortality rate have been dramatic; in technically developed nations, less than one child in one hundred dies in the first year of life. New diagnostic procedures based on microelectronic technologies have permitted medical professionals to see and test the functions of parts of the body that had previously been hidden. Chemotherapy developments have resulted in the effective treatment of diseases that had previously been untreatable. Synthetic organs and microelectronic prosthetic devices have successfully replaced parts of the human body. Biofeedback techniques have been used as preventive measures and as methods of monitoring and controlling prosthetic limbs and braces. Advanced technologies such as lasers have been adapted by the medical profession for use as surgical tools. Whole new areas of medical science such as genetic engineering, biomedical engineering, biomedical technology, and rehabilitation medicine have been developed as new research areas and have been applied to the medical and health fields (Weil, 1982).

During the same period, the United States population has become increasingly health conscious, manifesting a greater interest in the fields of health and medicine and have become better educated about such issues as the potential negative effects of smoking, excessive drinking, and food additives. Diet, exercise, and a return to natural foods have taken on greater importance, not only with medical professionals, but also with an increasing number of general citizens. The concept of preventive health care has taken root and is receiving greater attention. This attention to healthy life styles has, in turn, contributed to the increase in the average life span of the general population.

These and other developments in the medical and health related fields have been expensive. The development of new advanced technological diagnostic and treatment devices and the need for trained technicians to operate them have accounted for a considerable amount of the rise in medical and health-related costs. Approximately 10% of the gross national product in the mid-1980s was spent on health care and related medical research. Current projections indicate that this figure will rise to approximately 20% of the gross national product by the turn of the century. Also, increasing numbers of individuals have been employed in the medical and health industries. This trend of an increasing number of workers in these fields is predicted to continue into and expand in the 21st century (Cetron & O'Toole, 1982).

Continued research, development, and application of new advanced technologies are projected to result in spectacular growth in the medical and health fields in the early part of the 21st century. These new developments will serve to alter the life styles of the citizens of that future age. One of the primary changes that is projected to occur during this period is an alteration in the current concept of medicine and mental health treatment. Western medicine in general has traditionally been disease-oriented, a situation in which treatment is not begun until the patient has been ill or disabled, although there has been more recent interest in preventive medicine. Projections for medical and health services in the 21st century indicate that a preventive or "health-oriented" approach to treatment will replace the current disease-oriented one. This new focus on wellness and prevention is attributed to the fact that, in the Information Age, the fields of medicine and health will be responsible for the prevention, diagnosis, and treatment of disease in a world radically different from that of today; a world of advanced technologies, of changes in demography, and of new medical, scientific, and engineering developments.

The area of mental health, particularly the fields of psychiatry, psychology, and psychotherapy, will also be affected by this philosophical change and will stress the prevention and early treatment of disorders. Currently, the basic approach focuses on dealing with the presenting symptoms and on attempting to modify or change those maladaptive behaviors and attitudes by stressing that the current habits, frustrations, problem identifications, and behaviors are the direct result of prior events over which the client has had little or no control. Futurists project a switch in the mental health fields to a new future-oriented approach aimed at the prevention and early treatment of mental disorders. The emphasis will focus the client's attention on what will probably occur in the future, drawing thoughts away from the client's personal desires or biases about the future and away from dwelling on the past (Lesse, 1978). The Information Age implies rapid and continual change, an ever-increasing variety of new advanced technologies, and almost unlimited access to information. These dynamics and others of the 21st century can cause feelings of uncertainty, lack of control over one's destiny, uneasiness, and anomie in those individuals who merely focus on the present and the past while ignoring or rejecting the future. The projected future-oriented philosophy in the fields of mental health will be directed toward preventing and treating early these and other possible reations of tomorrow's citizen in the world of the Information Age.

Computers and other microelectronic technologies are foreseen as playing a far more significant role in the delivery of medical and mental services in the 21st century. Although this is already occurring, current projections indicate that a great many of the technical functions currently being performed by physicians and allied health professionals will be taken over by advanced computers with artificially intelligent expert systems and large storage capabilities. Two of the areas in which these developments are predicted to occur first are in the maintenance of patients' care histories and in patient diagnosis.

The rapidity of new developments in the medical and health fields makes it almost impossible for the medical and health professional to keep abreast of them. The current solution to this dilemma has been to train and develop increasing numbers of specialists whose expertise is limited to one very specific area of diagnosis and treatment. Although this approach has resulted in a higher level of advanced "state-of-the-art" care, it has also created a fragmented view of the patient. Further, the speed with which new treatments and developments have occurred has made it difficult even for these specialists to keep up. The problem, therefore, is one of accessing and using ever-growing amounts of information. The information explosion will increasingly affect the medical profession, just as it will the rest of society in the Information Age. The use of current and future computer technologies is viewed as the only viable solution to the dilemma of information overload in the medical and health professions.

Computer technologies are predicted to perform, or at least form the basis of, most of the medical and mental health patient diagnoses in the 21st century. The computer equipped with artifically intelligent expert systems brings to the diagnostic process three key elements: extensive memory, logic and probability, and objectivity. A computer diagnostic system would contain all of the known information of the medical and health professions, the collective memory and knowledge of all medical practitioners. This data base could be updated as soon as a new disease, treatment, or procedure was developed, and the new information would then be integrated into the existing memory file. This data base would also contain the full medical, familial, and health history of the patient from the time of birth or, in many instances, from the neonatal period. All of this information would be used by the computer system to diagnose the presenting problem of a patient and to suggest the variety of treatment approaches that have previously proven effective in ameliorating the condition. Upon the receipt of further information about the reaction of the patient to the treatment plan, the computer system would adjust the suggested prescription(s). Thus, the memory capacity and almost instantaneous processing of patient information by the computer would provide a solution to the information overload currently plaguing the medical profession (Medicine in the post-physician era, 1978).

Computers also bring the important element of neutrality to the diagnostic situation. They are always rational and objective. They cannot be influenced, as human physicians and diagnosticians can, by personal emotions, feelings, or personal physical health when making a diagnosis. Although this may seem to some individuals like a cold approach to patient diagnosis, a computer system brings the important element of objective consistency and an assurance of no diagnoses based on emotion.

In the mental health fields, computer diagnosis has already begun to prove effective. Current research has shown that a comprehensive battery of diagnostic tests can be administered to a client on a computer terminal in a much shorter period of time than when administered to a client by a human diagnostician. The results of the computer diagnosis are generally available to the practitioner within one minute after the testing is completed. Current studies have found that most clients taking diagnostic tests on a computer enjoyed the experience. They tended to be more relaxed and did not view the experience as threatening or as having the degree of social stigma that often occurs when a client is interviewed and tested by a human practitioner. Since the diagnostic testing is usually completed at one sitting, most clients feel that they are receiving individual and prompt attention. The problem of visual observations during the testing situation have been negated by directly observing the computer diagnostic process or by means of a videotaped record, which is viewed by the professional at a later time. Current projections indicate that the use of computer systems will become the principal method of mental health diagnosis employed in the 21st century.

Some medical and health futurists also forecast the use of microelectronic telecommunication systems interfaced with the home computer Net Console as the basic component of preventive and diagnostic services in the 21st century. The Net Console, with its interactive multisensory communication and television capabilities, will allow the citizens of the Information Age to receive much of their medical care from their homes. Sensing devices will monitor the individual's vital signs and general physiological condition. This information would then be transmitted instantaneously to the master medical computer, where it would be integrated into that individual's case history file. A visual examination of the individual could also be conducted by a medical professional through the interactive television system. Skin attached or implanted vaccine and medicine pouches could also be activated by the practitioner electronically through this system, permitting the professional to alter the dosage or to change the patient's medication from a remote site. The patient would only go to the physician's office, to a medical center, or to a hospital if the computer diagnosis indicated the need for more intensive evaluation or treatment. It is also predicted that the interactive multisensory Net Console system will allow patients to receive individual or group therapy in their homes. This type of electronic medical monitoring and assessment would occur at a reduced cost and with less inconvenience to the patient. Current projections indicate that this type of electronic medical and health service delivery will be a pervasive component of the home computer Net Console in the 21st century.

Biomedical and rehabilitation engineering has made huge strides in recent years in the development of synthetic organs, mirocelectric prosthetic devices and braces, sensory enhancement artifices, and electronic environmental control and self-care tools. Futurists' medical and health projections indicate that these developments will continue and will become even more spectacular in the 21st century due to the development of new advanced technologies. Current predictions forecast that robotics and bionics will become important medical, health, and rehabilitation treatment tools in the next decades. Bionics will play an important role in the design and production of artifical appendages such as legs, arms, and fingers, units which will be controlled through the use of biofeedback techniques. Robotic braces, prostheses, and transportation devices will provide mobility and self-care functions to individuals previously immobile or dependent. These units will employ advanced computer systems and many will be controlled by means of biofeedback or interactive voice systems. One example of an early form of such a device is the robotic arm that was recently developed for the Veterans Administration. This voice controlled unit permits a quadriplegic to perform such self-care activities as grooming and feeding. It is also sensitive enough to allow the user to type and thus, to control a computer's input device including a keyboard. The robotic arm design made several "improvements" in the human arm; six fingers with two opposing thumbs for better grasp and manipulation, sensors in the fingers to provide greater fine motor control, and a 360-degree arm rotation. Due to these changes in the structure of the robotic arm, the user can achieve with one robotic arm almost the degree of control, grasp and release, and movement that the average person can with two natural arms. The fields of bionics and robotics, then, are seen as being technological normalization devices for the physically handicapped, the disabled, and the aged in the 21st century (Jaffe, 1987).

Biomedical and rehabilitation engineering are predicted to become increasingly important branches of medical science in the next decades, particularly in the development of synthetic body parts. Already medical scientists in this field have produced functional artifical hearts. Within the next decade, medical projections indicate that this field will develop artificial colons and a synthetic blood substitute. As with other technological developments, this field is projected to grow exponentially in the 21st century. Current forecasts indicate that the synthetic body replacements that will become available to the medical and rehabilitation professions during the next century will include artificial blood vessels, limbs, extremities, skin, ears, kidneys, livers, and tongues. Further, many medical futurists project the availability of the artificial womb, a device which will not primarilly be developed for the convenience of the general female population, but for use in cases of high risk pregnancies. Development in pharmacology will make the implantation of these synthetic body parts rather routine with little risk of infection or body rejection.

The pharmaceutical industry has made great strides in the development of vaccines and medications that have eradicated the danger of many previously untreatable diseases and disorders. As with other areas of medical and health sciences, this industry is projected to experience continued growth with major breakthoughs anticipated in the 21st century. It is predicted that skin patch and skin implanted techniques for injecting vaccines and medications will become the most common form of chemotherapy delivery in the next decades for children, the aged, and those with chronic health disorders. These chemotherapy pouches would hold a year's supply of medication and would release a prescribed dosage directly into the blood stream or into the skin at predetermined intervals. They would also be able to hold and individually release up to a dozen different medications. The diabetic user of such a chemotherapy delivery system would not have to administer insulin daily since the skin implanted medical pouch would release the physician's prescribed dosage directly into the blood stream either at predetermined times or based on the body's insulin level as read by an implanted insulin sensitive microchip. The interactive telecommunication capabilities of the home computer Net Console would allow the attending physician to monitor the patient from a remote location and would permit the professional to change the dosage or the frequency of medication through the same system by transmitting an electronic command to the implanted medication pack. Newborns would receive either a skin patch or an implant before leaving the hospital. These units would contain all of the required immunization vaccines and would release them at the appropraite age. Early forms of these devices have already been developed and are currently being used by the medical profession in the treatment of such ailments as heart disorders.

It is projected that the pharmaceutical industry and its related research sciences will develop a whole host of new medications in the 21st century. These new chemotherapy techniques will ameliorate or assist the medical and health practioner in treating a variety of diseases and disorders. Medical forecasts indicate that a chemical cure for most forms of cancer will be developed early in the next century. Other areas of current research that are anticipated to result in a chemotherapy medication for the general population in the next few decades are a permanent stimulator of intelligence, the ability to lengthen or shorten memory, and chemicals to improve one's ability to learn facts and concepts. These medications are projected to be adminstered in the prenatal stage and probably during the first trimester. The development of these chemotherapy medications will raise some interesting questions in the Information Age for the field of special education, such as: what is "normal" intelligence, what constitutes developmental disabilities or mental retardation, and who is intellectually or learning disabled? Additional developments in this field that are predicted for the 21st century include: chemical cures for schizophrenia, chemical control of hypertension, chemical control of aggression, successful chemical treatment of depression, and chemical treatment to modify some forms of criminal behavior.

Genetic engineering is anticipated to become a major field of medical research and treatment in the 21st century and is expected to result in the evolution of new medications and vaccines using human hormones. As a result, current projections predict that genetic engineering developments will allow the control of growth and height, the retardation of the aging process, and the stimulation of human proteins to fight infections. Other forecasts of potential developments in this field include: the successful replacement of human organs with those of animals, in utero genetic modifications, and the ability to regenerate body limbs and extremities (Weil, 1982).

In summary of this section, the futurists' medical and health projections for the 21st century predict that greater attention will be focused on wellness and on preventive treatment. Microelectronic telecommunication systems will allow the home computer Net Console user to receive medical monitoring, diagnosis, and simple treatment in the home. Developments in biomedical and rehabilitation engineering will result in the replacement of certain body parts with synthetic ones using electronic technology-based interactive prosthetics and braces. New chemotherapy developments will ameliorate the effects of certain diseases and disorders and will permit greater control of the dosage and the time of adminstration of certain medications. Genetic engineering will allow new biological control of certain diseases and certain physical disabilities. The implications of these forecasts are that many disabled people can anticipate medical and health treatments that hold the potential of permitting them to move independently, communicate, sense, remember, and think in an improved manner. Certain of these developments may also require the fields of special education and rehabilitation to redefine the composition of the groups they serve in order to determine which individuals are disabled in the Information Age of the 21st century.

## EDUCATION

Historically our nation has viewed education as a system whose primary tasks are to pass on to future generations the values and mores of the society, to teach the basic academic skills so that all future citizens are literate and knowledgeable, and to prepare the young to take their places as employed and productive adults. Education has traditionally been viewed as the organizational structure that prepares the next generation to be our society's future. Although these lofty goals remain the basic tenets of education, our public and private educational institutions have recently come under increasing attack. There have been countless books, articles, and studies whose main purpose is to call our attention to the state of American education today. Major reports such as *A Nation at Risk* (National Commission on Excellence in Education, 1983; Technology Task Force, 1985), and *The Padieia Proposal* (Response to Mortimer Adler's Proposal, 1984) have all suggested one thing — the need for improving our current educational systems.

Although these and other reports and studies point out much that needs improvement in our educational institutions, it is not enough to attempt to correct only these identified deficits; the content and structure of today's educational programs must be examined as a whole. The current generation of students will not have to shape our nation's future in the latter part of the 20th century; they represent the first generation that will live most of their lives in the 21st century. Their world will be the world of the Information Age. Their future is tied to such dynamics as rapid and continuous change, instantaneous and almost unlimited access to information, advanced multisensory interactive world-wide communication systems, and a world served by advanced electronic technologies.

Educational futurists predict a variety of changes in the structure, content, populations served, and method(s) of instruction in the schools and other educational institutions of the 21st century. These projected alternatives for our society's educational organizations reflect the potential impact of the other projections that were discussed previously in this chapter. The decisions we make today will shape much of our nation's future, the world of our children. Unless we approach the revamping and revitalizing of our educational institutions with a forward-looking perspective, many of our positive future alternatives will vanish. For us to focus our attention totally upon our current educational crises is to renounce our responsibilities to our children and to limit both the scope and range of alternatives for their future. We must look at the world of tomorrow now, as we plan the future directions of our educational programs. We must also evaluate the educational futurists' alternative views of the role of education in the 21st century so that redesign of our educational system leads to the achievement of those projections. The actions we take today will directly affect whether or not we will have the type of educational programs and institutions that will meet the diverse needs of the citizens and children of the Information Age. They will also determine whether or not our children are adequately prepared to deal with the complexities of life in the 21st century.

The economic and employment projections of the 21st century will necessitate modifications in a number of the current practices of our educational institutions. As stated earlier, access to and the control of information constitutes economic power in the Information Age. The vast majority of workers will be employed in service and information processing jobs, whereas a decreasing percentage will be employed in the production of food and goods. Rapid technological development and the impact of advanced electronic technologies will require that the successful employees of the future be flexible, lifelong learners and that they be receptive to continuous change. These workers can expect to be retrained at least five to seven times during their employment careers, and the frequency and number of retrainings will be directly related to the exponential growth of new technological developments.

One of the results of these economic and employment predictions is that there must be close cooperation among schools, business and industry, and government (Abbott, 1982; Cetron, 1985; Sturdivant, 1983). Cooperative efforts between business and schools do exist today in many parts of the country; however, it is projected that in the 21st century these partnerships will become an integral element in both the operation and the role of schools in the future. The private sector, business and industry, will be an active participant in public education. It will provide financial support, instructional materials and equipment, and staff, and it will help determine the curricular goals.

The partnership between business and education will be a mutually beneficial and dependent arrangement. Educational institutions need financial assistance. Their current funding structure depends heavily upon the taxation of the local home owner. The demographic projections for the early part of the 21st century indicate that older citizens will constitute the majority of the total population. This group tends to have the least vested interest in public education, since their children have already matured. Government support for education has begun to decrease, a trend that is predicted to continue through the next few decades. Part of the reason for this is attributed to the fact that government spending priorities often reflect the needs and desires of its constituency. In the Information Age, the largest demographic constituency will be the older population. All of these factors indicate that educational systems will have to look to new sources of revenue to fund their programs. Business and industry represent the potential source of these needed revenues, and the establishment of a mutually beneficial partnership will do much to ameliorate the financial troubles of schools in the future.

Business and industry also have a great deal to gain from such cooperation since much of their economic viability will be determined by the success of the schools' educational training programs. They are dependent upon the schools to supply them with experienced and employable high school and college graduates, graduates who are prepared to be flexible lifelong learners. Since much of the economy of the 21st century will be related to the provision of services and information, they will also depend upon the educational institutions to graduate potential consumers of these service products, consumers who are technologically literate. Finally, business and industry will need the schools to assist them in retraining their current employees, particularly those who require further education in order to benefit from new job-related skill training. The revenues that the private sector pays for this retraining also represents an additional source of income for schools. Because of the necessity for schools and companies to be cost-effective, much of the training that students of all ages will receive will not be in the classroom as we know it today. The instructional site will vary with the needs of the individual and with the objectives to be achieved. Technology will be used to educate in the home, on the work site, or in meeting places (the redesigned school of today that will be more cost and energy effective). Knowledge and training will occur across miles from experts and data bases, from interactive television or computer teleconferencing, and from simulators. The approaches and medium for instruction will be based on individual learning approaches and objectives. Education must make significant changes and take on active partnerships in order to survive.

Vocational education has experienced particular difficulty in keeping abreast of new technologies. The equipment required to teach employment related skills is expensive and quickly becomes obsolete due to the speed with which new technologies are developed. Further, it has become increasingly difficult for schools to retrain their vocational education teachers in the use of new equipment and techniques. Business and industry, however, must maintain "state-of-the-art" technology and techniques in order to remain fiscally solvent. Therefore, educational futurists project that the private sector will become the primary source of vocational educational equipment for the schools, in whatever form. Further, individuals from business and industry will be called upon to provide specific skill instruction to students. It is predicted that this instruction will primarily occur in two ways. In the first instance, private sector employees will provide training to vocational educators in the use of new technologies and techniques. It can be anticipated that the private sector will share with schools the latest simulation vocational training materials and techniques such as interactive video and laser disc instructional programs. They will also provide some direct vocational skill instruction to students in the schools, generally on a part-time basis. Representatives of the private sector will assist educators in designing and updating curricula in order to reflect the continuous changes in the world of work and in society as a whole. Not only does this type of private sector involvement assist the schools, it also assists business and industry by allowing them to invest in their corporate future.

The second manner in which the private sector is projected to cooperate with schools is to provide on-the-job training to students in a work-study type of arrangement. In these instances, students would spend part of the day in school or at home for instruction in the academic areas. The remainder of the day would be spent in a business setting where they would receive specific employment skill training. Most educational futurists predict that all students, including the college bound, will participate in this type of work-study program. The rationale offered for this forecast is that one of the objectives of the educational systems and of the private sector is to have all graduates become productive employees and that, in the rapidly changing world of the Information Age, students must develop the employment skills and attitudes that are required of the successful worker of that era while they are still in school.

Cooperative partnerships between educational institutions and the private sector will probably result in a decrease in the number of four year colleges. Many of the jobs that will develop in the 21st century will require only a two-year post-secondary school education. Specific job skill training and retraining will be provided by business and industry either directly or through contracts with schools. Public education will help to evolve the basis for the development of job skills, which will be a combined effort and responsibility of education and business. Further, an increased number of private sector companies are predicted to provide financial support to employees to assist them in attending higher education institutions on a part-time basis. The company would, therefore, direct the employee into the specific educational program that would enhance the worker's skills and that would meet the training needs of the firm. This factor would probably mean a decrease in the number of college students enrolled in liberal arts programs.

Special education's vocational and rehabilitation programs will also benefit from the projected cooperative partnership between business and schools. All vocational training assistance mentioned previously will be available to the handicapped student. Further, an increased number of sheltered workshop and special vocational training programs will be located in business settings, rather than in separate simulated environments. The handicapped and disabled participant will not only receive training but will also be paid for the actual work produced. Such joint private sector and special education programs have increasingly begun to appear throughout the country. They have proven to be the most beneficial form of vocational education for the handicapped student. Further, the cooperative sheltered workshop programs have benefited both business and the disabled worker. The handicapped worker is receiving pay for gainful employment, and the business is receiving a viable product. Further, the current social security disability laws covers the insurance liabilities and fringe benefits of the sheltered workshop employees, thus removing this cost from the employer. It is projected that this type of cooperative special education and private sector arrangement will continue and expand in the next decades. One such program, an example of how far this type of cooperation can develop, is located in Sweden (Zimmer, 1985). Private industry built a totally robotic production plant. The employees who control the robots by pushing the appropriate buttons to start or stop them are all mentally handicapped adults functioning within the trainable to moderate range. This situation is mutually beneficial because the handicapped workers are gainfully employed and the company is producing a cost-effective product.

Another manner in which the private sector is projected to benefit the fields of special education and rehabilitation is in the development of new adaptive electronic communication devices and in prosthetic self-help, mobility, and environmental control devices. Business and industry have become increasingly involved in the development of these electronic prosthetic tools in recent years. In certain instances, this has been due to the altruistic interests of certain companies; however, increasing numbers of companies have become active developers of these systems because of their interest in their temporarily and permanently disabled employees (First annual conference on the employment of the disabled, 1987). Electronic technology and adaptive communication devices developed for the handicapped can also be used successfully by the private sector to permit their valued disabled employees to either return to work or to work from their homes. This trend is expected to continue and grow in the next decades because of the projected shift in demographics. An increased number of private sector employees will be older in the early part of the 21st century and, as a result, will have a greater need for such electronic prosthetic devices. Not only will older employees use these devices to maintain productivity on the job but they will represent an increasingly larger percentage of the potential consumer market for service and information products. Therefore, the private sector's cooperation in developing these devices is, for them, an investment in their corporate futures.

The predicted changes in the nation's demography in the 21st century will also affect the structure of education. As mentioned earlier, the older and aging will become an increasingly larger precentage of the total population. This group tends to have the greater amount of leisure time and, as present trends indicate, some people use that time to go back to school in order to pursue topics of personal interest or to attain a degree. As a result, schools will increase the scope and variety of their adult educational program options. As the pre-college population continues to decline in percentage of the total population, adult education will become a more important component of the total educational system. It is also predicted that older citizens will use their home computer Net Consoles to participate in interactive adult education courses offered electronically by schools, colleges, and universities. Open universities based on telecommunications are already in operation around the world. Further, the increased availability of adult education offerings, both day and evening as well as telecommunication opportunities, will reinvolve the older population in the schools and provide them with a new vested interest in the maintenance of quality programs: a trend that can be noted in most colleges across the country.

Another demographic factor that will have direct impact on education in the Information Age is the projected increase in the percentage of women who work. As mentioned earlier, approximately 75% of all women are anticipated to be employed, either full or part-time, by the turn of the century. This will create a demand for increased numbers of preschool and child care programs. Business and industry will be pressured by these workers to institute directly or to subcontract for such preschool programs. Alternative child care services are being developed today, as are flexible work hours and home-work stations. As a result of this demographic projection, education futurists predict that schools will, either independently or on a subcontractual basis with the private sector, provide infant care, child care, and preschool programs as a part of their total educational structure. Thus, the demographic impact of the aging of our society, the increase in the number of working women, and the economic implications of the private sector's retraining requirements indicate that education will be providing services to multiple segments of society in the 21st century. It will provide instruction to citizens of all ages, and the scope of its programs will extend "from womb to tomb."

A final demographic factor that will have impact upon the schools of the future deals with the issues of volunteers. Traditionally, women have constituted the majority of the volunteers who provide assistance to schools and teachers and who provide individual tutorial help to students. Since 75% of women are predicted to be employed in the Information Age, schools will have to find another group to furnish these volunteer services. Educational futurists predict that the older segment of the population, in particular those individuals who are either fully or partially retired, will provide these services in the future, a service that this group now provides in many communities. Not only would these citizens have the time to devote to such activities, but they would bring to the schools and to the entire instructional program all of their rich and varied life experiences. Certain futurists, therefore, view the schools of the future as the societal structure that will provide the "extended family" experience to children.

The structure of educational institutions is projected to change in the 21st century. Most educational futurists predict that both the length of the school days and the annual school calendar will be expanded in the next decades. This is viewed as being in direct response to a number of factors including: increasing emphasis on excellence in education, increasing complexities in the daily living skills required of life in the Information Age, financial implications, the projected changes in the nation's demography, and the availability of technology for telecommunications. One of the major criticisms of education today, as evidenced in the content of the reports cited at the beginning of this section, is the continued high national rate of functional illiteracy among secondary school graduates. This illiteracy breeds functional and fiscal dependency in our increasingly complex society. As a result, the general public is demanding that schools strive to decrease this illiteracy rate and serve as the vehicle to remove the problem from society as a whole. The concept of illiteracy is further complicated by the fact that a new form of literacy is becoming crucial to functional independence in the Information Age — technological literacy. Today's students will have to learn these technological and information-processing skills in order to function independently in the coming decades. They will have to learn how to communicate with others and how to search, locate, and use information data bases through artifically intelligent computer systems.

As a result, technological literacy is rapidly becoming the fourth "R" in education. Further, since current projections indicate an exponential growth in new and advanced technologies, the concept of technological literacy will be continually changing in the world of the 21st century. Therefore, in order to improve basic literacy and to provide for a technological literacy, schools of the future will have to expand the amount of time devoted to instruction by lengthening both the school day and the school year.

As mentioned earlier, the variety of skills that the potential employee of the future must bring to the work place will become increasingly complex and demanding. Private industry wants schools to produce graduates who are flexible, lifelong learners and who have mastered the appropriate worker attitude and interpersonal skills required to make them productive employees. Increasing numbers of educators today are complaining that there is not enough time in the school schedule to teach all of the subjects and concepts currently required. In order to implement comprehensive future-oriented prevocational and vocational technology programs in the schools, it will be necessary either to remove some of the current curriculum requirements or to extend both the school day and the school year. Projections indicate that the latter alternative will be chosen by the schools of the future.

Colleges and universities learned many years ago that it is not cost-effective to allow their physical plant to remain vacant for one quarter of the year. Public schools, however, do not tend to make such efficient use of their facilities. Greater fiscal accountability and a decreasing revenue base will act as the most powerful incentives for schools to extend the school day, to increase their adult education programs, and to extend the school year. Further, considering the fact that a great majority of school systems are projected to offer full-year preschool and child care programs, which will be partially subsidized by contracts with the private sector, the financial incentive to extend the school day and the school year will become more attractive. Finally, if schools are to provide retraining services to the private sector for a tuition charge in the future, they will have to offer instructional programs that correspond to the hours of the employee's work day during the entire year.

The demographic projection that at least three-quarters of the women in the 21st century will be employed either on a part or full-time basis presents another reason for educational systems to extend the school day and the school year. Increasing numbers of families will require custodial care for their children during the time that both parents are at work. Since these individuals represent an active and vocal constituency among school voters, and since the appeal for such an extension of the school day and school year will appeal to them, and since the private sector will probably support these requests, schools will be increasingly pressured to take such action. Finally, it have been projected that increased numbers of parents may remove their children from private schools if the public schools offered such expanded instructional programs, a factor that is important to school systems experiencing the phenomenon of declining pupil enrollment, school closings, and staff layoffs.

Education futurists projections indicate that there will be fewer four year colleges and universities in the 21st century. This prediction reflects a number of factors related to several other forecasts. The changing employment requirements of business and industry in the service economy of the Information Age will result in the need for an increased number of workers with specific technological skills. Current educational projections indicate that two-year post-secondary school institutions will serve as the primary vehicles for providing much of this instruction in the future. In many instances, these schools will offer work-study programs in cooperation with the private sector. The prediction that increasing numbers of post-secondary school students will be employed while attending institutions of higher learning portends an increase in the number that will participate in collegiate external degree programs (EDPs). Students enrolled in EDP programs spend little or no time on campus and receive instruction through correspondence curriculums or media presentations. Lecture and tutorial assistance is generally provided through mass media such as radio and television. In the past few years there has been a significant increase in the number of schools offering EDP programs. Educational futurists predict that this trend will continue and become a major component of post-secondary school education in the next decades. Should this projection come in fruition, it is predicted that there will be a commensurate decrease in the number of residential colleges and universities. A final factor that is predicted to effect four year colleges and universities in the Information Age is the projected impact of new and advanced microelectronic telecommunication systems. The growth of the video and laser disc industry will provide the capability for individuals to "attend" lectures at home. Further, the home computer Net Console system is foreseen as one of the primary delivery systems of post-secondary school education in the Information Age. The use of this approach would permit students to interactively participate in classes, receive tutorial assistance, and take examinations from their home computer console. All of these factors have contributed to the projection by educational futurists that there will be fewer four year colleges and universities and, in particular, residential schools in the 21st century. They also provide support for the contention that the number of two-year post-secondary schools that offer specific technical training will increase during the same period.

Current and future microelectronic technologies are predicted to have significant impact on the schools of the Information Age. Although computers and related technologies are increasingly used in education today, it is predicted that these and other new advanced technology systems will form the backbone of instruction and school administration in the 21st century. Part of this projection by educational futurists is based upon the belief that schools of the future will stress individual learning plans for all students as opposed to the group instructional approach utilized today (Cetron, 1985; Dillon & Wright, 1982). Students will move through a predetermined scope and sequence of skills at their own pace. Each child will have specific learning objectives for each academic subject. Student progress will be monitored by the teacher on a master computer control unit. As predicted with the medical and health industries, the schools of the 21st century will also use computers to adminster the majority of the educational diagnostic, ability, and achievement tests given to students. These expert computer systems will quickly provide the instructor with a diagnostic summary and a list of suggested learning objectives. The academic program and past educational records of each student will also be maintained in the master computer's memory. These computer systems, which will be equipped with artifically intelligent expert systems, will integrate the diagnostic data, the student's current performance level, and the student's past academic history in order to provide the teacher with suggested educational prescriptions (including a specific sequence of performance objectives as well as methods and materials designed to meet the student's individual learning style and major learning modality). Each student's plan will be determined on the basis of computerized achievement and ability diagnostic tests, past academic history, and teacher and parent input.

Computers and other electronic technologies will become essential components of school administration, record keeping, and teacher training in the 21st century. Although increasing numbers of school administrators are currently using computers to perform many of the tasks previously done by hand, the computer with expert business, projective, and educational systems will become the basic tool of school administrations in the Information Age. Computers and related electronic technologies will be used for school management in the same manner as they are used by business and industry. All aspects of the school program including student and staff scheduling, staff and student attendance, personnel records, student and staff medical records, negotiations, accounting, inventory and maintenance control, caferteria management and control, fiscal and budgetary predictions and projections, negotiations, transportation, correspondence, adult education, and extracurricular activity will be processed and the records maintained on computer systems. Staff meetings within the school system and on regional, state, and national levels will be conducted through the use of computerized teleconferencing systems. Mail and memorandums will be transmitted electronically. Mandated state and federal reports will also be developed on computer and transmitted electronically. All student records will be maintained on the master computer system and electronically forwarded to the pupil's teacher upon request. Further, in the event that a student moves, his or her entire educational history will be electronically transmitted to the receiving school anywhere in the nation. Educational futurists, therefore, predict that the use of the computer and other electronic technologies will permit the school administrator of the 21st century to have more time to devote to supervision, curriculum development, and the instruction of students.

Teacher training programs will also be affected by the impact of computers and related technologies in the Information Age. The application of interactive multisensory teleconferencing systems will allow teachers to participate in teacher training programs either at school or at their own home computer console. Video and laser disc systems will permit them to practice and receive immediate feedback on their newly acquired skills in interactive multisensory simulations. Electronic teleconferencing systems will also allow teachers to share their knowledge and techniques with other educators throughout the nation. Finally, they will be able to interactively participate in college proficiency unit (CPU) and graduate study programs at home through their Net Console. In the era of the 21st century, an age in which the knowledge base doubles annually and in which new advanced technologies develop exponentially, the computer and related electronic technology systems will provide the only cost-effective and timesaving methods to provide in-service and advanced study training programs to teachers.

Projections about the schools of the future indicate that the vast majority of the academic instructional materials provided to students will be electroinc, primarily in the form of computer-assisted instructional software and through access to information data bases. The video and laser disc will come into increased use as simulation tools that permit pupils to apply newly mastered skills to real life situations. Emphasis in the schools of the future will be on performance and criterion-referenced evaluation of pupil skill mastery. The objectives of educational programs in the Information Age, therefore, will be to equip students with the functional academic and technological literacy skills that are required in a world of continuous change and instantaneous access to almost unlimited information.

Most educational futurists predict that electronic textbooks will become the principle form of academic instructional material used in schools in the Information Age. As a result, the printed textbook will gradually become "a thing of the past." The knowledge data base of most areas will be expanding at such a rapid pace that it will be impossible for the publishing industry to provide current and topical instructional texts in any other format. Currently, it takes most educational publishers three to five years to produce a textbook, longer for a comprehevsive textbook series. In many subjects such as science, the material presented in the text is obsolete at the time of publication. Electronic textbooks can be updated continuously and economically as the knowledge base changes and grows. In the world of the Information Age, a world of continuous and rapid growth in the knowledge base, the use of electronic instructional materials will be the only way in which schools can hope to provide their students with cost-effective and topically relevent textbooks.

Instruction in technological literacy is predicted to become one of the core curricula in the school of the future. Students will receive instruction in the use of a variety of advanced technology communication, environmental control, self-care, and recreation systems. They will be exposed not only to computers but also to robots, artifical intelligence systems, video and laser discs, and a variety of electronic interactive and multisensory communication systems as a part of their normal program of instruction. All pupils will be required to receive instruction in electronic communication and teleconferencing since the ability to communicate with a computer and with other individuals through a computer will constitute basic daily living and employment skills in the 21st century. They will also have to develop the skills required to distinguish between human and machine intelligence as they communicate electronically. Large electronic data bases will be commonly used as reading and research sources and will lead to the school's increasing use of these and other "electronic libraries." These data bases and the multisensory capabilities of interactive communication systems will provide students with access to all of the knowledge of society through their classroom computer learning station. Functional daily living systems such as word processing will become standard instructional materials in every classroom at all instructional levels. Inductive reasoning, as opposed to deductive reasoning, will be stressed in order to prepare students to solve problems in an era of constantly expanding amounts of electronic information. The recreational uses of technology will also be included as a component of the basic technological literacy program.

Educational futurists forecast that electronic communication technologies will extend the classroom into the home in the 21st century. The home computer Net Console interactively linked to the classroom and to the school's "electronic library" will serve as the student home learning station. With the projected extension of both the school day and the school year, it is predicted that many students may attend school one or two days per week from their home computer console. Independent research, tutoring, and homework are foreseen as occurring on a regular basis through the home computer terminal. Electronic bulletin boards and teleconferencing systems will allow students to locate and interact with mentors throughout the nation who will assist them in their independent study and research. These systems will also permit students to form national study clubs with other pupils who have similar interests. Most educational futurists do not foresee students studying totally at home in the Information Age. Certain classes and programs of study are best conducted in the school's facilities. Further, the social interaction among pupils is considered to be an essential element in a total educational program. Finally, the instructional interaction with a human teacher cannot be replaced by an electronic communication system.

The use of the Net Console student learning station will, however, prove to be an essential educational delivery system for those students who cannot attend school, and it may solve many of the problems of rural educational systems. Electronic home teaching will permit pupils who cannot physically attend school due to health or distance problems to participate fully in their school's instructional program from their home computer terminal. They will be able to interactively join in the daily instruction provided in their classroom and to interactively communicate with their teachers and fellow students. Since the Net Console is a multisensory interactive communication system, the classroom teacher will be able to continuously monitor and supervise the student's classroom performance. Thus, the advanced technologies of the 21st century are not predicted to cause the demise of the school. Students will increasingly use the home computer Net Console to study and research from home; however, the vast majority of educational futurists stress the fact that, in their opinions, advanced technological interactive communication systems cannot and will not replace the interpersonal learning environment of the school. They foresee these electronic tools as supportive instructional alternatives strengthening the educational programs of the Information Age (Cetron, 1985; Shane & Tabler, 1981).

Educational futurists predict that the teaching profession as a whole will change its structure, organization, and instructional methodologies in the 21st century because of many of the factors already discussed (Cetron, 1985; Friedman, 1985; Koehn, 1986; Larick & Fischer, 1986; Shane & Tabler, 1981). The development of advanced artifically intelligent expert educational computer systems will allow teachers to be assigned to the type of educational program and instructional presentation that reflects their individual teaching strengths and preferences. (Similarly, students will be assigned to instructional groups based upon their preferred learning styles.) Teachers skilled in diagnostic and prescriptive processes will be assigned to activities such as establishing pupils' instructional schedules, reviewing student progress, and establishing the academic scope and sequence of the learning or performance objectives for individual pupils. Teachers with particular skills in working cooperatively with colleagues will be assigned to teaching teams. Teachers with strengths in conducting small group learning experiences will be assigned to such settings. Teachers skilled in larger group instruction and in discovery experimentation approaches will, likewise, receive assignments that capitalize on these strengths. Thus, teachers and students will be matched to the instructional method of presentation that most closely reflects their individual teaching and learning strengths. The teaching profession in the Information Age, therefore, will follow the trend anticipated in the private sector, and teachers will increasingly become instructional specialists.

The predicted increased use by 21st century schools of artifically intelligent computers with expert systems will also assist in improving the evaluation of teachers and teacher teams. Supervision and evaluation techniques employed by educational systems today tend to be subjective and rely heavily upon a few annual classroom observations. The computer, with its capability of maintaining records for all students, will provide administrators with empirical data regarding the effectiveness of the instructional programs of individual teachers, of teaching teams, and of individual schools as evidenced by measured student achievement. The prescriptive and pupil monitoring capabilities of the computer will identify the needs of individual students and classes and will provide information as to whether these needs were met by the instructional staff.

Educational futurists also predict that there will be significant changes in teacher preparation programs in the 21st century. Prospective teachers will begin their intern programs earlier, often in their second year of undergraduate studies. They will be placed in schools working with individual teachers or teacher teams. These student teachers will be provided the opportunity to learn the best teaching methods from master teachers in real classroom situations. Thus, teacher training programs will stress more practical experiences and fewer theoretical courses. It is believed that educators should be as technically proficient in their field as are employees in the private sector. Although intern programs are employed today in an increasing number of teacher training institutions, the intern program projected for the future will have an important additional objective; it will allow the prospective teacher to evaluate prior to graduation whether or not teaching should be their chosen career and permit them to change majors before graduation. It will also allow schools to evaluate the potential of these prospective teachers, to identify their strength mode of instruction, and to select the most qualified for employment. Further, directed teaching experiences will not end at graduation but will be ongoing throughout the individual's teaching career. This program will be essential if teachers are to keep up with the contantly changing society and the skills and knowledge necessary to function successfully in that society. Since technology will become such an essential component of education in the future, courses in the instructional and management use of current and future advanced technologies will be mandated for all prospective teachers.

The close and mutually beneficial partnership between schools and the private sector, as predicted by educational futurists for the 21st century, is anticipated to result in higher teacher salaries, flexible work schedules, and more effective teaching. Current projections forecast that teachers will receive salaries nearly commensurate with those of other professionals in the coming decades. Master teachers will be sought after by business and industry to provide retraining to their employees. Since these programs will often occur on a contractual basis in the schools, this will provide additional revenues to educational systems, funds that can, and often will, be used to retain these valued educators through salary incentives. This partnership is also predicted to result in the application of performance standards, the basis of employee evaluation in the private sector, to the evaluation of teachers. As a result, merit pay is foreseen as resulting from stricter educational supervision and evaluation standards. Further, the addition of the expanded school day and school year, the impact of private sector training programs, and the increase of adult education offerings are expected to result in flexible work schedules for many teachers in the future.

In the 21st century there will be a closer cooperation between educational institutions and the private sector. Business and industry will provide funding, staff, and equipment to schools. In turn, schools will offer retraining programs on a contractual or tuition basis to private sector employees. Schools will provide educational services to citizens of all ages by offering preschool and adult education programs; they will literally provide instruction from "womb to tomb." Each pupil will have an individual learning plan composed of specific performance objectives. The preference learning style of students will be electronically matched to the instructional strength of teachers. Advanced electronic technologies will dramatically change the manner in which students receive instruction and the manner in which educational decisions are made by both administrators and teachers. Study from the home computer Net Console will become more common, and the homebound and those students in certain rural areas will interactively receive daily instruction at home via the interactive Net Console.

## Summary

■ We are rapidly moving into a new era — the Information Age — which will be marked by rapid and continuous change and almost unlimited amounts of information to absorb. The disabled students of today will live most of their lives in the 21st century, and we must prepare them for the complexities of life in this enviroment.

■ The philosophy of health services will change from a concept of "sickness" to one of "wellness." Simultaneously, developments in bionics, robotics, and medicine will allow many disabled people to function more independently than has ever been possible before.

■ The Net Console, an electronic communication system of vast proportions and far-reaching capabilities, will remove many of the existing barriers to independent living for special needs people. Among its many benefits, it will permit improved communication, greater individual control of the environment, and access to health care from the home.

■ The economy of the western world will continue to move in the direction of increased services and decreased manufacturing. Many of these jobs will be able to be performed from the home, using the Net Console, allowing many more disabled people access to full employment.

■ It is expected that most people will have to be retrained for different types of jobs a number of times in their careers. Therefore, citizens of the 21st century will have to develop the willingness to learn new things throughout their lives if they are to be successful employees.

■ A closer partnership will develop between the private sector and the educational world. Business and industry will provide funding, equipment, and vocational education to schools, and in return receive well-trained employees. Technological literacy will become one of the most vital needs of education in the future.

# CHAPTER 3

# The Potential Impact of Advanced Technologies upon Special Education

U ntil the time of the computer and related microelectronic technologies, all human developments were mechanical in nature. True,
many previous inventions were dramatic and had significant impact
upon human society, but they were primarily labor saving or entertainment devices. For example, the printing press altered and improved the
method of written communication and of information storage, the automobile improved the method and speed of travel, the movie cinema
brought multisensory entertainment to the general population, and the
telephone improved the speed of interpersonal communication while
transcending geographic limitations. The entire Industrial Age resulted
in the development of increasingly sophisticated mechanical labor-
saving tools, which, among other things, improved productivity, decreased the amount of human physical labor required to produce goods
and food, raised the average economic level of most citizens, increased
the average life span, shortened the work week, and increased the
general population's amount of leisure time. Nevertheless, it is only with
the invention of the computer and related microelectronic technologies
that the human race has developed tools that assist people in thinking
and in processing information, tools that, for the first time, can extend
our intellects (Hamrin, 1981). Further, these microelectronic tools directly
assist in the development and design of newer and more advanced technologies and applications. They are, in fact, causative factors in the
exponential growth projected for the 21st century. Modern historians
often marvel at the speed with which developments occurred during the

Industrial Age, in particular during the last 100 years. Future historians will, in all likelihood, view that period of industrial growth as having been rather lethargic and as having had less impact on human development than will the current and projected advanced electronic technologies of the Information Age.

The term "advanced electronic technology" is a difficult one to define. Every development in microelectronics advances from the previous model or system. The term "advanced" in this instance is a relative one and, therefore, refers to the most recent development or the "state of the art," a state that will soon change due to some new developments. Thus, the microcomputers of today are advancements of the computers of five years ago. As a matter of fact, today's microcomputers have a memory capacity greater than those of the large main frame computers of a decade ago. One of the difficulties, therefore, in defining the term "advanced" in the field of microelectronics and interactive telecommunications is the speed with which new developments occur. New advancements are made in these fields almost daily. Some, of course, represent improvements in existing systems, while others represent entirely new systems, capabilities, and applications. As mentioned previously, these technologies assist us in thinking and in simulating alternative solutions; therefore, they contribute to the rapid development of new systems because they permit scientists, engineers, and programmers to consider and experiment with new theories, dimensions, designs, and applications never before deemed possible.

The term "advanced electronic technology," as used here, refers to research trends in the development, design, and application of microelectronic and related telecommunication systems. These trends translate into goals toward which the technology field is working but which may not be fully realized for decades. Many of these systems now exist in a primitive form or are only theories. Nevertheless, scientists and researchers in the field predict that these advanced electronic technologies will become a reality, will become the tools of daily living during the 21st century. They are the technologies of the next generation, the technologies of our children.

There are four major areas of advanced electronic technology and related applications that appear to have particular relevance to disabled people and that should receive consideration in today's design of special educational and vocational programs. These four areas are artificial intelligence and expert systems, robotics, interactive multisensory simulation, and interactive communication systems. As mentioned earlier, primitive versions or theoretical designs of these systems do exist today; however, they only portend the true applications and impact they will have in the world of the 21st century. The following sections briefly explain each of these advanced electronic technologies and the directions in which current research is headed. Also presented are some possible implications of these advanced technologies for the educational and vocational preparation of today's disabled children and young adults. Further, the use of these future technology systems by teachers, related service specialists, and administrators in the fields of special education and rehabilitation are examined.

## ARTIFICIAL INTELLIGENCE

The all too common reaction to the words "artificial intelligence" is the immediate assumption that scientists and research engineers are creating machines that will replace humans, machines whose thinking processes are superior to that of human beings. The typical scenario portrayed in science fiction, in general literature, in movies, and on television depicts a superior, intelligent machine, usually a computer, as a sinister force, one which is a threat to mankind. For some unexplained reason, artificially intelligent computers make excellent villains and, like their evil human counterparts, are usually defeated in the end by the identification and exploitation of some flaw, often a lack of emotion or a total reliance on pure logic.

Despite its entertainment value, this unfortunate and all too common depiction of artificial intelligence is totally erroneous. Yes, artificial intelligence research is directed toward developing advanced computer systems that "think"; however, to date, no one has been able to define exactly what human thinking is. Therefore, the issue has become, How does one design a machine that replicates and is equal to, much less superior to, the human brain with its complex structure? What is the essential element that constitutes true intelligence? Is it memory, logic, concept formation, language, sensation, perception, or emotion? This list could go on and on and not provide any answer to the question of how one creates an artificially intelligent computer.

The central objective of artificial intelligence research is not to create a machine that replicates the human brain and thinking process but to create a complex computer system that will learn. More and more researchers agree that the definition of an intelligent machine is one which learns how to learn, a system that can learn from past experience and apply it to new situations. These researchers are, however, taking a variety of approaches to the problem of designing a computer system that learns. Two approaches center around the debate over whether this learning should be based on deductive or inductive reasoning in order for a computer system to be considered intelligent. A third approach assumes that, to be intelligent, a machine must be able to sense and to use the information received from its senses to locomote. In this third area of research, the senses being considered are not only those processed by humans but also include other machine senses such as radar and sonar.

Despite the differences in approach, all researchers seem to agree that the artificially intelligent computer, one that learns how to learn, will not be a replication of the human brain or the human thinking process. It will, when developed, be the first alien intelligence the human race encounters. It will be a silicon based intelligence system, as opposed to the carbon based intelligence of humans. The artificially intelligent computer may be as complex as that of the human brain, but it will "think" in a totally different manner. The purpose of this research, and of artificial intelligence in general, is not to compete with human intelligence but rather to be an ancillary system, one which assists and enhances the human ability to think, solve problems, and create. Artificial intelligence research, when viewed in this light, is directed toward developing intelligent computer systems that will amplify human thought, not systems that will replace it.

Artificial intelligence research began little more than 25 years ago and, like the other advanced technologies projected for the Information Age, is only in its infancy. Initially the field was organized into two divergent avenues of endeavor, the theory mode and the performance mode. A third rather distinct area of thought and direction was begun by the Japanese in the early 1980s with their national effort directed toward the development of the Fifth Generation computer system. All of these continuing research approaches will contribute essential elements to the ultimate development of the artificially intelligent computer systems that will form the basis of information processing and communication in the 21st century.

The theory mode of research can most simply be described as viewing artificial intelligence as a branch of psychology. The purpose of this approach is to use the computer to assist in understanding the operation of the human mind by programming the computer to perform tasks in a manner similar to the ways in which humans perform them. Researchers in this area are attempting to discover and model how people think; that is, to establish the basic relationships among logic, intuition, and inference. One of the most promising areas of the theory mode of research is natural-language analysis, a system that would allow a person to talk to a computer in a natural linguistic format. An outgrowth of natural-language analysis is translational processing, a system that would allow a computer to move between different forms of information, such as from speech to the written word, a task performed easily by most people.

The performance mode of artificial intelligence research is directed toward programming a computer to do very complex things that would usually be performed either by a person or by a group of people. The objective of this approach is to have the intelligent computer system perform these complex tasks in ways that would not normally be performed or would not normally be considered by the human being. This area of research is developing applications known as expert systems and novice systems (Haigh, Gerbner, & Byrne, 1981).

## Natural-Language Analysis and Translational Processing

One of the most frustrating things for most computer users is to be forced to interact with, or converse with, a computer in an unnatural manner. Users find that they are forced to question a computer using "computerese" rather than in a normal conversational format. Natural-language analysis research is directed toward developing intelligent computer systems that will permit users to ask questions in their natural linguistic or inner language systems.

The difficulty in developing such a natural-language analysis system is that, currently, computers and people think and communicate in totally different manners. Their inner language systems are totally different. When people communicate with a computer, they must translate their linguistic questions or directions into the linguistic system the computer understands, that is, into a computer language. In the same manner, people must translate what a computer says into human language systems. Thus, computer users must conform to the rules of the computer. This situation may not be readily apparent, since software programs are already written in a computer language by a programmer and since the software accessed by a user has been translated into a human language. This software, however, is not true interpersonal communication with a computer; the user is communicating through another person, the computer programmer, who has already performed the direct communication with the machine. Artificially intelligent natural-language analysis implies that users will not be totally dependent upon prewritten software to communicate with a computer but will be able to do so in their own language systems whenever and for whatever reason they desire. When developed, this new system will serve humanity in the Information Age by permitting users to access and understand large data bases at one time. It will serve as an essential component of the Net Console and the grid, (Chapter 2).

Currently, computers use language systems based on pure logic and "if-then" rules. They use very specific syntax and have very limited vocabularies and restricted grammar. What this implies is that a computer can understand a question or a command only when it is presented in a rigid and prescribed format. This is even true, to some extent, with our current software; the user must respond in a very specific format because any other response will not be understood by the computer.

Human language and communication differs dramatically from the current computer languages. Grammatical rules and syntax are far more extensive, and both communication and comprehension are influenced by a host of factors that include, but are not limited to, the following: the individual's past experience, idiomatic meaning, innuendo, inference, context clues, voice tone and inflection, social setting, and body language. Comprehension among people is very much dependent upon stored memory associations; when a word or phrase is heard or read, meaning is attached to it or associated with it based upon the individual's inner language system of past experiences. Thus, two people can hear the same thing and attach totally different meanings to what was heard. Human beings, as a result, have enough trouble communicating among themselves. It is any wonder that creating an artificially intelligent natural-language computer system is such a formidable task?

One of the basic problems of the logic and "if-then" rules currently governing computer languages is that they are all form and no content. Even when one equips a computer with an extensive "human" vocabulary, such as a comprehensive spelling correction program, the machine has no understanding of the words with which it works. The key to natural-language analysis, therefore, is to equip the computer with the capability to attach meaning to the words and phrases that are presented to it in either a spoken or written format. Further, this artificially intelligent system must be able to understand the word within the context that it has been presented. As the messages given to the computer become more complex and vague, the requirements of the system increase.

Primitive forms of natural-language analysis systems exist today, but they are extremely expensive and require extensive memory depositories. These systems do not, in and of themselves, "understand" natural human language. They provide a translation of the human vocabulary into a language the computer can understand; they translate from human language into machine language. Although these systems do allow the user to use human language to communicate with the computer, the user is still restricted in the vocabulary that can be employed. Even in these systems, the machine is dictating the format and scope of the vocabulary that must be used in order for it to comprehend the communication. Therefore, these systems are not truly artificially intelligent.

Researchers project that a truly artificially intelligent natural-language analysis system will not be available until the early part of the 21st century. They also suggest that this system will have both speech recognition and speech output capabilities so that an individual will be able to talk with a computer in a manner similar to the way in which conversations are held with other people. Further, they suggest that these systems will be able to adapt to the individual language pattern of the user; that is, they will be able to modify themselves to accommodate the unique inner language pattern of the user. Nevertheless, the importance of this area of artificial intelligence research must not be overlooked today simply because the final product has not yet been fully developed. Today's students will live in the time when such a system is a tool of daily living. Therefore, students must be prepared by our current educational and vocational programs to use natural-language analysis systems to their full advantage.

Translational processing is directed toward developing systems that allow computers simply to manipulate information that is presented in differing formats, such as moving from the spoken word to a graphic display or to written text. These tasks are very easy for most people since most individuals have multisensory capabilities. Because of past experience and training, people move between different forms of information and translate from one mode to another almost automatically. Examples of this type of activity are writing what is heard or understanding the meaning or emotional intent of a picture.

These tasks are highly difficult for a computer and transcend the capabilities of today's systems. The ability to move between different forms of information would constitute a powerful and essential role for artificial intelligence. The task would require a high degree of discrimination and interpretation on the part of the machine, a capability that only human beings currently possess. People have the ability to conceptualize and reconceptualize on a variety of levels and to employ a variety of information-processing techniques.

Researchers in the area of artificial intelligence predict that translational processing will be fully developed at about the same time as natural-language analysis, about the beginning of, or early in, the 21st century. The development of these capabilities will allow the advanced computer systems of the future to deal with information as people do, an essential element in the development of the Net Console and the world grid (Cain, 1985b). It will allow computers to perceive information, either as a whole or in its parts, and recombine it to provide meaning very rapidly. It will also permit these computer systems to extract meaning from large amounts of written materials, to obtain meaning from pictures, and to translate voice to text or text to voice. The combination of natural-language analysis abilities with translational processing will enable the advanced computers of the 21st century to truly interact with people in a personal and conversational manner.

## Expert and Novice Systems

Expert systems allow computers to perform problem solving tasks in specific areas. They contain a data base of knowledge which human experts would take years to acquire, and also contain the rules of analysis and logic that human experts use to solve real-life situations. Already, such expert systems have been developed and have proven to be as effective as their human counterparts, analyzing the symptoms and test results of human patients and offering diagnoses. These systems can be very accurate because each contains a vast memory of information about symptoms and the meaning of human medical test results, a memory base greater than that of any individual physician; and they are able to apply the analytic and logical reasoning processes derived from a variety of human medical experts.

We all use experts. We go to doctors when we feel ill, to attorneys when we require legal assistance, and to auto mechanics when our cars do not run properly. We consult experts because they have more knowledge then we do; therefore, they can help us solve problems by providing advice. These experts do not solve our problems, they only provide knowledge and information so that we can make decisions.

Expert systems, also referred to as knowledge-based programming, provide the same type of assistance to people. Based on extensive, instantly accessed knowledge, they assist us by providing the best solution, a decision we can either accept or reject (Williams, 1982). The difference between a human expert and an expert system is primarily the amount of information available. An expert system contains large amounts of information superior to that available at any one time to any individual human expert (even though this information may be organized in rule form). These expert systems also contain a compilation of special techniques for applying the proper rules at the proper time, rules which have been gathered from the experience of a large variety of human experts and amassed into the system.

Expert systems interact with the user so that the solution to the presenting problem is personalized. They help us find appropriate answers to questions by using rule-based, highly structured analysis and inductive judgment of the information on a subject that is contained in the computer's memory. The suggested solution to the problem is personalized through the system's experience with the user. Thus, the information we provide to the program and the answers we offer to the system's questions will become essential factors in its development of the final suggested solution. Each additional piece of information that provides the system with another variable to consider is integrated into its memory and compared to its extensive knowledge base of information about the subject. The implication of the continued development of expert systems, and of their integration with natural-language analysis and translational processing techniques, is that the future user of these artificially intelligent systems, interacting via some device such as the Net Console, will be able to obtain expert advice about an almost unlimited variety of subjects in a personal and conversational manner.

The concept of novice systems is an offshoot of expert systems, one that is more interactive and one that considers more highly the level of expertise of the user. As the daily information base with which we have to deal continues to increase and change, we find it increasingly difficult to cope with the information or to make decisions about a problem. The deeper we move into the Information Age, the greater this problem will become. As mentioned in Chapter 2, a constantly growing and changing base of information can cause people to suffer from "information overload" and "communication pollution." Some individuals will become so overwhelmed by the amount of information that they will not know how to begin to solve a problem or even what questions to ask the electronic data base in order to receive assistance.

A novice system will be designed to recognize that the user is having difficulties and will act as a guide through the information base. These systems will assist individuals in forming personally useful questions and in understanding what type of answers they are really seeking. These systems will provide assistance in interacting with both expert systems and large electronic data bases of information. The novice systems of the Information Age will be able to recognize an individual's level of comprehension and to tailor the learning experience to the needs of that individual. Researchers predict that the novice systems of the 21st century will build their own bodies of knowledge based upon past experience and will have the ability to improve and redefine the information base of an organization or of an individual in order to reflect rapidly changing variables and sources of information. These systems will also be integrated with natural-language analysis, translational processing, and expert systems.

### Fifth Generation Processing Systems

The fifth generation processing systems are the most recent and most ambitious entry into the research and development of artificially intelligent computer system thus far. The inception of this program in the early 1980s represented a national effort on the part of Japan, and to a certain extent the United States, to be the first "real" postindustrial society to consciously act upon the realization that economic power in the world of the 21st century is based upon the control of and access to knowledge, information, and intelligence. Subsequent to the establishment of these efforts, France and Great Britain, among other industrial nations, have begun national programs directed toward the development of new knowledge-based electronic technologies.

The fifth generation approach to the development of artificial intelligence is comprehensive. It seeks to develop not only the necessary software but is also concerned with the design and structure of the next generation of computers that will run these artificially intelligent systems. Reseachers, therefore, are attempting to develop machines for the 21st century; machines that will amplify and augment human thought and intelligence. Researchers are investigating all of the efforts already mentioned, and are doing so in a coordinated and integrated manner. One of their central goals is to develop the machine and the system that will be able to accomodate, process, and communicate all of the exponentially expanding knowledge that will become available in the Information Age.

These projects are requiring comprehensive national efforts involving the human and economic resources of governments and the private sector. They reflect the importance of designing artificially intelligent computers and related electronic communication systems that will be required as the basic electronic components of information processing in the 21st century. Researchers are striving to develop computer systems that can learn from past experience, make decisions, associate, make inferences, understand both oral and written language and pictures, and converse with people in their natural languages (Cain, 1985).

### Some Implications of Artificial Intelligence for Disabled People

Artificially intelligent computers, systems that will form the basic electronic components of knowledge processing and communication in the 21st century, portend a number of implications for today's various disabled groups. These implications must be considered today by special educators, support service personnel, rehabilitation professionals, and parents as they begin to design new intervention programs and curricula to prepare these special students to live, work, and enjoy leisure activities in the Information Age. These instructional programs must be started now if these students are to take maximum advantage of the benefits of such advanced technology systems. Artificially intelligent computers have the capability to be important learning, training and retraining, communication, compensation, and prosthetic tools for special needs populations in the Information Age; however, unless appropriate instructional programs are instituted immediately to prepare disabled individuals to use such advanced technology systems, these groups will, in all probability, become more isolated and removed from the mainstream of the society of the future.

One of the most significant implications of artificial intelligence is that people will be communicating with computers just as they do with other individuals. Thus, today's disabled students will have to learn how to deal with the society of the future and with its institutions through the use of nonhuman computer-controlled communication technologies. Further, they will have to understand the similarities and differences between human intelligence and the artificial intelligence of these new advanced technology systems. Computers that have the capability to communicate with the user in a natural human language format can easily be confused with a human. Many of us have received phone calls from a "person" attempting to sell us a product, only to discover that the "person" is actually a computer program with an electronically controlled dialing system. The current computer telephone systems are not interactive; they only deliver a message and cannot respond to the individual receiving the call. What will happen when the artificially intelligent computer with voice input and human-sounding voice output not only communicates with a person in a natural human language format but does so in a truly interactive way? Unless today's various disabled individuals are prepared for this eventuality, they may not be able to distinguish between a human and a machine interactive message. In most instances, this will be very important if humans are not to be controlled by machines. Therefore, one implication of artificial intelligence for today's special education and rehabilitation curricula is that these students must be provided with a series of sequential instructional activities that will require them to find ways to discriminate between a machine-delivered and a human communication (just as educators in the past have had to teach that which is seen on television is not necessarily true). Instructional equipment that could be used to foster such learning activities would include items such as "talking" toys, tape recorded messages, records, cartoons, radio and television, telephones, computers with voice output, and so forth. The purpose of these types of activities is to help students begin to distinguish between interpersonal human messages, interpersonal messages delivered by machine, and one-way messages delivered by machine. The ability of the handicapped individual to distinguish between human and artificial intelligence communications is a crucial skill for them to master in order to be able to function appropriately in the world of the 21st century.

Natural-language analysis and translational processing capabilities imply that the computer user of the Information Age will be able to input information and ask questions of the system in a human language format. The ability of the individual to have some form of an interactive linguistic system therefore becomes extremely important. These new advanced technology systems will allow individuals to communicate in their strength modality and will, of course, be able to be controlled through any conceivable form of prosthetic interface. One of the most important elements of these new advanced systems, however, is that they will be able to modify themselves so that they can "understand" the inner language system of the individual. In other words, these computers will become personalized and be able to receive information from and provide information to the user in that person's unique linguistic style.

Many disabled individuals with either receptive or expressive linguistic problems or with limited linguistic abilities are now forced to translate messages into and out of their internal language systems when communicating with others. This causes them to focus on the process rather than on the content of the communication. As a result, the meaning of the message is often lost or misinterpreted. Given artificially intelligent systems, the computer will perform this "translation" task and will free the user to concentrate on the content of what is being transmitted or received. Natural-language analysis means that the computer will be able to communicate not only in the language of the general population but also in the individual user's "natural" or inner language, which provides the possibility of breaking down the communication barriers that now exist between the severely handicapped and the general population.

The translation capabilities of these new advanced computer systems will allow disabled persons to use machines to translate for them when they communicate with another individual or with an electronic data base. Since these artificially intelligent machines will form one othe the basic components of the Net Console, the disabled individuals, will be able to let the computer perform the actual process of communication either from their homes or from any other computer station. Further, since these systems will have the ability to modify themselves to the inner language systems of the users, they can act as the universal personalized translation vehicle for these individuals.

The natural-language analysis and translational processing abilities of the artificially intelligent computers of the 21st century will also be able to provide disabled users with information in a format that accurately reflects their current intellectual capabilities, knowledge base, and level of performance. Since machines will learn from people and will modify their responses and mode of communication as needed, they will be able to act as prosthetic devices and will be able to provide information and communication that matches the individual's linguistic receptive and expressive needs. Every time the user's response indicates there is a problem in some aspect of the communication process, the system will modify itself in order to make an individual accommodation.

Expert and novice artificially intelligent systems will provide the disabled user of the Information Age with individual assistance in simulating and in solving the variety of everyday problems. Natural-language analysis and translational processing capabilities of the computer systems of the Information Age will enable the handicapped individual to receive and transmit information in a manner that is personally important and that can be readily comprehended. The expert and novice systems will provide the continuous and individualized counseling that will allow disabled people to cope and to make appropriate daily living decisions, thereby increasing their potential for independent living.

The ability of the disabled individual of the Information Age to access expert systems in order to receive counseling and assistance may be important for another reason. The computer is neutral and impartial while, at the same time, being interpersonal. It passes no judgment by means of facial expression, body language, tone of voice, or response content. As a result, these artificially intelligent systems may prove to be less inhibiting to the disabled user than a human expert or counselor might be. The computer system does not care what the intellectual, physical, neurological, or emotional problems of the user are; these machines are personally modifiable servants whose only purpose is to offer their users assistance.

The Information Age implies that the knowledge base will be expanding and changing daily. Since many disabled individuals have difficulty in processing data and in learning new information, these expert and novice systems will provide them with personal assistance in coping with the vast amounts of information that will be available and in using that information to personal advantage. The novice systems will be particularly helpful in this task. These systems will also modify themselves to the specific needs of the handicapped user by presenting information through the individuals strength modality and reflecting the individual's inner language system.

Expert and novice systems will thus be able to assist disabled workers of the 21st century in dealing with the retraining demands of the job market. These systems will be able to tailor the learning experience to the individual's level of understanding and, through the Net Console, provide the user with multisensory and interactive retraining simulations. Further, artificially intelligent systems will allow disabled individuals of the 21st century to be lifelong learners. These individuals will be able to investigate and learn the same topics as their nonhandicapped neighbors. They will be able to enjoy the full variety of interactive entertainment and cultural events. All of these activities will be available to the disabled through the home Net Console, tailored to their particular cognitive and communication needs.

Further, artificially intelligent computer systems will also prove to be important management tools for professionals engaged in special education or rehabilitation. Natural-language analysis and transitional processing systems will permit these professionals to seek information and will provide them with guidance as to how to frame a question in order to receive the desired information. The information gathered through this process could then be analyzed by an expert system. It is anticipated that the use of these systems will permit professionals more time to devote to the instructional process since the computer will be able to perform much of the time-consuming paper work.

The diagnostic and prescriptive process will be enhanced through the use of artificially intelligent computer systems in a manner similar to that of the medical profession. Expert systems would contain all information regarding educational diagnoses and achievement test results. This information could then be applied to an individual child's educational history and current performance levels, and the expert system would provide the professional with an individualized educational prescriptive recommendation. Expert systems would also monitor development and learning, providing continuous records of each child's progress, and then providing the professional with updated analyses and prescriptions. The translational processing aspect of this advanced computer system, therefore, would assist the professional in sifting through vast amounts of data locate, retrieve, and analyze the desired information.

## ROBOTICS

As with artificial intelligence, the field of robotics tends to be misunderstood by the general population. Robots have fared little better than artificial intelligence in our literature and in mass media presentations. Although they have been depicted as evil or unwitting villains in many scenarios, they have also been portrayed as humorous, as evidenced by the popularity of the characters C3PO and R2D2 from the motion picture *Star Wars*. The actual robots of today are considerably more primitive than those depicted by the entertainment industry; however, to many individuals in manufacturing industries, robots have come to mean unemployment. Robots have been viewed by workers as a dark and threatening development, a dystopian force used by employers to render jobs obolete. Other individuals' views of the development of robots tend to be utopian; they see robotic as the creation of obedient electronic slaves that will obey every wish and that will free humans from the necessity of performing any distasteful labor.

The development of robotics portends neither a utopian nor a dystopian potential for the society of the 21st century, but will result in a complex combination of both of these future perspectives. This technology, like any other, is neither inherently good nor inherently evil. Robots are merely neutral tools whose use by us can create either benefits or barriers for ourselves and others. Technological change is taking place so rapidly that it is often difficult to know who is in charge of these developments. The frightening answer may be that there is no one in charge — that there is no master plan, no one at the helm, no one considering the alternative dystopian implications of change — just innovation for its own sake.

The term robot is derived from the play *R.U.R.* written by the Czechoslovakian playwright Karel Capek in 1920 (Albus, 1983). Rossum's Universal Robots (R.U.R.) were depicted as being chemically developed robots. The term robot is taken from the Czechoslovakian word "robata," which means forced labor. *R.U.R.* expresses many of the fears the general public harbors toward robots. In the play, robots become increasingly more intelligent and sophisticated and eventually turn against human beings. In *R.U.R.*, robots were constructed to look and act like human beings; whereas, in reality modern robots are distinctly unhuman in appearance. (Most industrial robots resemble units of automatic machinery or mobile carts.)

Robots are most simply defined as computer-driven mechanical devices which can be programmed to perform some act of manipulation or locomotion under automatic control. They are computers in forms that imitate human bodily movements, often surpassing the human, and as such, are one of the truly interactive technologies, technologies that link man and machine to the benefit of both. Generally speaking, a robot is any machine that performs a task previously assigned to a person. It is self-operating and is "intelligent" in that it is controlled by a microcomputer. Thus, any of the advanced technological artificial intelligence developments previously discussed would have applications to the robots of the 21st century. The primary barrier to the full utilization of robots with exceptional individuals lies in the current state of development of the robots' "mechanical minds," the microprocessors. Further, if we are to truly realize the potential of this technology with the various disabled groups, we will have to further apply artificial intelligence in our robotic designs.

Industry is the area in which robots have made the greatest impact, particularly in the area of manufacturing (Philbin, 1986). Robots have successfully replaced humans or taken on tasks that are uncomfortable or dangerous for people. Since robots can be designed in an almost unlimited variety of sizes and shapes, and since they can work in environments hostile to people, they can perform assignments that would be difficult or dangerous for humans. They tend to be insensitive to elements such as toxic chemicals, heat, fumes, and radioactivity. Further, robots can be moved from one job to another and can be reprogrammed to learn a new task, often by being led or directed by a human.

The application of robotics in industrial settings has proven to be cost effective for both business and industry. Robots can not only work in dangerous environments, but they can work multiple shifts, seven days a week. They work tirelessly with great precision, and their error rates are lower than those of fellow human workers because they do not become distracted, daydream, or talk with other employees on the job. Although they can break down, robots do not take vacations, sick leave, or coffee and lunch breaks. Further, robots do not have unions, go on strike, receive fringe benefits, or require the employer to pay social security or workman's compensation (Coates, 1983).

It must be remembered, however, that today's industrial robots tend to be rather primitive and costly. Their development has been slow compared to other micorelectronic advanced technology systems. The research and development of robotic technology has not been as vigorously pursued in the United States as it has been in Japan. Unless the pace of robotic research increases, many of the developments required to create domestic robot units and truly productive industrial machines will not occur for many years. Thus, robots remain rather limited in their usefulness, especially since they must be programmed to perform a specific function in a very precise manner. Further, the materials with which most industrial robots work must be coordinated in a very precise manner since robots do not have the sensory capabilities required to adjust to changes in the work situation. Very frequently the entire work environment must be redesigned in order to accommodate robots and allow them to perform at maximum efficiency. Many of these accommodations have to be made in order to protect human workers from the danger a "blind" industrial robot may present in the work setting.

In order for robots to become more adaptable, their ability to "sense" must be vastly improved. Robots, however, will not be limited to the human senses and will have special sensory capabilities such as sonar, radiation detectors, infrared sensors, radar, and ultraviolate sensors. Most engineers in the field of robotics consider the development of an interactive visual sense to be the most important of all senses for robots. Sight will permit robots to react and adjust to small changes in the work environment and will provide them with the capability to perform general purpose domestic tasks. It will also give robots the ability to locomote in an uncontrolled or independent manner, perceiving objects in their way and moving around them from one point to another. Most current vision systems use solid-state television cameras as robot eyes, which provide information to the microcomputer brain. Other visual systems being researched include three-dimensional stereoscopic systems, infrared units, and laser light systems. One of the greatest limitations to the development of interactive senses in robots, such as vision, is the current state of development of the microprocessor, the robot's "mechanical brain." In order for robots of the future to have truly independent capabilities, they must be able to learn from past experience and to attach meaning to what is sensed, abilities associated with the development of artificially intelligent computer systems. Without an artificially intelligent microelectronic "brain," the sensory capabilities of robots will remain rather limited.

Many robots, particularly those used in training and education, have speech capabilities. The speech is preprogrammed and, therefore, is usually not interactive. However, these robots can be programmed to deliver a preprogrammed message in response to a specific stimulus such as a certain frequency sound or a specific intensity of light. The voice quality of most of these units tends to be artificial since the words are made up of phonemes stored in memory; however, inflection can be added through the use of the appropriate word spacing and the volume of a specific phoneme. Therefore, the speech patterns of robots can be programmed to do things such as ask questions. The addition of artificially intelligent natural-language analysis and translational processing to the robot's microprocessor "brain" will allow the human user to communicate with the robot in natural human speech and in an interactive manner.

Some robots have been provided with a rudimentary sense of touch that allows them to feel and to form an image of what is being felt. Certain units have been equipped with an artificial "skin" and finger sensors. Recent developments in interactive voice input have provided robots, like other microelectronic technologies, with the ability to "hear" and to respond to an individual's specific voice pattern. New developments in advanced computer technology can be expected to provide future robots with improved interactive sensory capabilities and with entirely new senses (Higgins, 1986).

Robots have been increasingly used in a variety of educational settings and have proven to be very effective tutors and teachers (Freeman & Mulkowsky, 1982). By combining the interactive capabilities of computer, voice input and output, and the mobility and flexibility of a robot, these units have been used for a variety of instructional purposes. Robots are extremely effective in assisting children to perform tasks, to master concepts such as estimating distance or establishing position in space, and to develop concepts such as laterality and directionality. Since they can be equipped with the latest forms of instructional software, robots can serve as interactive tutors in a manner similar to the microcomputer. Many of these units have the capability of storing a student's educational history and can maintain a record of correct and incorrect responses for future analysis by the human teacher. Further, some of the experimental instructional robot models have the ability to recognize individual students' voice prints and, therefore, can respond to each child interactively in a personal manner. These robot teachers tend to be nonthreatening and, therefore, have shown themselves to be very effective with a number of disabled groups. The capability of robots to be programmed to perform a task exactly, consistently, and tirelessly has made them effective in providing sensory stimulation and patterning of young developmentally delayed and multihandicapped children. They have also served as interactive models for older handicapped students. For example, robots have been used to provide speech as well as physical and occupational therapy models for people such as adult stroke victims. Students who have been exposed to these robot tutors or trainers have not only gained a deeper understanding of an advanced technology that will become a daily living tool of their future, but have also benefited from the mobile and interactive instructional capabilities of these electronic technologies.

One of the criticisms of robotics, particularly in business and industry, is that they have and will continue to cause widespread unemployment. It is true that the use of robots in the manufacturing industries in the United States, in Japan, and in other industrialized nations has resulted in a decrease in the number of blue collar operator jobs (Kornbluh, 1982). However, it must be realized that the number of individuals entering the workforce in the 21st century, the era in which the use of robots is predicted to become common, will be decreased due to changes in demography (see Chapter 2). A smaller percentage of younger individuals will be required to support a growing percentage of older citizens in the Information Age; therefore, futurists predict that the increasing use of robots in the coming decades may prove to be the only cost effective way in which to provide manufactured goods, food, and certain services to the general population.

The use of robots to date has, in fact, created jobs and established entirely new industries (Albus, 1983). Someone must design, build, install, program, and repair robots. Plants have to be converted to a robot-based operation. Current industry estimates indicate that converting the world's industrial plants to a robot labor force will take decades and will employ millions of individuals. It is projected that the robotics industry will employ at least as many people as the computer and automobile industries do today. Robotics, like all other advanced electronic technologies, will grow and develop exponentially and will, in all probability, result in industries and in applications not yet envisioned.

Research engineers and scientists in the field of robotics predict that this advanced technology will become an important element in the economy of the 21st century and that robots will also become domestic tools of daily living and mobility. Yes, in this future era of the Information Age, we will have robots that will do windows. Again, it must be stressed that these robots will have artificial intelligence capabilities in their mechanical "brains" and, therefore, will be able to interact with their users in a natural human language format. They will also have fully developed and interactive senses including vision, touch, and hearing as well as machine senses such as sonar, radar, and infrared sensors. These senory developments will continue to increase, become more sophisticated, and result in more complex capabilities. These robotic units will be able to learn from past experience and to acquire new skills by analyzing tasks on their own. The robots of the future will be fast, accurate, and dexterous workers whose interactive capabilities will make them obedient and patient electronic slaves of humanity (Cornish, 1983).

It is projected that factory robots of the 21st century will perform most, if not all, of the operations that now require human skills. Robots in these automatic factories will be able to reproduce, repair themselves, and produce parts for other automatic factories. It is felt that these automatic factories and their potential for manufacturing components for other automatic factories will result in greater productivity and provide a simultaneous reduction in the cost of the final product. It is projected that robot "farmers" and "miners" will work the surface and the seabed in the coming decades. Robot cars and other transportation systems will convey the citizens of the future quickly and safely and at a greatly reduced rate of fuel consumption. Robotic appliances and domestic units will provide their users with obedient and intelligent interactive electronic servants in the 21st century. It is further projected that prosthetic and compensatory robotic devices will provide disabled and aged users with greater environmental control and independence. The potential dangers of nuclear power, chemical, and biomedical industries will be lessened by using robots to handle toxic materials. Robots will become increasingly important to the exploration of space and in the development of space stations and other human habitats in outer space.

### Some Implicatons of Robotics for Disabled People

The development of robots with artificially intelligent microprocessors, or machine "brains," implies that these systems of the 21st century will have more effective, natural, and interactive communication with people and will, therefore, allow the disabled individuals to "speak with" and command robots. The addition of natural-language analysis and translational processing capabilities will permit the handicapped users of the Information Age to communicate with robots in their personal and natural linguistic systems. This implies that the intelligent robot of the future will be able to adapt the interactive, receptive, and expressive communication processes to the individual's natural pattern of communication, and to modify the process so that it is attuned to the user's personal inner language system. Any consistent pattern of sound or touch, therefore, will be interpreted by the intelligent robot as a command or a communication. Other developments in the field of biomedical engineering, such as skin galvanized interfaces, eye-pointing control, and biofeedback computer and robot interfaces, will permit the nonlinguistic or severely physically impaired person to take advantage of the capabilities of robots. Thus, these advanced interface devices will permit most, if not all, disabled individuals of the coming decades to use robotic capabilities for environmental control, self-care, mobility, recreation, and employment. The prosthetic and compensatory applications of robotic technology will thus permit these individuals to become more independent in the era of the Information Age.

Many researchers in the field of designing more natural human-machine interfaces believe that these systems will be developed for three separate groups, all of whom have the same needs: permanently handicapped, temporarily disabled, and aged people who have disabilities due to aging (hearing, vision, memory loss, and so forth). Since aged individuals will represent a growing majority of the general population in the early 21st century and many of them may have a disability, researchers feel confident that such interface systems will be marketed at a price that these user groups can afford; based on the economic law of supply and demand. Further, since they will be easier for everyone to use, these new electronic interface units will prove beneficial to the general population, thus bringing down the cost even more.

As mentioned in Chapter 2, the Net Console, in addition to being the interactive home communication technology of the Information Age, is envisioned as the interactive domestic intelligent computer system that will control the environmental maintenance units, appliances, and robots. General purpose and specific task domestic robots will perform such basic home support tasks as cleaning, cooking, home maintenance, and repair. Under the direction of the master Net Console, these robots will respond to natural language communication or the advanced adaptive interface control units of the user. Since robots will have advanced sensory capabilities and be able to learn from past experience, they will be able to adapt their services to the specific needs of the disabled user at any point in time. With the Net Console's large storage systems and the ability to monitor and control complex functions and multiple activities, it will serve as the central control for all domestic functions in the home of the 21st century.

General purpose robot servants will also assist disabled users in basic self-care. The advanced sensory capabilities of these future units will allow them to perform very delicate fine motor tasks and, thus, will permit them to provide "humanlike" care to the user. These advanced and artificially intelligent robots will be able to provide services such as grooming, assisting in personal hygiene, feeding, individualizing physical and speech therapy, and performing basic medical care. The ability of these robots to learn from past experience, to communicate and be controlled through the natural language system of the user, and to modify themselves to the personal needs of their owner will permit them to respond to unanticipated situations such as an emergency. The interactive knowledge base and expert system elements of the master control Net Console will further provide these electronic servants with expert information as it is required. Since these robots will be under the direct control of the user, they will act as prosthetic or compensatory extensions of the individual and will, therefore, provide greater ability for users to care for themselves in the future of the Information Age.

An issue related to these advanced domestic and self-care robots of the 21st century is their design. Should these units be anthropomorphic, or humanlike, or should they resemble machines? Although this question may not immediately appear germane to a discussion of some of the implications of robotics for the disabled individual, it may be very important for some disabled people. The thought of anthropomorphic artificially intelligent robots is disquieting to many individuals who apparently perceive such machines as a personal threat; they would, after all, resemble humans and would talk, act and move like them. Robots that look like machines, such as R2D2 of *Star Wars*, are often viewed as being less of a personal threat, although they would have the same capabilities as the anthropomorphic units. An issue already discussed in this chapter dealt with the importance of disabled students learning to distinguish between artificial intelligence and human intelligence in order to function efficiently and independently in the Information Age. How much more difficult might it become for certain disabled people to make such a distinction if artificially intelligent robots looked and acted like human beings? Further, current research in the use of educational and experimental robots with certain disabled people shows that the least threatening units were those that looked and sounded like machines. On the other hand, anthropomorphic robots might prove to be very beneficial to some disabled people. Because the robots could be controlled and would look humanlike, disabled users might feel that they were more independent and less reliant on machines for daily living and self-care activities. The issue of the design of the domestic, general purpose robots of the 21st century will have to be carefully researched and evaluated so that the units constructed will meet the emotional and personal preference needs of the disabled people served by them. Further, different models will have to be designed for different special needs groups. Although this issue is one which will not have to be faced for a few decades, investigation into the implications of the design of robots should begin now.

The development of robotic mobility and transportation devices holds great promise for certain disabled people. These personally interactive units would permit the user to be independently mobile in the home and in the community at large. The advanced sensory capabilities of these robots would mean that they could compensate for any sensory deficit of their users. Their artificially intelligent microprocessors would allow them to plan the trip and to transport the disabled user almost anywhere in the community in total safety. These robotic units would, of course, interactively respond to the inner language communication of their owners and, as a result, would permit them to become independent in their ability to move about the home or through the general community.

The use of robotic trainers and "therapists" will provide enhanced physical and speech rehabilitation services to people who are handicapped, or disabled temporarily, or due to age. These units could provide such services in the user's home and would contain artificially intelligent expert systems that would monitor the client's responses and allow the robots to modify their own actions appropriately. Through the advanced sensory ability of the robot and the multisensory interactive nature of the Net Console control unit, these machines would be able to communicate with the human medical practitioner or therapist in order to provide diagnostic information and to receive new or modified treatment instructions. These robots are envisioned as being a part of the home technology medical treatment program described in Chapter 2. The advanced and artificially intelligent robot trainers and "therapists" are not intended to, and will not, replace the human practitioner; rather, they will act as intelligent extensions of the medical personnel.

Researchers project the development of interactive robotic braces and other prosthetic devices that will permit many physically disabled individuals to gain or regain control of their bodies. It is anticipated that these robotic units will be controlled by the individual through such means as nervous system control, galvanic skin interfaces, and biofeedback controllers. These units can act as prosthetic replacements for missing parts of the body and will also be able to serve as both implanted and external robotic braces. The artificially intelligent microprocessor components of these prosthetic robots will allow them to respond personally to commands and to modify their response to the individual user; that is, to learn through experience with the user.

One important caution should be raised concerning the use of robots by disabled people in the Information Age: the more dependent these people become on machines, even artificially intelligent robots and computers, the more susceptible they will be to a loss of their functional ability due to machine or power failure. Although this situation is true for everyone using these machines, special needs people may, and probably will, be more dependent upon these robots as prosthetic and compensatory aids; therefore, they will be less able to marshall alternative resources. We are seeing increased evidence of this phenomenon, particularly with physically and health-disabled adults and with certain of our aged citizens. For example, the breakdown of wheelchairs and other mobility devices, communication boards, and specially modified automobiles can pose almost insurmountable problems for these people. A nonfunctional telephone or the loss of electric power can create life-threatening situations for some of them. Many robotic scientists have pointed out that the more complex the robot becomes, like other advanced technologies, the more likely it may be to make mistakes or break down. Therefore, the greater the dependence of exceptional populations in the future on intelligent robots and other advanced technology systems for essential and, in many instances, life-sustaining daily functions, the more devastating the implications of such systems' failures. An intelligent and expert robot cannot help anyone if it does not work.

## INTERACTIVE MULTISENSORY SIMULATION

We have become a simulation society, a fact that many of us either ignore or take for granted. An increasing number of our basic manufactured products and foods are mere simulations of the real thing. Simulation can be most easily defined as an attempt or effort to re-create the preceived world around us, including both natural experiences and fantasies. Plastic, for example, is a re-creation of natural resources. We place aluminium siding that simulates wooden shingles on our homes since this synthetic product provides better insulation and holds up better against the elements. We desire to simulate or achieve the visual effect of "wood" and, therefore, manufacture the synthetic in that manner. Television and movies often portray situations that simulate real-life experiences or fantasies. We evaluate movie and television special effects by the measure of how "realistic" the scene was, even when the scene depicted was futuristic or imaginary. Prosthetic devices simulate human limbs and extremities. Biomedical engineering seeks to simulate the natural functions of the human body and genetic engineering seeks to simulate the body itself. Pharmacology research seeks to develop synthetic chemotherapies that either replicate the human body, natural organic, or inorganic materials. Simulation and simulated materials permeate our lives in uncounted ways. Simulation, therefore, is an integral part of our lives and will become an even more sophisticated and important element in the future world of the Information Age.

The purpose of simulation is not to interpret events and activities in the world around us in the way that television reconstructs events. The television news programs do not show us an exact event or even a simulation of that event. The news shows present a synopsis, or recounting, of the events that the show's producer and writers consider to be the most salient elements of the incident being broadcast. The viewer is unable to judge whether or not the report is, in fact, an accurate summary of what actually occurred. However, most viewers will accept the synopsis as reported. The instant replay at sports events is a similar form of condensation since the replay only focuses attention on one apsect of a larger event.

Simulation, on the other hand, is an attempt to create an exact or "real" duplicate of the original situation, one which has minimal divergence. The more realistic the simulation, the better. Thus, a simulation on television would, in fact, be a show which attempted to replicate an event or situation in the exact sequence and time in which it originally occurred.

The computer is an electronic technology which permits the user to interactively simulate real-life or fantasy experiences. Many other forms of simulation are passive in that they only permit the user to view the replication of the original. Computer simulations, on the other hand, require the active participation of the user in order for the simulation to proceed to completion. Consider the area of problem solving. Problem solving in real-life situations is active and involves the realities of cause and effect. There is a specific reaction or response for every action taken to solve a problem; choosing an alternative action yields a different response. How often have we said to ourselves, "If only I had done this rather than that?" Computer problem-solving software provides the user with simulated cause-and-effect experiences. These programs are interactive in that, for every specific action or response chosen, the computer gives a specific response. Thus, a different choice made by the user results in a different computer response. Should the user not like the computer's response to their selected action, they can change their selection and receive a different response from the computer system. Users are solving problems in a manner that simulates the way people really make choices, by means of cause and effect, or as some have phrased it, "the school of hard knocks." These systems, therefore, provide real-life cause-and-effect simulations that are personally interactive. Computers also permit multisensory interactive simulations since motor, visual graphics, print, and sound can be included in the software package. Further, the dynamic qualities of the computer allow users to match the modality of input and output to their personal preference.

Computer simulations also permit users to solve problems involving dangerous situations, ones which might not normally be experienced by individuals. By using the cause-and-effect method, users may explore such situations without personally endangering themselves. An excellent example of this is the computer simulation flight-training programs that are used with airplane pilots and astronauts. Computer flight simulators set in an actual replication of the cockpit of the airplane or the space shuttle allow the trainee to experience a variety of computer-simulated situations. Making a mistake, does not result in death or serious injury as it would in real life. An error made on the computer simulation simply teaches the user that you do not make that choice in that situation. It is cause-and-effect learning in a real-life computer-simulated experience. These simulation abilities of the computer truly make it a window to the real world and allow risk-free trial-and-error learning.

The attempt to develop artificially intelligent computers is actually an attempt to simulate human learning, problem-solving, and language in an advanced technology electronic machine. This is not to imply that artificial intelligence is an attempt to simulate the human brain; this is not the case. Biomedical or genetic engineering may attempt this simulation some day, but this is not the purpose of artificial intelligence research. Artificial intelligence research is attempting to simulate in a machine the human thinking processes. As mentioned previously, the artificially intelligent computer will probably think and function in a manner totally different from that of a human being; it will be an "alien" intelligence. It will, however, be simulating the human because it is thinking, solving problems, and using language. Thinking and language are pruely human functions. An advanced artificially intelligent computer that could solve problems and communicate would, therefore, be a simulation of a human. This is one of the benchmarks against which researchers hope to judge whether or not a computer is truly intelligent: Can it replicate human intellectual and linguistic functioning?

When a computer can learn from past experience and apply it to a new situation — one of the definitions of artificial intelligence — it is simulating the human. Expert systems — advanced computer simulations — attempt to solve a problem in a similar manner. The attempt to develop artificially intelligent computer language systems that will allow computers to interact with users in their natural language is an attempt to simulate the human linguistic system. Simply stated, artificially intelligent computers, therefore, will be simulations of the human thinking and linguistic processes. This fact does not change; even if these advanced computer systems perform certain tasks faster and more accurately than their human creators: the model upon which they were based is the human, so they are simulations of people.

The interactive linguistic abilities of the artificially intelligent computer will also make it a truly multisensory simulation vehicle. Individuals will be able to communicate with the computers in their personal language system, no matter what modality of communication or inner language system it is based on. The ability of the artificially intelligent computer to modify its responses to the current levels of intellectual functioning and experience of the user further enhances the multisensory interactive nature of the simulation. The addition of interactive language capabilities to the other graphic dynamics of these advanced computer systems will also make the simulation an interpersonal experience, one in which human and machine would interact in almost the same way that people interact.

The Net Console user of these artificially intelligent computers in the Information Age will therefore be able to simulate any experience, event, or fantasy contained in the huge data depository of the world grid. These simulations will be available to be created for historical, current, or future situations depending on the desire of the user. The simulations can be used to solve any variety of problems, be they personal, work related, environmental, and so on. These multisensory interactive simulations will permit the user to consider a variety of alternative solutions and to consider the steps required to achieve these solutions until the desired result is achieved, all without personal risk. This capabilities of advanced artificially intelligent computer systems of the 21st century will allow the individual to use interactive simulation as an essential tool for inductively solving problems in a world of almost unlimited information. The computer simulation can sift through volumes of information about a topic almost instantaneously, providing the user with the appropriate information in the user's personal language system and in an amount that can be personally comprehended. The situation being described is different from a computer search in which the user is simply attempting to find or gain information. In the artificially intelligent computer simulation of the Information Age, the user will be attempting to solve a problem. The presenting problem may, in fact, be a question of what information the individual needs to access at a specific point in time and for a specific purpose. Nevertheless, the ultimate purpose of these systems will be to interactively assist the user in finding a personally acceptable solution to a problem through the use of a multisensory simulation.

Robots, computers in "human" form, represent an attempt, then, to develop an advanced technology that replicates people. The intent is to simulate the human motor system and sensory abilities; the shape or design of the robot is not of concern, since to simulate human functions does not imply that the unit must look like a person. The current models of robots, units which look nothing like a person, have proven their ability to simulate human motor functions since they have been successful in replacing, or substituting for, humans in situations such as assembly lines. Although these robots must first be programmed to perform a task such as welding, a function previously performed by a human worker, once they have been "taught" this assignment they can do it with precision; they can simulate the human welder.

The current research into the development of sensory capabilities for robots also represents an attempt to simulate a human function. In this instance, the intent is to develop in a robot the ability to sense and learn from the environment the same way a person does. It will not matter whether or not the robot is using "human" senses, such as vision and touch, or whether it is using new modalities such as sonar and radar. The robot will be simulating a person because it will be performing a humanlike function; it will be sensing, processing, and using information from the environment. As humans create advanced technology systems, such as robots, they do attempt to improve on human motor and sensory capabilities. Robotic limbs do not have to resemble human limbs but can have "improvements" such as additional fingers or arms, in order to make the robot more functional in a given situation. The model upon which these systems are developed, however, is the human; therefore, the systems are simulations.

The addition of artificial intelligence to robots in the 21st century will combine the thinking, problem-solving, and interactive language capabilities of advanced computer systems with the motor and sensory capabilities of robots. This combination of two advanced technologies would more closely simulate a total human than would either system viewed separately. Would such a system be an exact replica of a human? The answer is no, of course, because these systems would be advanced electronic technology machines with silicon "brains," not biological simulations of a person as would be the case of a clone. Even so, these advanced robotic designs are modeled after the human and, therefore, will perform tasks that could be performed by a person. Since these systems would be interactively controlled by users, the robots could perform tasks as if the users were actually doing it themselves. It is this capability to simulate human sensory, motor, and mobility functions combined with thinking, problem solving, language, and ability to act as an extension of the human user that makes this type of projected advanced technology system such a potentially powerful and valuable tool for certain disabled and aged citizens of the Information Age. The model for the development of these systems must be human; such systems must have both artificial intelligence and a robotic body with its unique sensory system, or else they will not have the same compensatory and prosthetic potential for these special groups of people.

### Interactive Vidoedisc Systems

Interactive videodisc systems provide another tremendous potential for multisensory simulation. The simplest of these systems consists of a television monitor, a videodisc player, and an attached remote control key pad that operates the player. The videodisc itself looks something like a long-playing record with a 12-inch diameter and a surface that is thin, transparent, and flexible. Such a disc allows both optical and audio information to be stored in its memory. There are two types of videodisc players: optical or laser produced, and mechanical or stylus in groove. Videodiscs offer a number of advantages over videocassettes. In optical or laser production, videodiscs are able to store 54,000 still frames, individual pictures of information, or 30 minutes of regular video on one side of the disc. The types of video information which can be stored on the disc include almost any form of visual print materials, such as pages of books or records, pictures, and diagrams. The system can also store any form of regular video, such as reproductions of regular film, video footage, and animation. The cost of manufacturing the actual videodisc is very low compared to videotape or celluloid film. Finally, the videodisc can be connected to a computer for faster access to the 54,000 frames of information and for purposes of integrating these two powerful technologies. Mechanically reproduced discs are less versatile than laser discs in access of frames, type of frames, and amount of memory. Further, because they have grooves that are touched by a stylus, mechanical discs are less durable. The primary advantage of laser videodiscs, however, are the vast amounts of information that can be stored on them and the speed with which information can be called up on the screen for the viewer. The videodisc system can sift through the vast amounts of information stored in its 54,000 still frames or regular video and locate the one desired almost instantaneously. Encyclopedias or training manuals stored on videodisc could, for example, be a combination of passages of written material with still photographs, animation, film footage, diagrams, and actual demonstrations as illustrations. Auditory directions could also be included on the disc. The sequence of presentation could be predetermined in the program or could be interactive so that each selection made by the user would call up the next sequence of video and audio information. Further, computer commands can be recorded onto the disc so that it can be used interactively with a computer. The computer itself can be programmed to operate the videodisc system, allowing the user to control the display on the videodisc player from a computer terminal.

The integration of the videodisc and the computer provides for a truly interactive multisensory simulation system. The simulation abilities of the computer are enhanced by the storage, instant access, and visual and auditory display capabilities of the videodisc system. In such an interactive simulation, the problem-solving program of the computer can control the still picture, regular video, and audio aspects of the videodisc system. The user, therefore, will experience a response from the system that is visually and aurally realistic and that truly simulates a life situation. The branching abilities of the computer, the ability to move or jump to another part of a program based upon the response of the user, will allow the videodisc microprocessing system to be used for cause-and-effect problem-solving simulations.

The groups that have made the most use of this type of integrated computer-videodisc system have been the military, the government, business, and industry. The primary use of these systems has been to provide training simulations. The traditional classroom training programs supplemented by labs or field practicums were found to be too costly, so the military, the government, and business turned to the interactive multisensory system as an alternative. This new type of instruction allows the trainee to learn and practice new skills on the interactive computer-videodisc system after some basic instruction. The trainee can practice in a cause-and-effect simulation on the interactive system and learn through an "electronically real" cause-and-effect experience. Errors on these systems do not result in costly mistakes in injury. Trainees learn from their errors in the simulation by using the computer program to direct the videodisc display. Although the cost of producing these interactive training simulations is high, the use of these simulations results in an ultimate cost savings. Individuals trained on these systems tend to master skills faster and have better on-the-job performance.

The addition of artificial intelligence capabilities to the videodisc system in the coming decades will create a powerful and personal multisensory interactive simulation medium. This system will permit users to interact with the simulation in their personal language systems. The translational processing capabilities of artificial intelligence implies that these advanced technology interactive simulations will be able to move the videodisc presentation into the appropriate format for the individual user; that is, they could move from spoken word, to graphic display, to written text, or to video display. Expert systems will assist the individual in using this type of interactive simulation system to solve a variety of personal problems in a multisensory manner. Users will see and hear the results of individual choices, a factor that will greatly enhance their ability to judge whether the ultimate outcome meets their personal needs and whether the solution is perceived as right for them.

The novice system capabilities of artificial intelligence will have particular application in such an advanced computer-videodisc system. Simulations will be able to be personally modified to the needs of the user. These systems will be able to modify the specific response of the simulation to the intellectual and ability levels of the individual. Growth and greater understanding by the individual will therefore mean that there will be appropriate modifications in the simulation and in the responses to the user's input. This capability will allow simulations to be personally modified so that individuals with a variety of backgrounds, experiences, and abilities could use the same multisensory system and could each participate in a simulation that met their personal requirements.

The Net Console, with its interactive videodisc capabilities, will serve as the home computer multisensory simulation center. Since this station will be connected to the world grid, the user in the Information Age will be able to access any simulation experience available anywhere in the world. This huge data base with its artificially intelligent computer capabilities will be able to provide the home Net Console user of the 21st century with almost unlimited opportunities to use simulation experiences to solve problems, learn new information, train or retrain, and recreate. Each user in a family could have the simulation personally adapted to his or her personal needs and would be able to access the system using his or her personal inner language system. Further, the system could be controlled by any variety of input and output devices, including adaptive devices designed to assist the handicapped with access to the computer. Thus, the computer could be used for learning, communication, control of the environment, and as a prosthesis.

### Some Implications of Interactive Multisensory Stimulation for Disabled People

Interactive multisensory simulation holds great potential for disabled individuals in the 21st century. Integrated advanced electronic technology systems will offer the user unique opportunities for education, training, and retraining. The simulations that will provide these experiences will be personally interactive and will modify themselves to the individual abilities, needs, and intellectual capabilities of the user. The simulations will be linguistically interactive and will respond in a manner compatible with the inner language system of the individual. Given the reality that the successful employee of the Information Age will have to continually retrain in order to remain competitive and employable, the retraining simulations will prove to be extremely important to these individuals.

Interactive multisensory simulations will also greatly assist the disabled user in solving the variety of problems that are implicit in life in the Information Age. Simulations will assist them in coping with the vast amounts of constantly increasing information in order to reach a personal solution to problems. Daily living functional ability will be enhanced through the use of problem-solving simulations that will be able to be modified to the individual needs of the user. Through trial and error, users will be able to experience cause-and-effect decision making in the relative safety of their homes prior to having to apply their solutions in the world at large. Further, disabled individuals employed from their homes will be able to use these systems to solve work-related problems.

The computer-videodisc simulation component of the Net Console will allow disabled users to have a host of experiences they might never have had without this system. They will be able to simulate experiences such as traveling, attending cultural events, participating in sports, creating their own stories and fantasies, meeting persons from history, and so forth. These simulations will open a whole new world to these individuals. All of these activities and others will be available to all disabled people because the computer will adapt the simulation to individual levels of functioning, communicate in the appropriate inner language system, and be able to be controlled by any adaptive interfaces. These multisensory interactive simulations will provide the homebound individual with the ability to live through the multitude of opportunities that will be available to all citizens of the 21st century. These systems will provide them with meaningful and interesting recreational alternatives and will thus make their lives more full and satisfying.

## INTERACTIVE COMMUNICATION SYSTEMS

Communication has traditionally been a problem area for many disabled and aged people. Advanced electronic technology systems ease this process, but at the same time, they will make it more complex for many exceptional individuals. More information is not necessarily better information. It is not what one receives, but rather what one does with the information that is received that matters.

The issue becomes one of how the communication systems of the future will be delivered to the end user. We have the components available today and can apply them (if the general population accepts them as daily living technologies the same way they accepted the telephone, radio, and television). Our society has developed advanced technologies that have been utilized so far mostly by the government, business, and industry. Common acceptance by the average user, as in the past, comes at some later date.

Interactive, or two-way, communication systems do exist today. All of the technology — computers, video screens, videodiscs, telephones, and adaptive devices — are being used. The area that has changed and is expanding is the delivery system(s), or the ways in which these components are combined and utilized. One of the first ways in which electronic technologies were delivered to the end user was the telephone. Although this still remains the primary manner in which offices and homes are connected to electronic technologies, such as computers, newer systems have been developed that greatly expand communication. Telephone communication systems are basically still systems that can transmit voice or computer data, and yet these systems have already expanded to providing group conferencing, computer networking, and visualization of both information and human forms.

Cable television, or CATV, greatly expanded communication technology using many of the principles employed in telephone systems. This technology allows the user to receive both audio and visual information simultaneously, or in a unisensory manner. CATV also allows computer data transmission either to an individual location or to an interactive multiperson network structure. Today, cable television is commonly a one-way system in the home, and projections indicate that we will be able to receive up to 500 channels on the home cable television system in the immediate future. Current industry estimates predict that by the year 2000 more than 100 million households will have cable television; CATV will become a major information and communication delivery system — and not long after that two-way or "multi-way" communication will become commonplace in many homes (Jones, 1973; Martino, 1979).

Fiber optics, the newest form of connected communication lines, offers an even greater interactive transmitting capacity. Fiber optics consist of a core of transparent glass that is coated with a different, more reflective glass. Information is transmitted by a laser beam, a tightly focused beam of single wavelength light. Large quantities of information can be transmitted at great speed; in fact, one signal transmission over an optical fiber line, which is one-fifth the thickness of a human hair, could perform the work of 10,000 ordinary telephone wires. It can also provide transmitting services similar to that of cable television, but it can transmit 8,000 different channels at the same time. Audio, video, and computer data can be transmitted over optical fiber systems, and connected sites can communicate and access data either on a one-to-one basis or by an interconnected network. Optical fiber is highly durable and much less susceptible to damage or breakage than the current telephone or cable television lines. As a result of this, and of the much greater transmission capability, fiber optic lines are replacing these older systems. Experts in the communication industry predict that fiber optics will be the primary system of information transmission and overland communication in the 21st century (Martino, 1979).

By the year 2000 a new system of communication by satellite networks will distribute the benefits of the information revolution around the globe, making productivity and communication jumps possible even in isolated areas of the Third World (Shaw, 1986). One satellite can accommodate 33,000 voice circuits. These satellites can transmit audio, video, or computer data and can serve as interactive communication systems. Current plans call for a global system of twelve such communication satellites. This system will be able to send 36 billion bits of information per second, which could transmit the *Encyclopedia Britannica* three times every second. These satellite systems will, by the year 2000, have the channel transmission capacity equivalent to 22 thousand television channels. If every man, woman, and child in the nation spent four hours per day transmitting messages on either a teletype or computer terminal, the resulting message traffic would just about fill those 22 thousand satellite channels.

Current projections are that satellite networks will make small, inexpensive, independent ground receiver units possible. Data will also be sent across space using laser communications, a concept termed "the wired sky." Long range projections show that inhabited control centers in space will collect data from sensors and data banks and route the information to where it is needed. These space platforms will be able to transmit to and receive from a very small antenna, for example, a wrist radio receiver. Such satellite and space platform systems will provide the basic communication networks of the 21st century. These space systems will not replace land communication networks, such as fiber optic systems, but will serve as the basis of the world-wide communication and information network (Cornish, 1983; Haigh, Gerbner, & Byrne, 1981; Northwest Regional Lab Telecommunications Conference, 1985). They will be able to deliver audio, visual, and computer information almost instantaneously to anywhere in the world and will be able to accommodate the ever-expanding information and communication needs of the Information Age.

The information technologies of the 21st century will be interchangeable and will connect transmission and reception units such as typewriters, movies, radios, records, tapes, telephones, televisions, computers, home appliances, and robots. This interchangeable capability will, therefore, form the basis of the home Net Console. The home users of the Information Age will be able to use their console connected to the world-wide communication system for interactive communication, information retrieval and transmission, education and training, business, activities such as banking and shopping, recreation, and home control. They will be able to have interactive and multisensory information access and communication through Videotex data bases; a two-way, or networked, interactive system that uses a video display, such a television or a computer, local processing, and remote data base accessability. Such a capability will permit the user to receive information that is electronically published and to access such things as an electronic library. The implications for disabled people are obvious.

### Some Implications of Interactive Communication Systems for Disabled People

The interactive and multisensory communication systems projected for the Information Age will form the basis of information delivery in the 21st century. They will be able to accommodate the exponential increase in the information base and will be able to provide this information directly into the home via the Net Console.

The development of such a world-wide communication system with instantaneous two-way or multi-user network capabilities implies that the user of the future will have to have good communication skills. Although the artificial intelligence capabilities of the electronic communication network and of the home computer component of the Net Console will allow disabled users to communicate with others in their natural inner language system, and although these systems will permit the user to communicate in a uni- or multisensory modality, the user will have to possess good computer linguistic skills in order to take full advantage of these systems. This implies that the disabled students currently enrolled in special education programs must be helped to develop these linguistic and communication skills if they are to achieve the maximum benefits from the systems of the future.

Electronic publishing is already becoming a reality (Publish or perish, 1987; Edwards, 1983; Fuller, 1987). Electronic publishing will allow disabled individuals to access and receive what used to be only "print" materials through their most effective modality and have it communicated to them utilizing their personal inner language system. They will be able to use electronically published material to learn, receive daily news and information, train and recreate. In order for the disabled students of today to be able to benefit from these interactive and multisensory systems, they will have to develop a love for and an appreciation of learning. Further, they will have to understand that reading takes many forms and that it does not necessarily have to be only in printed form. If they are allowed the develop a distaste for reading today, for any number of reasons including unnecessary failure in school, they will be unwilling and unable to use the electronic publishing information systems of the Information Age.

The interactive communication systems projected for the 21st century hold great potential to serve as normalization and prosthetic daily living agents for disabled and aged people. If, however, disabled people are denied appropriate access to and education about these systems, the technology has the potential to serve as a barrier to the exceptional individual in the Information Age. It is essential, therefore, that today's special education and rehabilitation programs stress the development of appropriate linguistic and communication skills. Moreover, it is essential that students receive training on today's electronic technology systems using the available adaptive input and output devices and software. These students must have the appropriate skills, knowledge, and experiences to use the interactive communication technologies of the future.

## Summary

■ Artificial intelligence will make possible extensive training and re-training. It will allow disabled people, particularly those with cognitive or linguistic disabilities, to interact with others in a much improved manner.

■ Robots of the future will be more interactive, sensitive to environmental stimuli, and flexible. The refinement of robotics will allow disabled people much greater freedom and independence. Although robots often take away jobs from people, it is expected that the growth of the robotics industry will actually create a much larger number of jobs than it removes. It should also be kept in mind that robots are usually called upon to do things that humans either cannot do or prefer not to do.

■ Interactive multisensory simulation, an outgrowth of expanding technology in videodiscs and artificial intelligence, holds tremendous potential for disabled people. Simulations will be used for training, solving problems, and experiencing many aspects of life that otherwise would be beyond the abilities of many people.

■ The rapid development of interactive communication systems will bring the world into the home. Disabled individuals will have access as never before to vast amounts of information.

■ To interact with the technological systems of the future, it will be extremely important to have some linguistic concepts and capability to communicate. On the other hand, the development of artificial intelligence will allow individuals with extremely limited language ability to communicate more effectively than is now possible.

■ Since technological advances — artificial intelligence, expert systems, interactive technology — will allow computers to interact with a "human" manner, it will become more and more difficult to determine what is human and what is not. Special education students must be taught to distinguish between machines and people, much as they are now taught that what they see on television is not necessarily "real."

# PART II

# Technology in the Classroom — Designing Programs for Disabled People to Prepare Them for the World of Tomorrow

**P**art II of this book discusses the curricular implications of preparing today's disabled students for life in the Information Age. These curricular suggestions will be geared specifically to special education classroom programs and will provide today's educators with concrete methods for modifying their current programs in order to provide the types of instruction that will prepare their students for the Information Age.

Chapter 4 discusses some of the communication and linguistic components that can and must be introduced into today's curricula for all disabled people in order to prepare them for life in the 21st century. Particular emphasis is placed on the concept of "Technological Linguistics," the ability to receive and express information, to communicate with others through electronic technologies. The primarily purpose of this chapter is to suggest that, if disabled children do not gain experience today in electronic communication and information processing, they will be negatively affected in the world of the Information Age, the world of their future.

Chapter 5 focuses on the concept of using electronic technologies to assist in solving problems both today and in the future. The citizen of the 21st century will have to cope with more information than can be handled at one time. The issue of deductive reasoning (the current approach used in schools) versus inductive reasoning (the type of thinking and information processing that will be required in the Information Age) is discussed. This is not to say that deductive reasoning should not be approached, but that greater emphasis should be placed on the inductive process. The concept of using electronic simulations to assist in problem solving is also addressed. Specific instructional suggestions are provided to assist today's classroom teachers in using computer systems, software, and other electronic technologies to teach mild and moderately handicapped students of all disability areas the skills required for them to process information and to solve problems both today and in the future.

Chapter 6 focuses on how today's electronic technologies overcome physical and communication barriers. Having these children learn about and experience the dynamics of technology today will better prepare them to use the full potential of future advanced technologies. Also discussed in this chapter is the belief that handicapped students of varied disability groups who use these systems should also receive training in the use of the more traditional nonelectronic methods so that they are not fully dependent upon electronic machines. With the application of advanced technologies, the more sophisticated prosthetic alternatives become, the more susceptible their users are to power failure and system malfunction. Specific curricular suggestions are provided for designing an instructional program that integrates both traditional methods and electronic technology.

Chapter 7 suggests a series of curricular concepts that must be included in today's prevocational and vocational training programs in order to enhance the transition of the disabled student from today's schools into the world of work in the 21st century. The concepts of flexibility, retraining, and lifelong learning are stressed, as is the importance of developing collaborative programs involving the schools, community agencies, parents, government agencies, and business and industry.

Chapter 8 presents a series of curricular concepts and activities for all major groups of disabled people that can be taught in today's special education programs and that will prepare these students to use electronic technologies as positive leisure activities. The ideas that electronic technologies provide interactive, stimulating, and enjoyable recreational alternatives and that the systems of the 21st century will provide expanded opportunities for these types of experiences are explored.

# CHAPTER 4

# Designing a Communication Program for Disabled Students

C ommunication permits individuals to share ideas, feelings, needs, and desires. Communication can be primarily motoric, visual, or verbal-auditory, although it is usually multisensory. For example, besides listening to a person speak, one usually reads his or her body language. The ability to effectively communicate permits a person to be an integrated member of humanity. The lack of this ability leaves the individual totally isolated. As society has become more and more complex, the ability to communicate has become more and more important.

Anthropologists have shown that the more primitive the society, the less complex the manner of communication. Communication in primitive cultures is primarily visual and motoric, with limited verbal communication. As societies become more complex with greater emphasis on differentiated work roles, the amount of verbal communication increases, and the form of communcation changes. The more industrialized a society becomes, the more verbal and multisensory communication is required, until it is the dominant form of communication.

Today we are leaving that Industrial Age and entering the Information Age, an age that has information requirements far beyond that of the Industrial Age, both in amount and kind. Further, that size of the information base is growing at an increasing rate. This fact alone means that society must find new ways to store, access, and use information. Students of today are faced with living in a transition period between two ages and, in order to be successful, must learn to cope with both, to live in both, to change as the transition occurs, and to change rapidly.

This transition period will require not only the communication skills of today but also the acceptance of change, an educational system that is based on the need for continual change in both curricular areas and content, and a lifelong learning philosophy in all phases of education. We see signs of these changes today as people are returning to educational institutions for classes in work-related skills as well as in the use of advanced technologies from microcomputers to word processors to electronic bulletin boards. Even our retired older citizens are returning to school because they have witnessed the vast changes that have occurred in their lifetimes and they know and understand the importance of accepting change and of lifelong learning. Once, long ago, society accepted and valued the wisdom and historical memory of the aged. During the Industrial Age, we appeared to gradually lose that need and value for the role of the elderly. This has particularly become the case since World War II. Today we are entering a new era, the Information Age, in which the wisdom of older people can again become important because only they who have seen and experienced vast change can understand the need to accept change and to learn new ways, especially new ways to communicate. To better help us all project these needs into the future, we must look at the developmental sequence of communication in humans; then, in our imaginations we must project advanced communication needs that are surfacing as we enter the 21st century.

The observation of young children can provide insight into this developmental sequence of communication skills from the motoric to the verbal-auditory and multisensory levels. Infants rely primarily upon the motor system to receive information and learn about the world and people around them. Physical discomfort, such as hunger, will cause the child to cry. When the child's mother responds to this crying by feeding the child, the crying stops because the child's motor or physical needs have been met. Soon the child learns that if he or she cries, mother or father will respond by alleviating the physical discomfort, be it hunger or a wet diaper. The child is communicating with the parents; information is being received motorically and needs are being communicated "verbally," albeit in a primary way. At the same time, the child is learning about the world and about individuals, their roles, and relationships. The communication here is totally egocentric and simple since it always concerns the child's primary needs.

The development of visual ability in the infant brings with it another level of communication and a higher order of information-processing skills. The child is now able to associate the visual image of the mother and father with the previously experienced sound and alleviation of physical discomfort. The child is now able to direct the communication of needs to a specific person(s) rather than to the world at large as was previously the case. Although the communication message is still totally egocentric, it is specifically directed, and the response received is individually associated. The development of this visual ability also allows the child to begin to gain information about the world without having to touch the object. Most often, in the early stages the child will have to touch the object in order to learn about it; then the child will develop the ability to identify the object when seen. The development of this expanded information or data base in the child provides an expanded repertoire about which information can either be received or expressed. The child is now able to communicate desires by pointing to an object after visually identifying it. Then the child may gain the parent's attention by making specific sounds. This form of expressive communication, although remaining visual and motoric, is of a slightly higher order because the sound is specific to a general class of needs (hunger, wanting an object, and so on).

The last and most complex form of communication and information processing to develop in the child is the verbal-auditory system, which marks the transition from the prelinguistic stage to the linguistic one. The first sounds that the infant is usually able to make an association with are the sounds of the parents' voices. The child is soon able to derive understanding from the tone of the parents' voices. This attachment of meaning to tone of voice is generally developed from an association between the physical experience and the tone of the parents' voices. The child then expands this ability to other objects and people in the immediate environment. Auditory communication at this stage is receptive. The child makes an association between a sound and something that has been either felt or seen. The more frequently the child experiences the same sound association, the better able the child is to transfer this information to another similar situation. These motor, visual, and auditory experiences and the multisensory associations among them form the basis of the child's inner language system in which he or she will think or process information.

Speech is the last system to develop in children. As with other systems, it is developed in a trial-and-error associative manner. Most often, speech begins during the time when the child is babbling and experimenting with making sounds, particularly the plosive sounds. At some point, the parent will hear a plosive sound such as the "d" sound, and react as if the child was saying "Daddy." The parents positive response to the child's babbling is repeated every time the child makes a particular sound. Soon the child associates the production of a particular sound with the positive reaction and then with a particular person. As time goes on the child learns to modify the sound and to imitate the word the parents use. Thus, "d-d-d" becomes "da-da-da" and eventually is modified to "Daddy." Other words, usually nouns and names, are added to the child's vocabulary for important objects and people in the child's environment. The child associates the parent's word with the object and then the child begins to attempt to produce that sound in order to express a desire for that object. The sound produced by the child is gradually modified to more accurately imitate the manner in which the parent says the word until the child can correctly produce the sound or name of the object. Expressive language at this early stage is generally limited to nouns; verbs, adverbs, and adjectives are added much later. The linguistic expressions remain extremely egocentric at this early stage of speech.

The study of the development of language abilities in the young child shows that both receptive and expressive communication evolve from personal experience. The motor, visual, and auditory perceptions of the child form the basis of the inner language system. This inner language system allows the child to make sense of new experiences, since he or she can attach meaning to these new experiences by comparing them to past ones. The inner language system also allows the individual to derive meaning from communications made by other individuals. It is this unique and personal nature of inner language that accounts for the fact that different people will derive different meanings from the same communication. The meaning that is attached to the communication will depend upon the individual's past experiences. Thus, a color-blind person will attach a different meaning to the word "sunset" than will the color-seeing person.

A great amount of emphasis in special education programs is placed on improving linguistic decoding and expressive oral and written language skills of disabled students. The ultimate objective of these programs is to assist the students in acquiring better abilities in communication and in deriving meaning from the world around them. The better these students are able to communicate and to derive information from messages that are communicated to them, the better they are able to function in the world at large. As our society becomes more complex, and the larger its information base grows, the more important these linguistic abilities become to functional daily living. However, it should also be noted that instruction in the development of linguistic and communication skills must also not only focus on the process, but must also stress the methods and techniques of communication used by society. Therefore, a total program for disabled pupils in all categories must also stress the technologies society uses for communication and for information processing. Thus, students must receive instruction and become proficient in technological linguistics, the use of communication technologies of the present and of the future.

If we return to our analogy of the human development of language, we see that from this basic development of an inner language and expressive language system, development expands in many directions an an explosive rate. Disabilities, however, can cause language development to be delayed or become skewed. The new Infomation Age technologies have the capability to compensate for or be used as prosthetic devices for visual, auditory, or motoric deficiencies of disabled people. When this occurs, individuals are free to become more technologically literate. They can now learn to communicate more precisely, more effectively, alleviating many of the multiple interpretations of language, and learning to better interpret communication. Through the use of advanced computers, artificially intelligent expert systems, and simulation, disabled people can then attach many more new meanings to past experience, and as this past experience knowledge base increases, they can learn at an ever-increasing rate. Advanced technology systems involving telecommunications expands the possibility of increasing this knowledge base even further. The world then becomes the environment in which functioning and learning occurs and, as it occurs, realistic knowledge of the world grows and expands.

These communication technologies are also changing and will continue to change rapidly in the coming decades. Prior to the invention of the telegraph and the telephone, the primary forms of communication were direct face-to-face conversation and written communication. The telegraph and telephone dramatically changed communication and permitted oral expressive and receptive communication across great distances. These communication technologies have remained the primary form of long distance communication and information access. The development of mass media is another major development in communication that increased access to information. Although these mass media have brought great amounts of information into the home and the office, they are, however, passive communication media since persons can only receive information.

The computer related microcomputer-based technologies represent the next stage of development in communication technologies. The computer is most simply described as an information-processing machine that can be used as a communication tool; a linguistic device. Through the combination of telecommunication systems and computers, the user can not only send and receive information but can communicate with an individual or a group of individuals. The importance of this communication tool will grow as we move into the Information Age. As advanced technologies come into general use, one's ability to

effectively use this technology as a daily communication and information-processing device will determine in good measure how well one
will be able to function in the 21st century. Therefore, disabled students in special education programs today must become technologically literate and must learn to use these systems as communication tools.

Technological literacy for special education students must not be
viewed only as a desirable program enhancement. Rather, it must
become a core program permeating all curricular areas and extending
throughout the student's educational career, as do other programs of
instruction in the development of communication skills. It requires both
specific instruction in the use of the computer as a daily living tool for
communication and information processing and it must involve sub-
stantial hands-on experience. Our special education students must also
learn about the limitations and capabilities of computers. They must
learn about the social, educational, vocational, and recreational uses of
computers in society today and in the future. They must be helped to
understand how computers and related technologies are used for communication and for information processing. Their practical experiences
must be with the variety of computer systems and applications that are
used by the general society.


## TECHNOLOGICAL LINGUISTICS


An essential element in a technological literacy program for disabled students is the concept of the computer and related microcomputer technologies as communication tools and linguistic devices. One's
ability to effectively use these technologies as daily living tools is directly
related to one's ability to communicate with a computer system and
through a computer system to others. Thus, competency in the area of
computer technology is related to the disabled individual's proficiency
in the language system of these technologies.

The linguistic systems of computers and related technologies are
quite different from that of "natural" human speech. Technological
linguistics is a crucial concept that refers to how a person "talks" to a
computer and "receives" information from a computer. Although the artificially intelligent computer systems projected for the 21st century will be
able to modify their linguistic communication to the user based on that
person's inner language system, although they will be able to modify
input and output capabilities based on individual needs, the user will
still have to be proficient in technological linguistics. The user of these
advanced technology computer systems will be required to have the

ability to communicate with the computer system. One example of this concept can be found in how we use the personal banking card of today. Most banks now permit an individual to make banking transactions through the use of a banking machine. This machine is nothing more than a microcomputer that has been modified to the banking industry's needs. Although an individual may have a personal banking card and a personal identification number, he or she will be unable to make a banking transaction if the user is unable to communicate with the banking card machine. If the information requested is not entered correctly, or if the questions asked are now answered accurately, the user will be unable to complete the transaction. As a matter of fact, in certain instances, if the information is not entered properly, the machine will retain the card and not return it directly to the user. Thus, technological linguistics, or the ability to "talk" to the machine, is a prerequisite for making a banking transaction.

Technological linguistics is a crucial concept that refers to the language process of how a person "talks" to a computer, or to a computer-based machine, and how an individual "receives" information from such a system. This concept must not be confused with computer programming. In most instances in today's world, the user will never have to create a new program for the computer system. In tomorrow's world, very few persons will ever be required to have this skill since communication with the computer will only require the use of one's native language, and not "computerese." In other words, the user will have an increasingly large variety of software to use on the computer, or the individual will use authoring language systems to create new software to use on the system if there is a desire to design such a new program. These authoring language systems allow the individual to write a program using "natural" language commands.

Today, unfortunately, instruction in programming remains the primary form of instruction in too many computer literacy programs, a practice that is highly inefficient and that often results in a student "turning off" to technology instead of learning how this technology can be used to address particular needs. Of course, some students may want to learn to program for vocational or personal reasons and should be encouraged to do so; however, the majority of students do not have such a desire and, therefore, should not be forced to attempt to learn this skill. Furthermore, in the school curriculum, technological literacy should not even be approached as a course of instruction, but should be integrated into the total curriculum. Programming could be an elective, but only available if specific prerequisite skills and knowledge in the area of technology have been met.

Technological linguistics, therefore, is a functional skill that permits the individual to use the computer as a daily living information-processing and communication tool. Like oral language, it includes both expressive and receptive elements. It is a sensory language system employed by the computer user. It relates to the manner in which the individual communicates with the technology and through the technology with other individuals and data bases. Thus, the school system, including special education, must educate students to be bilingual, fluent in one's native language and in the language of technology.

The concepts of expressive and receptive technological lingusitics open language and communication alternatives for the disabled individual. The unique capabilities of computers and related microcomputer-based communication systems may prove to be a less complex system for many disabled students and, therefore, easier for them to learn and use — one which is particularly suited to their needs. It is definitely the one linguistic system that leaves the expresser and receiver in complete control of the communication process. These systems hold tremendous potential as compensatory learning and life-skill, prosthetic tools for disabled people and must be included in special education programs to provide school experiences in this linguistic system as part of the preparation for functioning in the increasingly computer-dependent society of the 21st century.

The effectiveness of the computer to serve as a linguistic alternative for the disabled individual is readily apparent to anyone who has watched a disabled child play a computer game. The symptoms of distractibility, short attention span, and low frustration levels, so typically manifested in the classroom, seem to miraculously disappear when the child is at a computer terminal. Although it must be admitted that the purpose of this activity is generally recreational rather than educational, the perceptual and motor skills required to operate the computer are no different than those used in instructional classroom activities. The ability of disabled children to use such a device whether for games or other purposes is indicative of the potential of technological linguistics to serve as a communication tool for them.

### Expressive Technological Linguistics

Expressive linguistics is a process significantly different from oral language. A computer is a memory and sequencing device and, as such, can perform these functions for the user. Further, the computer performs the actual transmission of information (speech) or the actual writing (motor) function for the user. Thus, the content of what is being communicated can be separated from the actual process of communication. The individual using a computer for expressive linguistic functions does not have to specifically attend to auditory-motor or visual-motor aspects of communication and can, therefore, give primary attention to the content of the message being communicated. Further, the message can be stored in the computer's memory until the time that the user is satisfied with the content of the message and is ready to output that information in whatever form.

Traditional oral or written language, on the other hand, requires that the individual devote attention to both the content of the message and the actual process of communicating that message. Speech requires that the person think of what will be said while actually producing the sounds. Further, the person must self-monitor what is being said by means of listening themselves. The more memory or sequencing problems a person has, the more difficult this task becomes. In a similar manner, writing requires that the individual attend to the formation of letters, spelling, grammar, and punctuation while at the same time attending to the content of the message.

These elements of expressive technological linguistics make this a language system that is conducive to the needs of many disabled people, particularly those individuals with expressive and central language dysfunctions, those who are physically disabled and those with sensory disabilities. Computers and related microcomputer-based systems, such as banking machines, can receive directions and information from the user in either a single modality or a multisensory manner, including voice activation, voice interactive systems, touch screens, keyboard and screen, hand held controller devices such as electronic pencils and joysticks, and the variety of other adaptive input devices. Thus, these factors make the computer an expressive language that can be readily adapted for use by disabled people, capitalizing on the strengths of the user and compensating for the individual's particular deficits. Therefore, disabled people can use their strength modalities to interact with the computer in order to transmit a message and allow the computer system to convert the message into one that can be understood by the receiver of the information. A blind individual can input information into a computer using either a Braille keyboard or a voice input system. The computer then translates the message into "normal" print or speech output while, at the same time, providing a soft Braille output for proof reading purposes if desired.

Expressive technological linguistics, as an element of a life skill technology proficiency curriculum, would include two major daily living competencies for disabled individuals: (a) to develop the student's ability to "communicate" with a computer using the variety of data entry and control devices that are currently available and as they become available in the future, and (b) to develop the student's ability to use the computer to "talk" with other individuals and with other data bases.

If we expect the handicapped to use computers and related micro-computer technology as a daily living tool in the 21st century, we must provide them with training and experience on these devices throughout their entire educational careers in order to develop in them an understanding about how to communicate with and through these systems. Here the emphasis is placed upon developing functional proficiency on a variety of computer entry devices so that the commands can be given to the system and information entered. Among the variety of computer and related electronic devices that should be included in such an instructional sequence of practical experiences are the following: calculators; digital watches; touch tone telephones; electronic banking machines; computer game devices; electronic pencils and other graphic input tools; computer keyboards, including prosthetically altered adaptive input devices; voice activated and voice interactive systems; electronic bulletin boards; electronic data bases; and acoustically coupled or modem-linked telephone systems.

A second element in developing the student's ability to "communicate" with a computer or with a microcomputer-based communication system focuses on the commands that must be used with such systems. An individual does not have to know how to program a computer in order to direct and control the machine; however, computers are exact and literal devices and, therefore, the commands given to the machine must be consistent and in a "language" the computer can understand. An individual, therefore, must learn the commands the computer and the software systems understand. There is a basic vocabulary of terms, such as "load," "run," "stop," and "save," that constitute the language of commanding a computer. Handicapped students must learn this relatively small but unique vocabulary if they are to use computers as daily living tools. These terms cannot simply be taught as vocabulary. These pupils must learn them while using computer systems. They must experience the computer's immediate and exact response to their commands as they are learning the meaning of these terms.

Handicapped students will also have to receive instruction in the use of computers and related microcomputer communication devices to speak with other people. This is becoming an increasingly important skill, and projections about the home Net Console of the 21st century indicate that it will become even more important in the Information Age. As was mentioned previously, expressive technological linguistics implies that the computer will perform the actual task of communication, whether it be on the screen, in print, by means of voice output, or by touch. This capability means that the disabled user will be able to devote almost complete attention to the content of the message while disregarding the actual motor task of speech or writing. This separation simplifies the expressive language process. Further, since the computer performs the actual task of communication, it becomes a compensatory tool for individuals who experience problems in language expression.

When one considers the variety of disabled people who have some degree of expressive language problems due to physical, neurological, or emotional problems, one begins to realize the potential of the computer as a compensatory or prosthetic expressive language tool. A computer can perform the short- and long-term memory, information sequencing, and motor functions that the human brain, nervous, and muscular systems previously had to perform. Further, it can perform the actual process of communication for the individual. Most importantly, the computer in this instance is a passive tool and, therefore, leaves the user in total control of the communication process. The computer will do nothing unless commanded to do so by the user.

On the other hand, oral conversation, even that on a telephone, is interactive. The person communicating is limited by the reactions of the person receiving the message. Therefore, the individual must attend to the process of communication, the reactions of the receiver of the message, as well as to the content of what is being communicated. This is a complex and difficult process for individuals with expressive or central language dysfunctions.

The use of electronic bulletin boards as a communication system, for example, simplifies the expressive communication process for the user. The individual can take as much time as is necessary to formulate the message to be communicated. The actual message will not be transmitted until the user is satisfied with the content. This information can be entered into the computer in the person's strength modality and with a variety of input devices. The use of electronic bulletin boards to communicate with others leaves the user in total control of the expressive language process. They are not limited by the reactions of the receiver.

Word processing provides another excellent example of the use of a computer as a compensatory expressive language tool and represents a basic daily living skill that should be introduced to many disabled people. Word processing provides individuals who have impaired written expression abilities or physical disabilities with a compensatory tool to overcome these limitations. Rather than focusing an inordinate amount of attention on the motor act of writing, word processing frees disabled individuals from this distraction and permits them to focus their attention on the quality of the message. Since the computer will store the message while it is being composed, the user can correct the message after having composed it or have the computer correct it using one of the checker softwares available (for example, syntax or spelling). Word processing can, therefore, form the basis of communication on electronic bulletin boards.

The computer is a particularly powerful expressive communication tool when it is interactively linked via telephone or cable television systems. These modifications permit not only interpersonal computer communication with others but also the performance of such daily living functions as shopping and banking from the home. Thus, physical barriers to communication are removed and distance limitations are negated. These factors can provide many disabled people with greater control of their lives and increased independence.

## RECEPTIVE TECHNOLOGICAL LINGUISTICS

Receptive technological linguistics is the process by which an individual "receives" information from a computer or from another person through a computer system. As with expressive technological linguistics, this sensory process is also significantly different from oral or written language. The unique memory, sequencing, and sensory display functions of a computer permit the disabled user to focus increased attention on comprehension rather than on the sensory-motor process of reception. Further, the memory capabilities of the computer make it a communication device that leaves the user in complete control of the reception process. Communication received through a computer can be reviewed by the individual at his or her own pace. The computer will retain the message in its memory until the user has indicated either that it has been comprehended and no longer must be retained or that a print copy is desired for further review. Thus, the use of the computer to receive information and messages leaves the individual in complete control of the process.

Receptive technological linguistics suggests the following daily living competency for inclusion in a life skill technical proficiency curriculum for disabled people: to develop their ability to "receive" and "process" information directly from a computer as well as from other people and resources through an interactive computer system.

This linguistic competency is one of the most crucial in the achievement of functional independence in the Information Age. The increasing use of computers by government, business and industry, science, medicine, and the mass media is causing an information explosion. The pressure to keep up and to deal with an information data base is constantly increasing. Although we are only in the early stages of this phenomenon, we can anticipate that further advances projected for the 21st century will result in a greater information glut. Therefore, today's disabled students will have to deal with much greater amounts of information than we deal with today. Those who have been trained to use the computer to receive and act on information will be best able to compete.

Receptive technological linguistics is the first step in learning how to manage the information revolution.

The dynamic elements of the computer make it a receptive linguistic machine particularly suited to the needs of disabled people. Data can be received from a computer in a visual mode, in an auditory or voice output mode, or in a tactile mode such as Braille print. Visual information can be presented in the form of print, print and graphics, or in a graphic manner exclusively. The message can be presented in one modality exclusively, in a multisequential format, or in a multisensory manner. The mode of computer presentation can be matched with the individual's learning or communication strength(s). This quality of the computer allows the disabled user to devote more attention to the content of the reception and less to the actual sensory-motor function. Thus, the teacher or disabled user can select and control how the information is presented, thereby compensating for deficits and capitalizing on sensory and learning preference strengths.

Receptive technological linguistics also implies that graphics, sound, or voice can be used to enhance the comprehension of a printed message by the disabled user. If the full benefits of the computer are to be realized in special education programs, then information presented to disabled students must not be mere reproductions of the pages of a book. The marriage of the computer and the videodisc greatly expands the multisensory transmission of information and improves comprehension. These systems combine the memory capabilities of the computer with the graphics and sound capabilities of the videodisc. When these systems are interactively merged, information can be presented through printed words coupled with video segments, such as video graphics, sound, or voice, to provide disabled students who have impaired reading abilities with an important alternative: they can comprehend complex concepts above their decoding reading level.

The computer is a passive communication device, one which leaves the user in total control of the receptive process. It can store tremendous amounts of information in its memory, and it does not present this information or any part of the message unless given a command to do so by the "receiver." Although these machines are passive communicators, they are also interactive since they respond immediately to commands and present exactly the information selected in the modality of presentation that has been selected by the user. These factors permit user, teacher, or therapist to control the rate of presentation, the amount of material, and the content of the information transmitted to them by the computer. Sensory overload can, therefore, be minimized because people control how quickly information is received from the computer as well as the actual mode of presentation. The disabled user can devote more attention to the message being received and less to the process of reception.

## CLASSROOM APPLICATIONS AND ACTIVITIES

A technological linguistic program should be implemented for all disabled students and should extend throughout their educational careers. It should be core element of study and, as such, should be integrated into all curricular areas rather than becoming a new and separate curriculum. The more disabled students use computers and related electronic communication tools, the better their chances of developing good and functional computer linguistic skills. The following suggestions about applications and activities that can be employed in instituting such a program are not intended to be a comprehensive discussion but will address some of the types of activities that can help disabled students learn these skills. It is hoped that these suggestions will stimulate the creative thinking of special educators, parents, and rehabilitation experts so that they will be able to expand on the basics and thus meet the individual needs of their disabled students or clients. Further, since this is such a rapidly developing field with new hardware, adaptive devices, and software becoming available constantly, professionals must stay abreast of these developments to take advantage of them in providing technological linguistics training.

One of the very first steps in implementing such a program is to conduct an evaluation of the disabled students. Such an evaluation is designed to identify the specific needs of the pupils in using the computer and related technologies as communication and information-processing tools. Therefore, the specific physical, neurological, and intellectual abilities of the students must be assessed in order to determine whether or not prosthetic input or output devices must be used in order to give them access to the computer and to determine the most effective interface between the individual and the machine. Therefore, the exact needs of the individual must be considered in determining which adaptive device to use or how to modify the device. Naturally the adaptive device must then be evaluated to determine if it is appropriate for a particular individual, in the case of severe impairment, or for a group of individuals where the impairment is not as severe. The importance of evaluating the individual needs and abilities first and then matching the adaptive device(s) to that individual cannot be stressed too greatly. It should never be the other way around; the device should never be purchased with just a general idea of how it might work. Purchasing an adaptive device without thorough evaluation of the individual's needs will cause great frustration for all concerned parties and will not be of the greatest benefit to the individual.

Physically and developmentally disabled individuals might require such adaptive input and output devices as modified keyboards or keyboard guards; pressure, touch, suck and puff, or sound microswitches; electronic communication boards; light emitting diodes (LEDs); scanning hardwares and software, tilt screens or voice synthesis output. Blind and visually impaired students may require Braille keyboards, voice activated systems, voice synthesis output, Braille printers, or large screens and printers. Neurologically impaired pupils may require the use of a computer that allows the input and output devices (joysticks, light pens, touch input devices) to be selected and modified for use by different students. Deaf and hearing impaired pupils should receive instruction in using the Tele-communication Teletypewriters for the Deaf (TTYs) and other augmented systems that allow them to communicate with the hearing world through the home telephone.

The first series of skills that students will have to master in techno-logical linguistics is how to command a computer in order to control a soft-ware, how to get a response from the machine, and how to enter data into it. This includes the use of the keyboard or some adaptive input device. Because increasing numbers of computer access devices found in the general community use a calculator or a touchtone telephone as a data entry device, most mild and moderately impaired students should also receive instruction in the use of these tools as a part of learning how to input information into a computer. For example, the touchtone telephone type of entry format is used with electronic banking. Since a technological linguistics program has as its ultimate goal the development of functional daily living skills, it is, therefore, important that students receive experiences on the variety of input and output devices that are currently used in the community.

Disabled students should also receive training in how to use touch pads and the touch screens. Although these can be very effective adaptive input devices for certain disabled pupils, the reason for their inclusion in data entry training for all disabled students is entirely different. These touch devices provide students with another form of expressive communication, computer art. They can use these devices to create designs, to draw pictures, and to communicate feelings. The production of such art is personally rewarding and the artwork can either be saved in memory for future viewing or be printed using the printer. The use of these systems also provides students with a better understanding of how to control, interact with, and receive information from a computer. The use of these touch input devices are fun and allow the user to explore the computer and its dynamics. Children with physical, perceptual, or sensory-motor disabilities often find the computer and touch pad to be an easier tool for creating art than the more traditional materials of paint and crayons. The use of a computer to create art has also proven to be a very effective teaching tool with emotionally disturbed, linguistically impaired, and autistic pupils. These students are able to express themselves and their feelings through this medium. Since the computer is noncritical, it poses no threat to them in creating their pictures.

Computer game and control devices, such as joysticks and paddles, should also be included in the instructional program. These devices can provide access to computers for some students and assist others in learning how to control a computer for linguistic purposes. Aside from being entertaining and fun, these computer devices allow students to learn additional ways in which they can "talk" to a computer. Further, these adaptive devices help them to develop eye-hand coordination skills. This ability becomes increasingly important as students progress to the use of instructional software, word processing, and electronic communication systems.

Another important device to which some disabled students should be exposed is the mouse, a hand-manipulated and button-activated computer controller based on surface contact. Increasing numbers of computer systems are being designed which use these input and control devices in connection with icons, windows, and mouse activated menus. Therefore, the purpose of a technological literacy program is to develop functional life skills, and since the mouse and related software are being used increasingly in employment situations, it is important that disabled students, in particular the mild and moderately impaired pupils, receive instruction in the use of this technology and its related software. The more severely impaired students can use these software programs, involving mouse input, in connection with an adaptive firmware card.

Robots and microcomputer robotic toys represent another technology to which disabled students should be exposed. These systems provide the students with a basic understanding of how to communicate with and use this technology, a technology that will become increasingly important in the 21st century. Microcomputer robotic toys can also be very effective tools in assisting students in exploring their immediate environment. Young mild and moderately disabled pupils can use these machines to develop skills in estimating distance and position in space. They can also assist in the development of laterality and directionality. Electronic toys can also be employed in teaching number sequence. Larger instructional robots such as HERO 2000 or HERO 1 (Heath/ Zenith) have been used to provide sensory stimulation to infants and young children. They can easily be "taught" to move a child's limb, as in a patterning program, and can provide sound and voice stimulation. A robot performs its task exactly as it has been taught and, therefore, can provide consistent stimulation. Another group with whom educational robots have proven effective are emotionally disturbed and autistic children. For some reason, children view these robots as nonthreatening. They will imitate the behaviors of the robot and respond to its speech more readily than they will a human. The robot, therefore, serves as a role model for these students.

Low functioning developmentally delayed and very young children with other disabilities also receive instruction in controlling a computer and "talking" to it. Most programs for these children use the computer for sensory stimulation. Bright attractive graphics, sound, and voice output generally comprise the stimulation. The child is provided with some form of adaptive input device. Through trial and error, the child learns that when the controller is activated the computer responds. Such a sensory stimulation and awareness program has been used successfully with infants and very young children who have multiple handicaps. The computer stimulation can be varied by the teacher or parent through the use of an authoring language system such as MACS, the Multisensory Authoring Computer System developed by The Johns Hopkins University under a grant from the Department of Education. New stimulations, voice–picture associations, and sound–picture associations can be quickly and easily developed on this or some similar authoring system and, therefore, individualized materials can be generated for specific children.

There are numerous adaptive software programs that assist the linguistically impaired student with expressive communication. These systems have also proven effective in use with mentally disabled students. In certain instances, the software permits the user to identify a picture symbol on the screen and the computer will add the word or linguistic phrase associated with the symbol. Thus, through the identification of a series of symbols, the disabled user can communicate to another individual. Authoring language systems permit the teacher or parent to develop additional symbol-language associations rather easily. As a result, this type of communication program has proven to be very effective for use in total language communication curricula. Another version of this type of communication software allows the user to scan and select words. The computer program generates the word most likely to appear next in the phrase or sentence after the user has selected its first letter. If the word selected by the computer is incorrect, the user can enter the correct word through scanning; however, since the computer is very often correct in its choice, it greatly speeds up the communication process for the physically and severely linguistically impaired student. The computer with appropriate adaptive devices and communication software is very often a more effective electronic communication device for disabled students than stand-alone electronic communication boards because the computer has a greater memory capacity and more flexibility. For example, vocabulary can be continuously added to many computer programs as the user's linguistic system improves. Schools are increasingly employing programs like these since they permit the disabled user to communicate more precisely to other individuals and to the teacher by using either print or voice to add to the student's communication effectiveness. A copy of the program should also be used in the pupil's home to provide comprehensive and consistent electronic communication support for the child.

The use of word processing software is another important skill to be developed in children with disabilities, particularly those in the mild to moderate range of impairment. Simply stated, word processing is a program that uses a computer as an automated typewriter that allows editing prior to printing. It also allows a message to be entered or stored in the computer program's memory. This message can be entered using a standard keyboard or adapted input devices, thereby requiring no handwriting skill. At any time, the message can be loaded from memory and the data can be reviewed, corrected, or reordered either by the individual or by the computer through its software program. Many word processing programs also contain spelling and grammar correction units called "checkers." Threfore, the program can assist the disabled user in making corrections to the message, thus compensating for problems which the user may have in these areas. The final message can be transmitted to another individual in many forms including print or voice output. It can even be transmitted over long distances using telecommunication systems.

Since parts of the message can be stored in the computer's memory and recalled at any time, the disabled user can create the message at his or her own pace. Therefore, if the message is to be communicated to another individual through an electronic bulletin board, the user can take as much time as required to develop the message, even if it is days, and then command the computer to transmit it when the user is satisfied with the content. Word processing leaves the user in total control of the communication process. The computer and the software merely serve as obedient assistants to the disabled user.

Word processing can and should be introduced as soon as the disabled child begins to use symbolic representation as a form of expression. Young mildly disabled and slightly older moderately disabled children can manipulate symbols or words on the screen using simple word-processing systems. Further, these children should also be given experience in "saving" what was on the screen and in "calling it back" at some later time. This will help them develop an understanding of how they can compose a message at their individual pace. Finally, they should experience "sending" their completed message in some output format. Although the messages these children develop initially may be no more than a very short sentence, such experiences are essential building blocks in learning how to use word processing as a daily living expressive language tool.

Since word processing is a basic expressive technological linguistic skill, it should be developed as a disabled student progresses through his or her educational career. It can be used in almost all curricular areas and, therefore, should not be taught as a separate subject. It is important that these students understand the multitude of applications that this daily living skill holds for them, and they can best learn this by using it in a variety of ways and for a variety of academic subjects. It is a skill that will later assist them in getting a job and in functioning in general society. Further, when one considers the advanced computer and artificial intelligence systems projected for the 21st century, having this skill will take on even more importance to functional daily living in the Information Age.

There is no one word-processing system that is good for all disabled children. These systems vary in the complexity of commands and in the manner in which they allow the user to manipulate the message. Information from student evaluation will assist in determining which of these systems should be used with a particular child. As time goes on, however, and the students develop ever-increasing abilities in word processing, they should be introduced to more complex and sophisticated systems. Further, some of the older pupils will need to use more advanced systems as a component of prevocational and vocational training programs. Thus, students should not use one word processing system throughout their educational careers.

Although students should be encouraged to use word-processing systems as a basic form of writtern or alternative linguistic expression in all of their academic subjects, this is not to suggest that they should not also use the more traditional form of written communication in the classroom when possible; the development of this skill is still important. Nevertheless, students should use word processing as frequently as possible in order to provide them with the maximum amount of exposure to these systems throughout their educational careers. For many students, the use of these systems will prove to be an easier form of communication and, therefore, will allow them to devote more attention to the content of the instruction. For certain pupils, word processing may prove to be the only way they can communicate in a written format. Regardless of the ability level in handwriting, it must be remembered that the ability to use word processing is becoming an increasingly important functional daily living skill and will be even more important in the future. Electronic bulletin boards and related computer-based communication systems are increasingly used today in business and industry and, therefore, the development of the skills necessary to use these systems are often important in attaining a job. This is particularly true if a person must work from home. It is, therefore, essential that disabled students are provided experiences in using this form of electronic communication throughout their educational careers. Further, for many students with limited oral or written linguistic abilities, this electronic medium may be the only way in which they can efficiently and effectively communicate with the world at large.

Most schools and special education programs do not as yet have access to an electronic bulletin board. Although the cost of subscribing to these systems is not great, other instructional priorities always seem to take precedence. It seems that when new curricular directions are instituted, they are add-on items instead of integrated items. In the case of electronic bulletin boards, however, it is relatively easy to integrate their use into the curriculum. Prior to instituting the use of electronic bulletin boards, a simulated electronic bulletin board training system can be set up in the classroom, throughout a school, or throughout a school system by using word processing. Individual students create messages on the computer for other students or teachers. These messages can be saved on disk and later transmitted to individuals throughout the school system. The receiver would then decode the message and respond back to the original sender on the same disk. The use of such an electronic communication system provides disabled students with the needed experience in sending and receiving communication from another individual through a computer. Not only are such instructional exercises fun for students, but they can simulate in a cost effective manner the electronic bulletin board and the Net Console system projected for home use in the 21st century.

An extension of this concept, the electronic pen pal, can provide other linguistic and social benefits to students. A disabled student corresponds with a nondisabled student through word processing on the computer. Messages are sent and received via an electronic bulletin board. Not only does this approach provide disabled students with much needed experience in electronic communication, it can serve to enhance their linguistic skills. The nondisabled pen pal can serve as a linguistic model for the disabled child. Through such an electronic correspondance system, the disabled child can learn to modify his or her inaccurate linguistic patterns by noting how the received messages are composed. Over a period of time the disabled pen pal can modify his or her communication system so that it better reflects that of the nondisabled participant. A second important benefit of such a program is that the disabled child can develop social skills and competencies. The pen pals will communicate about things that interest them, things which very often transcend school issues and concerns. Through these communications, the handicapped participant will be developing social communication skills and, in many instances, social awareness that his or her condition had previously precluded.

Another receptive technological linguistic skill that disabled students will have to master is the use of electronic data bases to gain information. These would include such things as shopping and banking from home by means of telecommunications. In addition, it includes the ability to access data bases in order to locate and receive information. Students can learn to access and use data bases through direct access to the computer and through electronic bulletin boards within the classroom. For example, library data bases can be accessed through the electronic bulletin board from the classroom, opening up the entire world of available information. As in the case of using electronic bulletin boards to send and receive individual messages, data base access and usage will be an important functional daily living skill for these students to have in the Information Age, the era of the home Net Console.

Additional methods can be employed in special education and rehabilitation programs to provide disabled students with information retrieval training in somewhat of a simulated manner. Large telecommunication information data bases, such as the Encyclopedia Brittanica, work from a menu format. This means that the individual must make selections and answer questions in order to locate the desired information within the system. This process can be simulated in the classroom by using instructional and problem-solving software that uses a menu format. Other sources for training are large scope and sequence instructional software systems, systems which generally cover basic skill areas such as reading and mathematics. Disabled students can gain experience in using data base and menu formats by using these systems. The information can be provided to them as print on screen, printed copy, or voice output. Further, any adaptive output system such as Braille print, can be employed in order to accommodate the special needs of individual students. In addition to the academic training these students will gain in using these systems, they will be developing an essential receptive technological linguistic skill.

The use of functional daily living receptive skills can also be developed in a simulated manner in the classroom. There are many excellent computer-shopping and computer-banking programs currently available for use on a microcomputer. In addition to providing functional daily living skill training, the use of this type of software in special education will assist students in developing the concept of shopping and banking by means of a computer. Although these programs are not the same as accessing a shopping data base, they do provide simulated shopping and banking experience.

Few special education programs, schools, or school districts currently provide their students with access to these types of information data bases. Again, the issue is usually limited resources and a lack of understanding about the importance of the mastery of these skills. Although many nondisabled pupils can and may develop these skills in the relatively near future, the disabled students will need to be trained in how to use these systems and in how to receive and comprehend information from them as soon as possible; such skills provide the primary communication access that is not presently available to the vast majority of these individuals.

## Summary

■ Technological linguistics comprises three major elements: expressive, receptive, and compensatory linguistics.

■ Expressive linguistics refers to technological processes that perform memory and sequencing functions, as well as the actual transmission of information, allowing the individual to concentrate on the actual content of the message to be communicated.

■ Receptive linguistics is the process by which information is received by the individual using the technology. Advances being made now and that logically will continue to be made in the future will allow disabled individuals to concentrate on the actual content of the message being received rather than by the process of reception.

■ Compensatory linguistics involves technological compensation for the physical, neurological, or intellectual deficits of the individual user, through adaptive input and output devices.

■ These three major components of technological linguistics will become extremely important for people with disabilities to understand and utilize. Technological linguistics should be integrated into all areas of the education of all disabled students.

# CHAPTER 5

# Electronic Problem Solving in the Classroom

A lthough communicating with others and transmitting and receiving information through a computer are essential skills for disabled students to master, they represent only a part of the linguistic competencies required for them to function independently in an information technology society. Not only must they be able to access and manage information, they must develop the ability to use the computer and related electronic information technologies to solve daily living problems. Their ability to function independently in the technological society of the Information Age is directly related to their ability to use the technology to apply learned concepts to new situations in order to solve daily living problems.

It is important to remember that electronic technologies such as calculators, computers, and robots are man-made machines. Admittedly, they are becoming more sophisticated and complex and can perform many functions more efficiently and more quickly than a human. This reality will continue and the advanced electronic technologies of the 21st century will significantly widen the gap between the performance of machines and humans. Nevertheless, technologies, both of today and of the future, remain purely electronic servants, instruments designed to obey our commands. A calculator cannot solve a mathematical problem unless a person gives it the proper algorithmic command. An industrial robot cannot perform a factory task unless it is first trained in a specific function and then given a command to perform it. A computer cannot perform a task unless an individual gives it the proper commands.

Further, a computer does not make mistakes, although it can provide incorrect data. Errors are made by human operators either in information entry or in program commands. A technology-dependent society is not one in which electronic machines make the decisions. Rather, it is a society in which people use electronic machines to solve problems, manage information, and perform tasks.

Providing real-life problem-solving experiences for all disabled students has traditionally been a concern for the fields of special education and rehabilitation. Basically, school is not a microcosm of the world; rather it is an alien society because, too often, little occurs in the classroom setting that occurs in a student's experience outside of school. Further, once pupils leave school, there are few adult experiences that resemble those encountered in school, except perhaps those faced in a residential facility. The type of experiences we have been able to provide that come closest to bridging the gap between the school and the world as a whole has been through classroom simulations or visitations. The traditional use of textbooks, films, and filmstrips to provide simulation experiences are limiting because of the lack of interaction possible between these mediums and the student. Further, the increasing fiscal constraints of school systems have often impeded the creation of realistic environments that simulate real-life experiences and that permit students to play roles, make decisions, and evaluate probable consequences.

Special educators place great emphasis on providing students with a multitude of instructional opportunities to practice learned concepts in problem-solving situations that reflect real-life situations. The purpose of all of these programs is to assist students in making the transition from merely exhibiting academic mastery of concepts to actually applying these concepts in real life. Their ability to solve problems in life and to intellegently apply learned concepts is crucial to adult independence.

This concern with functional proficiency has not, of course, been limited to the education of disabled students. The applications of academic learning have been receiving more attention as the general public has become more aware of the difference between a student's academic grades and a student's ability or inability to manifest functional applications of these skills as adults. There have been countless books, articles, and studies published whose main purpose has been to call the public's attention to the state of American education today. The major reports all suggest one thing — the need for improvement in our current educational system. A common situation often cited is mathematical illiteracy. Schools have been graduating students who are able to compute basic mathematical algorithms but who are unable to functionally apply these concepts to such daily living situations as banking, family economics, balancing checkbooks, the use of credit cards, counting change, and so forth. If our public educational systems were properly teaching problem-solving in mathematics, we would probably not be experiencing such a growth in the personal financial consulting industry.

Programs designed to prepare disabled students, particularly mild and moderately impaired students, to be active and efficient problem solvers must not only teach them decision-making techniques but must also teach them the problem solving language of specific curricular areas. All too often, students can perform a specific skill in isolation, but they cannot transfer this skill to a real-life situation. Using the mathematics example, students have difficulty in applying math skills because they were not taught the utility of such concepts as "more than" and "less than" in reference to mathematical operations. Further, the students' difficulties in mastering these skills are often compounded by such demonstrated difficulties as impulsivity, distractibility, short attention span, poor organizational skills, and failure expectations. Despite the instructional difficulties, the ability to solve problems in life is crucial to their achieving adult independence, especially since our society continues to become more complex and requires us to make more and more decisions. Living in society will continue to become more complicated as we enter the 21st century, the era when our current population of disabled students will be adults. It is crucial, therefore, that they learn the language and skills of problem solving today.

The computer and related electronic technologies can provide these necessary personal and interactive problem-solving experiences to disabled students in the classroom. A computer data base does not have the updating limitations that textbooks, films, or filmstrips have. The computer data base can be inexpensively and frequently updated and, therefore, can provide students with topical simulation and problem-solving experiences. When one considers the length of time that it takes an educational textbook or film publisher to create a new instructional material, one realizes that many of the facts and situations depicted in the print materials and film are outdated at the time of publication. The technology of print or film does not allow for the rapid and frequent content changes necessary in our rapidly changing world. Besides, print and film materials are basically passive in the manner in which they impart information to students, and technology takes on special importance because of its interactive ability.

## COMPUTER SIMULATION AND PROBLEM SOVLING

The computer provides an important instructional alternative for teaching problem-solving techniques to students of all disability groups. It is a highly interactive medium, one which attends exclusively to the individual user. It permits student creativity, allows for self-monitoring, and provides continuous feedback. Most current instructional simulations, particularly those presented in print and on film, are passive; pupils are presented with a real-life situation, a series of related facts, and are then asked to solve the problem. Answers are usually evaluated as being right or wrong. Although the situation described in print or on film may reflect a situation that occurs in general society, it is a static and passive situation. Problem solving is the real world is active and personal, involving the realities of cause and effect. The decisions reached in real-life situations are generally evaluated on the basis of appropriateness rather than as being right and wrong. If a decision turns out not to be the most appropriate, the decision can be changed when the individual is faced with a similar situation, a process often referred to as "the school of hard knocks." Every decision in real-life situations has an effect, and it is the effect that the individual evaluates to determine whether the decision was personally appropriate. Other than carefully controlled classroom role-playing, only a computer-generated simulation can interact with a student in a cause-and-effect sequence, thereby providing a true representation in the classroom of how a learned concept might really be applied in daily life. Further, the personal risks in computer simulations are minimal, whereas those in real life are often critical. In a computer simulation, the student is allowed to go back and attempt the simulation as often as necessary until satisfied that the decision is the one most personally appropriate. Very seldom in real life is an individual able to try the same situation again; once the decision is reached, a person must live with the consequences. Some consequences of inappropriate behaviors can have permanent detrimental effects that prove to be very difficult to change.

An excellent example of how a computer can provide interpersonal cause-and-effect simulation is found in vocational training. Students can be placed in highly probable problem-solving situations on specific jobs. They can then investigate the possible consequences of a number of decisions prior to actually facing these situations. The computer simulation indicating the probable consequences of losing one's job is much less devastating than actually losing a job. This simulation, like all computer simulations, is highly personal in that each student decision or series of decisions creates specific reactions. The computer simulation could also retain a record of all student decisions in order to provide the instructor with a record of the specific sequence of decisions the student used. This feedback will assist the instructor in evaluating the progress of the student and in deciding what type of further instruction is required. Finally, the student can go through the simulation as many times as necessary in order to achieve an appropriate solution.

Each time that this occurs, the student learns and hones his or her decision-making skills.

Thus, the computer can provide the disabled student with personal and interactive problem-solving and simulation experiences in school. There is a great variety of microcomputer programs in a variety of formats that are currently available in a number of subject areas. Some of these problem-solving programs are even available in a game format. All of these systems, however, have certain common elements, and almost all are developed using branching techniques; that is, the student's specific response to a question or situation determines how the program continues. The decision the pupil makes determines what information the computer will present next. Thus, these programs are highly personal and can be used by a student multiple times, allowing the pupil to learn from the consequences of his or her actions. These problem-solving and simulation programs are very different from such programs as drill and practice. In drill and practice programs the student's response to a question is either right or wrong because these programs are primarily designed to reinforce concepts that have been taught or to provide practice in specific skills. Problem-solving and simulation programs, on the other hand, are designed to develop cause-and-effect learning and, therefore, do not have a right or wrong answer. They merely provide the student and teacher information about the consequences of a decision.

In certain instances, problem-solving software uses a reverse screen technique. These programs really represent the next step above drill and practice software. They all have one prerequisite — that the student be able to read. Many of these programs use a low reading level to present higher level situations and concepts. Students are presented with a word problem and asked to answer a question regarding something that is implied in the problem. If students give an incorrect answer, the program will reverse the screen to highlight, to focus a section of the problem that will help the student solve it. This process will continue until either the student solves the problem or until all pertinent data has been highlighted by the program. These reverse screen problem-solving programs have proven to be very effective in assisting students in developing functional mathematics, science, and health problem-solving abilities. They are generally used with students who have a least a second or third grade reading level. Students benefit from the reverse screen technique because the program shows them how or what to look for in order to solve a problem. The systems are also very effective in teaching the language of problem solving in particular subjects. Reverse screen problem-solving programs do tend to have one major drawback, they generally cannot be used multiple times by a student because they use only simple branching techniques (that is, the program branches to the next problem when the desired response is given by the student). Basically, however, the reverse screen sequence remains the same because the situations have specific right and wrong answers.

Many simulation and problem-solving programs that have been developed for use by disabled people rely heavily on still or animated graphics in order to present the problem or situation. The graphics are supported by print or voice, which are used to pose the situational questions. The use of graphics makes these problems considerably more realistic since they reflect situations in real life more accurately. Further, they do not rely heavily on the ability to read. In some instances, simple commands or responses must be read by the student, in some instances voice output accompanies the text, and in other instances a simple switch device can indicate yes or no, or be used to select the appropriate icon or picture response.

## Interactive Video Systems

Most problem-solving experiences in the school occur in the relative quiet of the classroom where the students attempt to solve written word problems. Real-life problem-solving situations seldom, if ever, occur in such an environment. Real experiences occur in a world with multisensory stimulation. As an example, classroom word problems simulating the application of shopping do not accurately reflect that total experience. Stores are noisy and visually stimulating with people, products, and displays vying for our attention simultaneously.

Special education programs have traditionally relied on films, filmstrips, audio tapes, and television to bring the real world into the classroom. Although these media do tend to accurately reflect the environment where the student will be required to solve problems, they cannot provide personal and interactive simulation experiences because they are passive activities. True learning requires the knowledge gained from cause-and-effect reasoning, not from outcomes predetermined by the producer of the instructional material, but from probable outcomes determined by the user.

Interactive computer-connected video systems can provide the necessary multisensory cause-and-effect simulations for disabled students in the classroom. Such an interactive video system is composed of videodiscs containing video and voice material controlled by a computer program. The student is seated at a microcomputer keyboard with video input provided by a television or monitor screen. Instructional materials in the form of computer texts, graphics, sound, and video segments are experienced by the student on the monitor screen. The instructional program, including branching options, are controlled by the computer. The student reacts through the keyboard to the simulation segment depicted on the monitor. Any adaptive input device can be used with such a system, thus making this electronic instructional modality applicable for use by students with most disabilities. Each student response generates a new video segment, thus simulating a cause-and-effect problem-solving situation.

A computer-generated interactive video system permits instructional variables to be presented in a multisensory manner. This modality of electronic simulation permits cause-and-effect learning to be experienced and allows the individual to vicariously "live" the experience. This dynamic aspect of computer technology has been a major aspect of our astronaut training program. Only the computer simulator can provide future space shuttle pilots with the multisensory experience of flying in space before actually being there. Although these computer simulations usually occur within some form of robotic training module, the actual simulation is computer controlled. This type of simulation is designed to train the individual in a safe environment. Another example is the type of computer simulation employed by the armed forces. Past experience has shown that the servicing of equipment, including advanced weapons systems, can be taught more efficiently and quickly through the use of computer simulations than by the more traditional directly supervised "hands-on" approach. Students are provided with traditional classroom training, are then directed to apply this training in a computer-simulated repair situation, and are finally permitted to practice and hone their skills on the simulated equipment until they show the appropriate skill level required to perform the task unassisted. Their progress and problems are monitored by the instructor, and individual assistance on the simulation is provided when required. The armed services have reported that students who participated in the simulated training repair experience manifested better skills than those trained in the more traditional methods. One cannot be harmed or damage equipment in a simulation, whereas one can be seriously injured or killed in the "real world."

The same technological applications of computer simulation used in astronaut training can and should be applied to the classroom instruction of disabled students. This technology permits the special educator to bring real-life problem-solving situations into the classroom, where consequences can be realistic but not devastating. These simulations are personal and interactive and can be provided at reasonable expense. They allow the student to personally interact with a situation and permit the pupil to directly manipulate the solution. The student can experience cause-and-effect learning at every level of the problem-solving sequence. These computer simulations can be easily and cheaply adapted to the course content.

## DISCOVERY LEARNING VIA COMPUTER

A major purpose in forming special programs and classes for disabled students is to create a learning environment that will support their individual learning styles and that will permit them to discover information and form concepts at their own pace. PL 94-142 and related legislation have provided funding to states and local school districts to achieve this goal. These publicly and often privately subsidized programs seek to focus attention on the students' learning strengths so that they can cope with their immediate environment and learn to express their own concepts and ideas. Unforunately, many of these well-intentioned program objectives are seldom achieved due to limitations in instructional materials available or the skills of the instructors. Most classroom materials used in special education programs remain in the form of print or graphics and, as such, fail to foster discovery-learning opportunities. These very same print and graphic materials resemble the instructional instruments that caused many of these children to experience failure at home or in school. Since these materials tend to be passive and to focus on the students' learning weaknesses, they inhibit the student's self-expression and ability to acheive academic success.

### Exploring the Environment

Students with disabilities can be provided with a true discovery-learning environment in their classrooms and at home through the use of a microcomputer and software. These systems permit children who have oral and written language problems or who have fine and gross motor problems to develop control of their immediate world, thereby assisting them in coping with daily living experiences. These electronic materials also permit them to control their learning environments and thus experience, think, and label in their own personal styles. Given the interactive nature of this technology and its ability to devote total attention to the user, it is an ideal tutor, teacher, and friend.

One excellent example of a program that permits exploratory learning in the student's immediate environment through electronic technology is LOGO. This computer language system was originally created by Seymour Papert, Harold Abelson, and Paul Godenberg and others at the Massachusetts Institute of Technology (MIT) as a part of a National Science Foundation research project. The program language was expressly developed for the purpose of creating a computer language that has it roots in the way children learn. The essential element of this discovery learning is that it permits children to learn about their immediate world through experimenting and through cause-and-effect learning. The freedom of children to explore, create, and self-correct is the most powerful aspect of discovery-learning programs. Since its development, many other instructional programs and games have been developed to aid children in exploring and learning about their world. LOGO, however, is the best known version of these systems.

The symbol most closely associated with LOGO is its "turtle graphics" or *Terrapin*. The *turtle* is represented on the computer screen by a small triangular figure. This emblem can be moved in four directions: forward, backward, right or left. The distance the turtle moves is controlled by placing a number, an indication of the number of moves desired by the user, after the command for the direction. Therefore, the command FORWARD 10 would move the turtle forward 10 spaces, and LEFT 30 would command the symbol to turn 30 degrees to the left. The turtle leaves a trail as it moves across the screen in response to the user's commands, thus creating the design of a geometric pattern. A series of commands are written into what is termed a *procedure*. The user can name or identify each procedure written and save it so that the specific design or program can be recalled from the computer's memory simply by telling the turtle to redraw that named procedure.

For some students, especially those in a sensory-motor stage of development, the LOGO turtle and its movements on the computer screen is too abstract. For these children, LOGO graphics can be performed by a robot that carries out directions in three dimensional space, or in the student's own environment. These robot devices can either be controlled by the computer as in the case of *Terrapin* LOGO, which can draw the designs in three dimensional space, or they can be in the form of a self-contained robot that is generally a battery powered toy. A task-analyzed program can then be developed to teach students that the computer screen is a representation of environmental space. The robot here is used for problem-solving situations involving spatial relationships as well as to assist the student in comprehending representations of the screen.

The process of commanding the turtle in the LOGO computer language is relatively simple, and its use permits children to explore their world in an electronic learning environment. Children are provided with an interactive environment that allows them to learn and solve problems on a computer. The students can control their rate of learning and teach themselves through their personal exploration. They can define problems according to their individual needs and past experiences and solve these problems in their personal style. There is no element of right or wrong in LOGO. The immediate feedback created by seeing the turtle train and the emerging design on the screen permits them to self-correct by modifying their procedure. The children are in total control of their learning. Further, these types of experiences are not only teaching problem-solving skills but are sensitizing students to the role of this electronic technology as a personal aid, an essential concept for them to develop in order to cope with the Information age of the 21st century.

The freedom of children to explore, create, and self-correct are LOGO's most powerful features. They can discover the unknown in their own way, moving from personal perspectives concepts, and language usage into new knowledge through trial and error. Later, this exploration takes the form of systematic planning. Errors in procedure becomes a means of learning rather than a failure experience. Students develop a sense of achievement since the computer never evaluates their efforts. The computer simply carries out their commands, helps them solve problems, and rewards their exploration by showing them their creation on the screen.

LOGO can be used as either an individual or a group learning and problem-solving experience. When used in a group setting, usually three or four students, the group cooperatively plans and solves a group-identified difficulty, design, or puzzle. Another variation of the group use of LOGO is to assign different groups of children a different aspect of a graphic, such as a house. When each group has completed its part, all aspects are combined to achieve composite design. Very often, the combination of the different parts will result in the need for the groups to redesign their sections, in order for the parts to fit together as a coordinated, finished product. Not only are these experiences fun for students, they teach group decision-making and cooperative planning techniques through electronic exploration on the computer. These group electronic decision-making techniques are important for children to learn, since the mastery of these techniques is necessary for individuals to be productive electronic workers in the world of the 21st century — a world with decentralized offices, home computer work stations, and electronic communication systems.

The use of LOGO by students fosters the development of analytical reasoning skills and logical sequencing. Students must plan the sequence of the turtle's moves that are required to achieve the desired result on the computer screen. They must use further problem-solving techniques to correct any errors in the graphics.

In summary, LOGO and other exploration software hold tremendous potential as teaching tools to foster the development of problem-solving skills in disabled students. They create an electronic learning environment that allows pupils to learn in their own style, discovering concepts and building on these discoveries. Their self-expression is immediately rewarded in the form of screen graphics. Self-monitoring and evaluation techniques are developed through the process of continuous feedback. LOGO and other exploration software permits these students to individualize and personalize problems by breaking them down into components that are within their personal repertoire of language and experience. They permit them to move from what they know to the unknown through exploration. Most importantly, LOGO and other exploration software help the mild and moderately disabled to discover their abilities, to be creative learners, and to be problem solvers. Students are highly motivated to use these electronic tools because they are never evaluated as right or wrong and can simply learn from the results of their own decisions.

### Discovery Learning Through Stories

Another excellent source of computer software that fosters discovery-learning and problem-solving skills in mild and moderately disabled children are computer software "books." These materials use graphics to tell a story and to support the written word. They are particularly effective for use with students who are experiencing reading problems because they allow the child to comprehend the content through graphic support. Students can read a software story in the same way they would read a printed book; however, it is the manipulative nature of these programs that allows them to foster the development of discovery-learning and problem-solving skills. This is especially true since computer software books permit the student to change the story by manipulating the picture and the print on the screen. They can, therefore, change the original story and create a new one, their personal story, just by making selections or exploring possible changes on the screen. These changes can be achieved by using a joystick, a mouse, a keyboard, or an adaptive input device. Any object, character, or background can be moved by the student throught the use of these input devices. Further, they can add characters or objects to a picture in order to further personalize their story. Finally, they can erase the original text and add their own text to create a totally new story that is personally meaningful to them. These new stories can then be saved on disc for future viewing or printed for a personal copy. In some instances, new graphics can be added either from commercially developed graphics discs or from graphics developed by the student. Student graphics can be developed by such devices as the Koala Pad or by other types of graphics input boards.

These transformable computer software "books" provide children with valuable experiences in discovery learning. They are able to express their feelings and ideas by creating a story or an entire book. They also learn problem-solving techniques because they have to plan the sequence of events and self-correct when they are not pleased with the results. This type of software further assists in the development of language and written expression skills. A child with limited linguistic ability can plan and tell his or her story with the same ease as the child with more advanced linguistic skills. These electronic instructional materials are extremely motivating because the pupils see the results of their ideas immediately. Again, there is no right or wrong. The computer merely obeys the children's directions and passes no judgment upon their product.

Computer software books also help to develop some problem-solving skills that will be important daily living tools in the 21st century. Many of the problems the individual of this future era will be required to solve will be of a linguistic nature involving the use of advanced electronic technologies. They will, for example, be required to solve work-related problems on the computer. Even though they will have the advantage of artificially intelligent systems, they will need the skills to solve problems and discover information on a computer.

### Discovery Learning Through Games

Certain electronic computer games, those designed for educational use as well as those designed for general commerical use, can also provide mild and moderately disabled students with excellent discovery-learning and problem-solving experiences. These programs require a student to solve a computer-generated problem through the use of cause-and-effect learning. In most instances, these programs can be played by the individual against the computer as well as against another player. Since most of these systems have multiple levels of skill, they can be used by students of different ability levels. Most of these educational and commerical games rely on graphics and, therefore, also provide the user with immediate visual feedback regarding the consequences of the decision.

Many educators frown upon the use of these educational and commercial games, claiming that the students who use them are only "playing." This is not necessarily an accurate perception. If the game is a planned activity leading toward a goal stated in the student's IEP, they can be excellent instructional tools. Students usually have to use logic and problem-solving techniques in order to play and complete many games. They can be entertaining and fun for the students while at the same time assist in developing specific skills. Remember, it is not a proven educational fact that students should not have fun or enjoy learning in school; it is only a misconception held by certain educators. Many mild and moderately impaired students are placed in special education programs because of prior school failure. This failure lowers self-esteem, heightens frustration levels, and often results in behavioral problems. Good quality computer games can and do serve as excellent instructional materials, which provide important experiences in problem solving, logic, and discovery learning. Their appropriate and planned use can do much to raise student's self-images while proving to them that they can learn and achieve.

The construction of these games is intended to have the user apply cause-and-effect problem-solving techniques in order to participate. Students discover that, for every action they take, there will be a reaction from the computer program. These are important learning experiences for pupils because they provide them with situations that closely resemble what happens in real life. When one considers that the individual living in the 21st century will have to use advanced computer technologies in order to solve a great number and variety of daily living problems, these learning experiences are extremely important. Further, it provides students with recreational alternatives, another important area of instruction for disabled children that is discussed in detail in Chapter 8. At this time, suffice it to say that both educational and certain home product commerical computer games have a very important role to play in the preparation of the disabled student for life in the Information Age and, therefore, should be integrated into a technological literacy program today.

## SOME FUTURE DIRECTIONS IN PROBLEM SOLVING

There are a number of projected developments in advanced electronic technology that will have significant impact on the education of disabled children and youth in future decades. These very same developments will also provide daily living problem-solving assistance to disabled people in the early part of the 21st century. Although these technological advances are projected, they are already in developmental stages.

One of the most significant advances that will have impact on problem-solving daily living applications and on problem-solving instruction of students will be the further development of artificially intelligent computer systems. Artificially intelligent systems will permit the development of new instructional software to provide multisensory and personally interactive experiences for disabled students in almost all categories. These systems will learn from past experience with the individual and will adapt themselves to the personal learning styles and inner language systems of the students. Thus, these instructional programs will be able to modify themselves, their language and content, to the unique learning needs of their disabled users and assist them in developing problem-solving skills through carefully sequenced strategies. These systems can also be used prosthetically to assist in the problem-solving process.

The fifth generation computer, which will run artificially intelligent software, will also offer new problem-solving opportunities for disabled students in the classroom. These systems will have large memory capacities and will often be networked within a school or classroom. They will provide students with the composite information and experiences of many other individuals and experts in any given area on an individually interactive basis. Since these systems will be able to modify themselves to the individual learning and inner language styles of the pupil, they will provide problem-solving computer learning experiences that are far more interactive and personal than today's systems. Further, these large multisensory expert systems will be able to assist the student in applying a concept in a cause-and-effect simulation of real life situations within the classroom. The graphics and sound capabilities of the next generation of computers will be far superior to todays machines. Further, the next generation of computers will have voice recognition and touch input capabilities. The voice output capabilities will sound human and the extensive memory capacities will allow them to contain an extensive vocabulary. These enhanced sensory capabilities will assist students in interacting with the computer in their preferential mode(s) of learning and with material that looks and sounds real.

Projected developments of new adaptive input and output devices should further expand the instructional opportunities for disabled students in all categories. Many of these new devices are currently being developed by biomedical and rehabilitation engineers and are being designed for use with disabled people. Further, the increasing percentage of the population that is aging has generated increased interest in developing new and more advanced adaptive devices for this population to use as prosthetics. Regardless of who develops these systems or for which group they are initially designed, they will have applications for disabled students both at school and at home. These developments will mean that many of the disabled students of today who are unable to access the computer will be able to do so in the future. One example of such a adaptive device currently in the research and developmental stages is a galvanic skin response input connection. This type of adaptive device would mean that a student would only have to think to control a computer. A change in body heat, which can be learned through biofeedback training, would activate the adaptive input device and allow the user to control the computer. Developments such as this will open up the computer to many disabled people and will simplify communication with the computer for others. The development of these adaptive systems and the impact of the next generatoin of computers with artificial intelligence will greatly expand the ability of disabled students to have personal electronic problem-solving experiences.

Developments in the interactive videodisc systems will also provide expanded real-life problem-solving experiences for disabled students. The development of these systems is currently underway, and it is projected that they will be available for home and school use early in the 1990s, though it will probably be a few more years before a large amount of software materials will be available for use in the schools. These systems will have extensive memories, excellent sound quality (equal to a very good stereo system today), and will be able to show print, pictures, graphics, animation, and film on the screen or monitor. They will be able to be used as self-contained interactive units, or they will be able to be used with a computer so that extensive branching can occur. The current projections are that the cost of such units will come down to well under $1,000. Publishers are already making plans to develop educational materials for these new systems and are discussing products such as an interactive encyclopedia that uses the voice, sound, graphics, animation, and film capabilities of the videodisc system. It would appear that this new advanced electronic media will provide expanded and new problem-solving and simulation opportunities to disabled students in the future because they will be more interactive and realistic than are the interactive videodiscs of today. Further, they will be integrated into the Net Console system of home, school, and work in the 21st century for lifelong learning.

All of the developments just mentioned will provide assistance to today's disabled students in problem solving in the Information Age of the 21st century. They will have to use these and other advanced technologies as tools of daily living. Theirs will be a far more complex society, one in which the information base will be growing and expanding exponentially. In such a complex world with a glut of information, disabled people will be required to make many decisions in order to be productive members of that society. The use of electronic problem solving will be vital, one skill that they and others can employ to cope and survive as independent or semi-independent citizens. Disabled people then, will have to be proficient in technological linguistics and be able to use these advanced technology tools and others such as the home Net Console. It is for this reason that it is so important that they receive instruction in the use of electronic tools for problem solving today.

## Summary

■ Computers, with their enormous data bases, graphics options, and interactive capabilities, are natural tools to help students learn to solve problems in their daily lives.

■ Because computers are going to become an essential component of everyday life for all of us, it will be critical to be able to solve problems using computers. Thus, it is critical to develop computer literacy to a level that will allow disabled people to problem solve with computers.

■ Interactive video technology, discovery learning software, and computer games are all important tools that should be utilized to their maximum degree in helping disabled students to prepare for their futures.

# CHAPTER 6

# Using Electronic Technology to Enhance Strengths and Compensate for Deficits

Although most individuals use the terms for compensation and prosthesis interchangeably, they do not mean the same thing. Compensation, as it is related to computers, refers to using these devices to make up for a deficit in an individual. In most instances these deficits are neurological or intellectual in nature. Prosthetics, on the other hand, refers to the use of computers and related electronic technologies as a prosthesis to replace or substitute for a physical or sensory dysfunction in an individual. An electronic prosthesis serves the same function for an individual as would a nonelectronic device such as an artificial arm, a wheelchair, or a brace.

Thus, an electronic prosthesis could serve two distinct types of function. First, it could be used to substitute for an individual's physical or sensory dysfunction in a specific area. An example of this application is the computer activated robotic arm that was developed for the Veterans Administration (Jaffe, 1987). This device allows quadriplegics to perform such basic functions as feeding. It is so flexible that it also allows them to perform functions such as typing, using a computer, and dialing a telephone. The key in this type of prosthetic application is that the device is used to replace a physical or sensory dysfunction in an individual. The electronic device does what the person cannot do. Another example of this type of application would be the electric wheelchair, especially in cases where the individual does not have the arm strength to propel a wheelchair.

These devices enhance an individual's physical or sensory dysfunction. In this type of application, other functional abilities of the individual are usually enhanced in order to substitute for or replace the area of dysfunction. Adaptive computer input and output usually fall into this category either when they enhance a physical or sensory dysfunction or when they use another ability of the individual to provide them access to a computer or related electronic device. An example of such a prosthetic adaptive device is the Braille keyboard and printer. These adaptive units allow blind and partially sighted individuals to interact with a computer in their written expressive and receptive language of Braille. These devices are using another ability, the tactile system, to substitute for the visual dysfunction in order to give the visually impaired individual access to the computer. The computer in turn could translate the Braille input message into a normal language output message for a sighted person, a translation function. Another example of this type of application is an electronic device called the "super phone." This electronic instrument allows a deaf individual to speak with a hearing person over the telephone. The deaf user types the message into the unit and the hearing person at the other end of the line receives that message either in print or in voice. In turn, the hearing individual either types or speaks a return message which is transmitted to the deaf user in the form of print on screen. These devices are really small one-function microcomputer telecommunication units that prosthetically use other functions of the deaf individual, vision and motor, to provide them access to a computer and to telecommunication with another individual.

Assistive and adaptive input and output devices provide access to computers and related electronic devices for many physically and sensorially impaired individuals: adaptive devices being those that can be purchased in off-the-shelf configurations; whereas assistive devices may be adaptive devices, modified adaptive devices, or developed by an interested individual or rehabilitative engineer. These latter devices are designed to meet specific assessed needs of an individual. Adaptive devices are designed to meet a generic need, such as voice output. Throughout this book, these terms have been used interchangeably. However, whether a device is adaptive or assistive, it must always meet the needs of the individual to be effective, because without the development of these devices for compensatory or prosthetic purposes, these individuals would be unable to use the power, applications, and communication potential of computers. Without such adaptive devices, whole segments of the disabled population would be excluded from access to important learning and daily living tools. Without the current and continued development of these adaptive prosthetic tools, a large portion of these special populations would be doomed to be "second class' citizens in the world of the 21st century.

The number of prosthetic assistive and adaptive devices grows annually. Each new development triggers a new direction for research and development, which results in new adaptations and other new developments. Further, as is the case with all computer and related electronic technologies, the cost to the consumer decreases with time and as new systems and applications are developed. Despite the number and variety of assistive and adaptive devices currently available for use by physically and sensorially disabled students, they tend to fall into several general categories: adaptive input switches and scanning devices, alternative keyboards, voice input, voice output, vision and touch output, and motoric output.

### Adaptive Input Switches and Scanning Devices

Some of the first prosthetic adaptive devices developed were a variety of switches that allow severely physically disabled and low functioning mentally challenged individuals to use the computer and related technologies. In all instances, the input of information or data is simplified so that a single switch allows a physically handicapped individual to control a computer. All of these switches are toggle or on-off switches. They can be operated by whatever physical ability the disabled user possesses. Therefore, any form of controlled muscle contraction, such as a brow wrinkle or an eye twitch, can control the computer. As a matter of fact, if an individual can breathe, they can control a computer through a "suck and puff" ability switch in which sucking activates one function (such as on) and blowing activates the opposite command. There are even switches under development that can be activated by thought processes such as changing skin temperature, a process achieved through biofeedback training. In most instances, these ability adaptive switches are coupled with special software that automatically scans all of the options available on the screen. The disabled user activates the adaptive ability switch at the time that the scanner points to the choice the individual desires. Such an adaptive switch device is generically termed a single switch scanner, and these systems can provide severely physically disabled individuals with full operation of a computer.

The Adaptive Firmware Card, from Adaptive Peripherals, expands the capabilities of the single switch scanner systems and actually serves as a keyboard emulator. The card allows the severely physically disabled individual to use adaptive ability switches to run general commercially-produced software by means of scanning in a manner similar to the single switch scanner. The adaptive firmware card, therefore, permits these handicapped individuals to use the same instructional, general purpose, and recreational software that their nondisabled peers use. It gives them the access to the entire world and the power over the computer that is available to all other individuals.

A recent development in scanning systems shows great promise for severely physically disabled and low functioning mentally challenged individuals. These scanning systems use what is termed "line of gaze" scanning. Whatever the handicapped person looks at is what is chosen from the computer screen. Thus, the individual controls the computer system by merely looking at it. In most instances, the individual is equipped with some form of photo cell or video device that is usually located around the eye in a unit that looks like eyeglasses. The device allows individuals to use the computer to learn, to communicate with others, and to control certain elements of their environment. This type of adaptive ability device holds great promise for severely disabled individuals, particularly those with degenerative neuromuscular disorders.

Adaptive ability switches and scanning devices are important access tools for severely physically disabled and low functioning mentally challenged individuals. They are prosthetic devices because they replace dysfunctional physical abilities and allow the individual to use other abilities, no matter how limited, to control and use computers and related electronic technologies. It can be anticipated that these devices and accompanying software will become more sophisticated in the future, allowing greater access to computers and related electronic technologies for these people.

### Alternate Keyboards

Adaptive keyboards are another type of prosthetic input device that makes the computer accessible to physically and sensorially disabled people. Keyboards are most simply defined as a series of electrical switches that, when activated, run and control a computer. The keyboard generally has a typewriter type of configuration of letters and many have a numeric pad that looks like a calculator. In addition, the keyboard may have a number of special "function" keys that allow an individual to give special commands to the computer. Each of the keys on the keyboard is an electrical switch that gives a specific command to the computer, such as, put the letter "a" in memory and on the screen.

Adaptive keyboards function in the same manner as traditional keyboards to control a computer. They are, however, specially adapted for use by physically and sensorially disabled individuals, and they provide prosthetic access to the computer as well as to the full functional control of the keyboard. They are prosthetic tools because they substitute for the dysfunction of individuals and allow them to maximize their abilities.

Some of the most common forms of adaptive keyboard devices have separated and enlarged keys that permit data entry and machine control by individuals with gross hand, foot, or arm movements. Another common variation of this type of modification is the template, a raised cover that goes over a standard keyboard. These templates not only assist individuals with gross hand motor control problems in gaining access to the computer but they also assist individuals who must use some form of pointing device, such as a head or mouth pointer, to activate the keys. The template simply deepens and, therefore, separates the keys to assist these individuals in data entry.

Another type of alternative keyboard is the Braille keyboard, designed for use by blind and visually impaired individuals. The letters and numbers on this keyboard are simply presented in Braille. They may be placed in the same position as the regular keyboard or may be organized more efficiently. In other instances, a Braillewriter is electronically activated and connected to the computer via input-output ports or through an additional board placed in the computer. Therefore, any blind individual who knows Braille can immediately have access to the computer for data entry. The only special training on the keyboard they will have to receive is in the new Braille symbols used for the function keys. The primary limitation to this type of prosthetic device is that it requires the visually impaired individual to know Braille. Not all blind and visually impaired people know Braille, particularly those who became disabled later in life. As voice input systems have become more functional, and as their price has decreased, they have begin to be an alternative to the Braille printer.

A final type of adaptive keyboard device is the touch-sensitive pad and the remote keyboard. Touch sensitive pads are membranes that cover or access the electric wires or switches that control the computer. The Touch Window (Sunburst Communications, Pleasantville, NY) is one type of touch sensitive system, one which, in its original configuration, allows the disabled user to draw on the screen or, with appropriate software, can become an alternative keyboard. Other systems contain the same functions and keys as the regular keyboard. Remote keyboards have been developed for individuals with very limited limb control, such as quadriplegics. These units are usually controlled by a joystick or by a series of push buttons that can be activated by a head or mouth pointer. They may be located anywhere within a specified distance from the computer, and they operate by infrared rays. This permits their use on the side of a device such as a wheelchair.

Alternate or adaptive keyboards are important prosthetic devices because they permit disabled individuals to gain access to and control a computer through a keyboard, thereby providing them with the same degree of flexibility as the user of a regular keyboard. These prosthetic tools are primarily used by physically disabled and people who are blind or visually impaired.

### Voice Input

Voice input is an important prosthetic and compensatory adaptive tool for disabled computer users in a number of different disability groups. These systems remain rather limited in their capabilities at the present time, although rapid advances are being made in the development of new systems. Despite the limitations of the current systems, they represent an adaptive input option that makes computer access and operation an easier task for many disabled individuals.

Voice input generally refers to the ability of a computer system to "listen" to a human voice and to respond to the commands given orally. The user speaks into an attached or internal microphone to give commands and information to the computer. The voice input device then sends electrical signals to the computer in a manner similar to the keyboard. Most voice input systems today require that the computer be "trained" to recognize the voice or oral expression of the individual user. These systems can be trained to understand any consistent sound that the individual can make and to use that sound as a computer command. Therefore, if the individual can consistently make the sound "ugh," and this is equated to the computer command "load," every time the individual makes that sound, the computer will load a program. Thus, the user of a voice input system does not have to have comprehensible speech in order to use these systems, they only have to be able to make consistent oral expressions and to understand that these expressions mean a special command to the computer system.

A limitation of many of these voice input systems is that they are personal once they have been "trained," and they cannot be used by another person unless that individual "trains" the system also. Further, these systems require that users be consistent in the manner in which they articulate commands to the computer. Any significant deviation in the way the voice command is given to the computer and the system will not recognize the user's voice pattern. For example, if an individual developed a heavy cold and attempted to use a voice command, it is highly probable that the computer would not recognize the voice and would not respond to the command without going through a retraining sequence. This would also hold true for those individuals with degenerative speech disorders. They would have to retrain the computer periodically to recognize their voices. Retraining, however, does not require as much time as the original training does.

There are voice recognition systems that have been developed that do not require the user to "train" the computer. These systems recognize a wide variety of voices and regional pronunciations. Unfortunately, to date, most of the systems within a reasonable price range will recognize only a very limited vocabulary of spoken words and phrases. This can be a rather severe limitation for the disabled individual who needs to control a computer by means of voice input. Further, these systems require that comprehensible words and phrases be used in the speech recognition system. This precludes the use of oral expressions by speech limited individuals. Other recently developed systems (i.e., for IBM) are not limited by the number of phrases or words because the words are recognized using phonetic analysis and can be modified to recognize any sound patterns. These most recent developments also recognize continuous speech instead of one word at a time. Unlike the voice recognition systems described earlier, these systems are not susceptible to minor variations in the voice quality of the user. Further, they can be used by more than one person without requiring individual "training" of the system.

Voice input devices represent important prosthetic tools for both physically disabled individuals with oral expressive abilities and people who are blind or visually impaired. They serve as compensatory tools for other disabled groups such as learning disabled, emotionally disturbed, and mentally retarded individuals. It can be expected that voice recognition systems will continue to be developed and will become more sophisticated because business and industry see great value in their development. As these new developments occur, they can be applied as prosthetic and compensatory tools for disabled people.

### Voice Output

Voice or speech output systems are also important prosthetic tools for a number of disabled groups. Those who would use these devices the most include: blind and visually impaired individuals, mentally challenged people, and certain physically disabled groups who cannot attend to the computer screen because of motor or muscle problems involving head control such as people with cerebral palsy. As with voice input, these sytems are also used as compensatory devices for learning disabled and mentally retarded individuals, compensatory because these electronic tools are used to make up for certain of their intellectual or neurological deficits.

Voice output systems allow the computer to reproduce relatively human-sounding speech either to communicate a program's outputs or to serve as an adaptive expressive communication device for individuals who have nonverbal or limited verbal skills. the voice output devices or peripherals can be located either within the computer itself, as is the case with computers such as Commodore and some Apple models, or they can be an external peripheral attachment, as with the ECHO (Street Electronics) system. The quality of the voice output varies depending upon the system. In some digitized systems, the voice is quite human sounding, and in some synthesized systems, the speech is very robotic sounding. Although voice output systems are either contained within the actual computer or added as an external peripheral, they can be controlled through the computer by the variety of adaptive ability switches that are currently available. Therefore, disabled individuals who have little or no expressive language ability, or who cannot maintain head control or eye contact with the screen, can use voice output systems to receive the information necessary to control the computer. In the same manner, they can, through adaptive switches, receive information directly from the computer or from another individual through the computer system.

Most voice output systems provide the user with information about what has occurred on the screen or about the results of the functioning of the computer. In this application, these systems act as prosthetic tools for disabled groups such as blind people. Users are able to receive information from the computer in their strength areas of learning or functioning or by using the computer system as a prosthetic device that performs the actual task of reading or visual decoding for them. This type of application provides the blind user with an important alternative to Braille output. When one considers the fact that many blind and visually impaired individuals do not read Braille, voice output represents the only way in which they can get information from the computer other than having the printout read to them by a sighted person. When applied in this manner, the voice output system is actually performing a sensory task that the disabled user cannot perform.

The second type of prosthetic application for voice output systems is as an expressive aid for limited verbal and nonverbal people. In these instances, the disabled user enters the message into the computer; then, when the message is complete and satisfactory, the user commands the machine to "speak" the message to another individual either directly or remotely through a telecommunication system. This is also a prosthetic application since the computer system is performing a physical and sensory task that the disabled user cannot perform. Further, this type of application allows the individual to use his or her areas of strength, motor and vision, to compose the communication for another individual.

Voice or speech output adaptive devices are important prosthetic alternatives for receiving information from a computer. As the quality of voice output becomes less robotic sounding, and as memory capacities of these new voice systems improve, these systems will have even greater impact upon the classroom and daily living functioning of disabled individuals.

## Vision and Touch Output

Vision output adaptive devices are designed to serve as prosthetic tools for blind and visually impaired individuals. Computers are designed to provide users with a great deal of visual information, either on the screen or in the form of print. This is a serious problem for individuals with visual deficits. Unless there is a modification in the manner in which visual information is displayed or printed out, the visually disabled will be unable to take full advantage of the computer as a classroom learning and functional daily living tool.

Adaptive vision devices provide the needed adaptation for blind and visually impaired people. First, there are computers that send text out to the printer for Braille output or to a "paperless" brailler. The paperless Braille system, also called soft-Braille, is an output plate that permits the user to read line by line what is contained in the computer's text and memory. This device does not provide a permanent Braille output but does allow a person to send and receive text either when connected to a computer or by means of a telephone.

The second major type of prosthetic vision output device is a system that either enlarges, brightens, or reverses the print on the screen. These systems are designed for use by visually impaired people. Some of these devices allow the user to scan print on a page by displaying a magnified version of the text on the computer's screen. In some cases, the entire screen is magnified. The user can also zoom in and magnify a portion of what is on the screen — called a "window." The print can even appear inverted or upside down. These applications mean that the visually impaired are no longer limited to the content of large print books and, with such a device, can read any book, magazine, or other print material they desire.

## Motoric Output

Using many of the input devices already mentioned, disabled individuals can control objects in their environment. For example, they can explore their environments by remote control robots. They can control the operation of any electrical appliance (e.g., range), power supply (e.g., lighting, heat), or communication device (e.g., television, telephone, telecommunications) within the home or office through the computer driven Net Console.

Computer chips will also be able, and to a certain extent are now able, to control artificial body parts, medication release into the body, and devices used for locomotion, such as wheelchairs and guided canes for individuals who are blind.

## POTENTIAL APPLICATIONS FOR PROSTHETIC TECHNOLOGY

Prosthetic devices of artificially intelligent computer systems will modify themselves, responding to the physical and sensory deficit needs of the user. The system will learn from the performance of the individual and, thus, vary the types of output provided to all disabled users based on individual needs in specific situations. As indicated earlier, for physically challenged people, these systems will operate prosthetic limbs more effectively than is done today. For those with health impairments, these systems will automatically administer medication and monitor vital signs. Systems are available to do this today but are basically in experimental stages.

These systems will be voice interactive so that they will be able to be used effectively by individuals with limited oral language ability. Since these systems will automatically learn from the individual, no "training" of the system to the voice or oral language pattern of the user will be necessary. If the user can only make sounds to communicate, these advanced systems will understand these sounds and will be able to interact with the user based upon these sounds. For emotionally disturbed individuals these systems will be able to sense the need for therapy and provide verbal suggestions or medication upon a physician's orders. For blind and visually impaired people, these systems will be able to provide verbal cues to go along with bionic eyes or visual sensing devices that send appropriate messages to the brain. For deaf and hearing impaired individuals, they will be able to provide auditory images to the brain and appropriate speech. Given the interactive nature of the Net Console and the fact that these units will be connected to expert medical systems and to the individual's attending physician's office and data base, these artificially intelligent systems will be further able to modify themselves based on the current needs of the physically or health disabled user. All of these prosthetic modifications to human functioning will open the way to effective learning either in the classroom, on the job, or in the home.

The interactive multisensory nature of the advanced computer systems projected for the early part of the 21st century, and the fact that the home Net Console will have an interactive video component, will make these systems particularly suited to disabled individuals as both compensatory and prosthetic tools. These units will be voice interactive with human voice and inflection patterns. Since the Net Console will serve as the primary station for home-work, communication, information searching and processing, environmental control, and recreation, these capabilities of advanced computer systems will become particularly important. The more they are modifiable to the needs of the user, the more efficient and effective they will be as assistive tools of daily living and learning. It is projected that these systems will have the capability to accommodate the full variety of adaptive and assistive input and output devices that will be available in the Information Age and, therefore, will be able to be used by all people with physical or sensory disabilities. Since these systems will serve as the control center for the home environment through the Net Console, and since they will have all of these personally modifiable characteristics, they will provide physically disabled individuals with almost total independent control of their home environment.

The Net Console will also serve another important prosthetic function for individuals who are homebound. This central home computer unit will be interactively linked to the world-wide network of information and communication. This grid will not only electronically provide the user with a variety of daily living functions such as shopping, banking, library access, and recreation, but it also will open up an electronic classroom encompassing the entire world. Individuals who are homebound today cannot perform these activities unless someone else assists them. The Net Console of the Information Age will permit them to perform these daily living and eduational functions independently. They may request assistance from an artificially intelligent expert system contained within the grid, but this assistance will only be to help them make personal decisions. This system will allow them to transcend the limitations of distance and travel and to function in an unrestricted manner. The Net Console will be acting in a prosthetic manner, performing the actual task of movement and travel, thus allowing them to concentrate on the decision-making and learning processes. Most importantly, this sytem will allow them to function in an independent manner, free to learn and to interact with others wherever they are located.

### Robots

Robots represent another form of advanced technology prosthetic tools for many disabled individuals in the 21st century. (Chapter 3 contains a detailed discussion of robotics.) These robots will be voice interactive and will be able to be controlled through direct verbal or visual command or through the Net Console's advanced computer system.

This implies that they will be able to be commanded by any disabled person regardless of their physical, sensory, or neurological limitations. Physically limited individuals with little or no linguistic abilities will be able to command their robot(s) through advanced technology adaptive control devices connected to a Net Console computer. These artificially intelligent electronic slaves will be able to perform many functions to assist the student in the classroom or in the home. Further, certain of these units will be mobile and sensitive enough to perform grooming, self-care, and basic medical care functions for individuals with extremely limited physical ability, either under the direction of that person or under the direction of the teacher, parent, or caretaker. Since the focus of control should eventually lie within the student, since these units will contain artificial intelligence, and since they will be controlled by the Net Console with its interactive communication and advanced artificial intelligence capabilities, robots will be able to respond to the personal inner language and oral expression systems of the user. Further, robots will be able to learn from the user and respond to particular needs whether based upon past experience, the current situation, or the personal needs of the user at a particular moment. The ultimate impact of advanced artificially intelligent robots will be their ability to serve as prosthetic extensions of their disabled users, particularly those individuals with physical or sensory deficits, allowing them to achieve a greater degree of independence for learning and for living in the Information Age. However, in order for disabled individuals to understand the functioning of robots and give them appropriate commands, they must learn the appropriate technological linguistics. Since the robot becomes an extension of the individual into space, important spatial concepts need to be learned along with reasoning and logic skills.

Computer-controlled cars and mobile robotic transportation devices hold the potential to be compensatory and prosthetic aids for disabled people in the Information Age and thus must be a consideration for the curriculum. Projections from the National Transportation Authority indicate that automobile transportation systems will be computer controlled by the early part of the 21st century. Should this prediction come to pass, such systems will serve as compensatory tools for many disabled individuals who are currently precluded from getting a driver's license or who experience extreme difficulty in mastering and performing basic transportation skills such as directionality or finding a specific location from a map. The projected systems would have nationwide, regional, and local computer-directed grids that would control individual vehicles and that would monitor the area's traffic patterns. Cars and trucks would be equipped with a computer, a sensor, and access to a "master" system. Once an individual entered a major traffic artery, the master computer grid would take control of the vehicle and monitor its progress by means of sensors and control strips embedded in the road. The individual's destination would be recorded in the vehicle's own computer and would be "read" by the master grid system. The system would place the vehicle in the appropriate lane and control it. The driver of the vehicle would regain control of the automobile or truck when the vehicle reached either its destination or a local road that was not controlled by the grid. If unable to take control at this point, the user's robot could be programmed or instructed to do so. All cars and trucks would also be equipped with computer-generated map devices — a few already are — that would show the driver exactly where he or she is as well as the most direct route to the final destination, indicating exactly the route to take to get there. This may sound like an ideal situation to many of us, particularly those of us who always seem to get lost. However, for many disabled people, this type of computer-controlled transportation system will be essential to getting around in the future, allowing them to travel independently, in safety, and with reduced anxiety.

Robotic mobility devices will serve as prosthetic transportation tools for the physically disabled and for some sensory impaired in the Information Age. One of the types of robots that has been proposed for the 21st century is a mobility robot that will transport the user. The automobile of the future is not a robot, although it would perform some robotic functions. The future automobile is simply an advanced ground vehicle that contains a computer system and that can be connected to a large computer-controlled grid. In many ways, the vehicle of the future is similar to the home Net Console in that it is controlled by the user and is connected to a large master computer grid or network. The robotic mobility devices projected for the Information Age will move and transport users. Basically, they could be considered as robotic wheelchairs. The concept of the robotic mobility device was initially proposed as an assistive device for aged and disabled users. Given the demographic projections for the 21st century that the percentage of the total population which is aging and aged will grow and the fact that life expectancy will continue to increase, it is highly probable that such robotic mobility devices will be commercially available in the Information Age. They would be voice interactive so that they could receive oral comments from the user. These mobility robots would also be able to be controlled by any type of adaptive ability interface which would be available at that time. These robotic systems would allow the user to control the destination of the device, but would allow the mobility robot to perform the actual task of locomotion and of sensing and moving around objects in order to reach the desired objective. These robotic systems, therefore, would prosthetically perform the sensory and mobility function for the handicapped and/or disabled user. The user would be in total control of the robotic mobility device and could stop it or redirect it at any point. These devices could be designed in almost any form, depending upon the needs of the user, but most would probably resemble the current wheelchair.

## ALTERNATE PERSPECTIVES ON ELECTRONIC COMPENSATION

The potential of computers and related technologies to serve as compensatory and prosthetic tools for the handicapped and disabled are great. It is predicted that the disabled will increasingly use advanced technologies for daily living functions and will, therefore, come to depend on these electronic tools as compensatory and prosthetic devices.

Although the use of computers and related electronic tehcnologies as compensatory and prosthetic tools expands and enhances the learning and performance capabilities of the disabled, these applications may prove to be barriers as well as benefits. This possibility may become even more of a factor for the disabled people living in the future world of the Information Age because they will make even greater use of advanced technologies such as compensatory and prosthetic tools. The more dependent disabled people are on computers and related electronic technologies, the more susceptible they are to the loss of functional ability due to machine or power failure. This reality will become more pronounced and a greater danger in the 21st century when these special groups rely even more on the use of the advanced electronic technologies to assist them in daily living functioning. Although the concern about the failure of these electronic devices due to breakdown or power failure is a reality for all citizens, these exceptional populations may, and probably will, be more dependent upon advanced technological compensatory and prosthetic systems and, therefore, less able to marshall alternative resources.

We are witnessing increasing evidence of this phenomenon today, particularly with physically and health disabled people and with certain of our aged citizens. For example, broken electric wheelchairs and other powered mobility devices, communication boards, and specially modified automobiles can pose almost insurmountable problems to these groups. A nonfunctional telephone or the loss of electric power today can cause life-threatening situations. Health disabled individuals using medical support systems powered by electricity are in specific life-threatening danger during a power failure unless they have some form of a generator as a backup system. This is one of the reasons that hospitals have generator systems that can be used in just such an emergency. However, the average special needs citizen who uses electronic technologies or electric machines for compensatory, prosthetic, or life support functions generally does not have the luxury of such a back-up system.

An intelligent and expert electronic machine cannot help you if it does not work. These special needs groups are usually less equipped and less able to cope with the impact of machine or power failure than the nondisabled. Their alternative options and their exercising these alternative modes of functioning will, in good measure, be determined by their abilities and by their experiences with nonelectronic tools of daily functioning. If an individual has been able to achieve functional independence using electronic devices, he or she may have no one to turn to in order to gain assistance, especially if the home Net Console communication system malfunctions and the person cannot contact another individual for assistance.

Thus, the need arises for our educational system to consider teaching alternative systems for what to do when electronic systems fail. In some instances, electronic backup systems must be installed and appropriate procedures taught. In other instances, procedures for reactivating the system must be learned by the user. Machine or power failures are realities, realities that must be addressed and prepared for now. We cannot afford to wait until such an event occurs because that will be too late. We must begin today to prepare and train the disabled students in our special education programs about how to cope with such a possibility so that they can select alternatives in the event of such machine or power failures in the future.

## THE IMPORTANCE OF BASIC SKILLS

Computers and related electronic technologies will never provide all of the solutions to the problems of disabled individuals. The compensatory and prosthetic applications of these systems today show great promise in assisting special needs groups in using their areas of strength and in becoming more independent. The future of advanced technologies and the impact of the Information Age indicate further applications for these groups; however, these electronic devices are not the total answer. They further the functional abilities of the disabled people who use them, but they are not and were never meant to replace the more traditional forms of training and instruction in communication, learning, mobility, and self-care. They are supplements to these programs, alternatives. In fact, the most effective programs are those that continue training and instruction in the more traditional methods and also integrate the new alternatives provided by computers and related technologies.

Special educators and speech, occupational, and physical therapists have developed proven and effective programs to assist disabled individuals in using strengths and in functioning independently to their maximum potential. These programs were in existence long before the development of electronic compensatory and prosthetic alternatives. If disabled students are proficient in these skills, they will be able to cope in a situation of machine or power failuer in the future. Computers and related technologies are not a panacea; they do not solve all of the problems of disabled people through their compensatory and prosthetic applications. They are important tools of learning and daily functioning, and we can expect that they will play more important roles in the lives of disabled individuals in the Information Age. These devices should be used to augment individuals' strengths; at the same time, these people must rely on themselves to do all that they can. Therefore, it is extremely important that today's disabled students continue to receive training and instruction in the more traditional methods of communication, learning, mobility, and self-care.

## THE FUTURE

The current compensatory and prosthetic applications of the computer and related electronic technologies are essential elements in a technological literacy program for all disabled students. The compensatory elements allow the technology to enhance student skills and to make up for student learning and performance deficits. The adaptive prosthetic elements of the technology allow students with physical or sensory deficits to gain access to the power of the computer and to use this electronic device as a classroom learning, functional daily living, and communication tool.

We have come far in the compensatory and prosthetic uses of the computer in special education. Some of the breakthroughs for individual students are amazing. We now have devices that permit blind students to "see" the screen display and output of the computer; deaf students can communicate with other hearing individuals over the telephone; physically disabled students, even those who are severely limited, can gain access to the computer to communicate with others and to control their environment; and those with limited or nonverbal capabilities become capable of speaking. These systems have done much to improve the educational programs of these students and have become essential learning tools for many. Through the use of these devices, many children are achieving near their potential for the first time in their educational careers. These devices have permitted other more disabled children to participate more fully in an instructional program for the first time. These are accomplishments not even envisioned ten years ago in the fields of special education and rehabilitation. To many parents and professionals, they are electronic miracles that permit their disabled children to function in a more independent manner both in school and at home.

Although the present is bright, the future is even brighter and more spectacular. We have only touched the tip of the iceberg in the use of computers and related electronic technologies as compensatory and prosthetic tools for disabled people. The coming decades of the 21st century hold the potential for dramatic breakthroughs in the use of advanced electronic technologies to assist disabled individuals. These devices will serve as both compensatory and prosthetic tools for these populations and will, for many currently disabled people, serve as the vehicles that will take the limitations out of their particular disability. One of the reasons why such a growth in the compensatory and prosthetic applications of advanced technologies is forseen for the coming decades is due to the demographic projections regarding the increase in life expectancy and thus in the number of older citizens in the near future. An aging society with advanced technological capabilities will require the development of new and more advanced compensatory and prosthetic applications. Since the needs of aging individuals are very similar to that of disabled people, it is believed that developments made for this population will have immediate application to disabled groups of the 21st century.

## Summary

■ Prosthetics substitute for an individual's physical or sensory dysfunction.

■ Electronic prostheses are becoming more and more refined, a trend which is expected to continue indefinitely. Such development will allow disabled individuals to function more effectively than has been possible in the past.

■ Adaptive input switches allow low functioning individuals to communicate electronically via a single switch. Although there are a great many such switches for a large number of different applications, they are all basically on-off switches.

■ Alternative keyboards are essentially regular keyboards that are adapted in some manner to act as a prosthetic device for handicapped people.

■ Voice input allows a computer to "listen" to and interpret human voice. Although voice input is still in its initial stages, it is expected eventually to be able to "learn" to recognize any consistent sound, whether or not the same sound is recognizable to human ears, and thus will be particularly useful for people with limited communicative abilities.

■ Voice output systems allow a computer to produce relatively human-sounding speech. Such systems will be especially valuable for people with visual impairments, limited or poor motor control, and mental disabilities. These systems can be used either to provide the user with information about what is actually appearing on the computer screen, or as an expressive aid for individuals with poor communicative abilities.

■ Vision output adaptive devices allow visually impaired individuals to obtain a great deal of visual information otherwise inaccessible to them. Such adaptations usually involve either a modification in the printer (Braille) or in the screen itself (increased brightness, size, change in color).

■ The use of robots as prosthetic devices is expected to expand tremendously into such areas as transportation, personal hygiene, messenger and delivery services, and medical service delivery.

■ The future potential for prosthetic applications with disabled people is staggering. Along with such vast potential goes the possibility of devastating consequences in the event of failure of such systems. Therefore, it is very important to continue to train our special students in traditional skills, to avoid their becoming totally dependent upon devices that might fail and leave them helpless.

# CHAPTER 7

# Designing a Vocational Program to Prepare Disabled Students for Employment in the 21st Century

The achievement of functional independence by disabled people in the 21st century will be determined in good measure by their ability to find and maintain consistent employment. The job situation in the Information Age will be drastically different from that of today, both in the types of jobs and in the employment requirements and characteristics. Business and industry will take on a major role in both the vocational preparation and the retraining programs of the future and will form cooperative relationships with educational institutions in order to provide these services to students and to displaced workers. Cooperative or work-study programs should become the primary form of vocational preparation; making the transition from school to work will become less discernible.

The control and use of information will be the primary economic resource in the 21st century. The majority of jobs will be in information processing, communications technologies, and service industries, with a simultaneous decrease in the number of jobs in manufacturing industries. An increased number of employees will work from their home Net Console or from local offices due to the decentralization of large business complexes and the application of electronic technology systems for communication among workers and management. Further, there will be an increase in the number of individuals engaged in home or regional cottage industries.

Perhaps one of the most significant changes in the employment requirements in the Information Age will be the demand for alterations in employee characteristics. The disabled workers of the future will have to be retrained a minimum of six times in their employment careers. Flexibility and adaptability will be essential characteristics of the successful employee. As a result, today's prevocational and vocational programs for disabled students must stress the development of general employment and work attitude skills, rather than the current trend of training for a specific job or industry, and must prepare students to accept change as a "way of life."

The reality of change is not only an important concept for students to master but also for all educators. Never again will educators be able to teach the same skills and concepts in the same ways. Educators must accept the fact that curricula and teaching methodologies will change. Therefore, if educators are to prepare today's students for the changing world ahead, then educators must also change.

## PREVOCATIONAL AND VOCATIONAL PREPARATION — AN HISTORICAL PERSPECTIVE

In order to appreciate how today's special education prevocational and vocational programs will have to be modified in order to prepare the current generation of special education students for employment in the early part of the 21st century, we should briefly review the history of training for disabled people. The manner in which disabled people fit into adult society has been determined as much by the attitudes of the culture towards them as by economic factors.

Disabled people in the earliest human societies were either abandoned to die or killed outright. There were some changes once society became primarily agricultural. However, many of the attitudes and modes of treatment of disabled people continued, with very few differences, until the Industrial Age. Some of the superstitious attitudes and practices manifested in primitive tribes and in the Middle Ages even persist to some degree in today's advanced technical society. Cultural and religious belief(s) have done little to alleviate the problems of disabled people and have often served as the societal focus used to persecute them and remove them from the view of others.

The next major stage in human history that changed the treatment of disabled people by society was the growth of cities and the movement of increasing numbers of the total population from rural areas to urban settings. Cities gained in importance as the economic centers of society, and jobs became increasingly specialized and diversified. At the same time, the use of machines as labor-saving and goods-producing devices was growing, as was the use of scientific study and methods to solve problems and to discover new information. These factors were significant for changing the way in which disabled people were viewed and treated by other members of society and in their ability to find an economic place in the world.

The consolidation of an increasingly larger percentage of the population into urban communities also meant that the disabled population was being consolidated into the same central urban locations, and thus, disabled people were more visible to the general population. This visibility represents one of the most significant benchmarks in the treatment of disabled people by society in the history of the human race; it forced the general population to become aware of these special needs groups and of the diversity of their membership. This is not meant to imply that the treatment and attitude towards these special groups necessarily improved or that they were accepted by the general population of that society. As a matter of fact, unfortunately, greater visibility resulted in a regeneration and reinforcement of many of the fears and superstitions that had been manifested in the previous stages of the human race.

The shift of the general population to urban centers also caused an increased need for interpersonal communication. This increased communication resulted in a greater interchange of ideas and information and served to spur the development of systematic methods of scientific investigation and analysis in order to solve problems, to gain new information, and to create new machines and technologies. The development of systematic scientific investigation had a direct impact on the lives of disabled people and began to replace superstition as the way in which they were viewed by certain segments of the general population.

The greater visibility of disabled people in urban centers with large populations and the continuing development of scientific investigation combined to cause a number of changes in the treatment of disabled people, particularly the more severely and overtly impaired. First, the growing scientific community began to recognize and accept the fact that the conditions which affected these individuals were medical and biological rather than the result of some curse or other superstitious cause. Second, there was increasing pressure from the general public to remove these overtly disabled individuals from the general society. As a result, many severely disabled people were placed in institutions, which served to remove them from the general population in response to public pressure but which also placed them in environments where they could be studied more efficiently. These institutions were, in most instances, poorly kept, and the treatment afforded the inmates was often inhumane. Other less severely disabled people were placed in pauper prisons. Although these individuals were removed and isolated from general society, this was an important turning point in that the scientific and medical communities began to recognize that these disabled individuals suffered from medical and biological problems. As a result, a systematic investigation into the causative factors of these disorders was begun, and a classification system was designed. Further, certain members of these communities began to investigate alternatives for disabled people in institutions. New ideas were implemented and found to be successful, as were the attempts to design training and, in some instances, educational programs. These programs, however, were designed to support scientific research, and not necessarily to improve the functional abilities of disabled people.

The specialization of employment due to urbanization and industrialization created a change in the employment picture for disabled people, particularly those with mild and minimal disabilities. In an agrarian society, these individuals could be absorbed into an economy if they could perform some or all of the general tasks required in the production of food; however, in the urban and manufacturing setting with its increasing demand for specialists, these disabled people faced a different problem. They had to be either able to learn a specific job or able to find some lower level nonskilled form of employment. Training for specialized employment generally occurred in an on-the-job situation. The higher-functioning individual often did master the on-the-job training required to gain factory employment; however, the more specialized jobs became, the more they required good communication skills and a considerable amount of thinking and decision making skill. It also became apparent that some of the key requirements necessary for them to gain employment, besides the intellectual and motor skills required to perform the task, were the abilities to follow directions and to interact with fellow employees, the employer, and the supervisor in an appropriate manner.

Mild and moderately disabled individuals who were unable to achieve success in the manufacturing industry really had only two other employment alternatives. The first was to enter a family business if the individual's family was involved in a self-owned service occupation. In these situations, the pressure to master a task within a specified period of time and at a specified skill level was not present since the employer was in fact a member of the family. In fact, this type of family-sponsored employment situation was similar to today's concept of a sheltered workshop. It was never anticipated that the disabled individual would take over the family business, as was usually the case with nondisabled children in family businesses; rather, the person was given some menial tasks that were a benefit to the family and that made the disabled individual feel like a contributing member.

The second alternative was to seek some form of low level or nonskilled employment. This tended to be the type of employment that was viewed as being undesirable by the nondisabled job seeker, since its level of pay and opportunity for promotion was considerably lower than that in the goods-producing industries. The handicapped worker always worked under the supervision of a nondisabled individual, and it was not uncommon to find the disabled person exploited by the supervisor.

This general pattern of treatment and employability of disabled people continued until World War II, when many members of the armed forces returned to this country with a disability; thus causing a greater acceptance of people with handicapping conditions. This acceptance was one impetus for the next major development: the admission of certain disabled children into public school special education programs. Another push for these programs came about because many disabled children were enrolled in school under compulsory attendance laws. These children were generally in the mild to moderately impaired range. Some severely disabled children received education and training; but, for the most part, this training took place in institutions or in special schools, such as schools for the blind. The vast majority of children with severe disabilities, however, did not attend school. During these early post World War II days, in almost every instance, disabled children in public school special education programs were placed in self-contained classes. For the most part, these public school special education classes were created in urban areas since this was where the largest population of disabled people was found. This pattern of education of the handicapped continued up until the enactment of PL 94-142, when the rights of all handicapped to receive a free and appropriate education was first affirmed and the concept of "least restrictive" environment was first introduced.

The importance of establishing public special education programs for disabled people is twofold. First, systematic programs of instruction and theories of intervention were established to teach disabled students basic academic skills as well as other academic subjects, skills which were becoming increasingly important for survival in an increasingly complex society. Second, attention began to be given to the question of what will happen to these students after they leave the public school system. This led to the establishment of prevocational and vocational programs and centers for disabled students. It was recognized that certain of the lower level moderately impaired students would never be able to achieve independent employment and living or be able to take advantage of the prevocational and vocational programs established for higher functioning individuals. As a result, the concept of sheltered workshops was introduced at a post-secondary level, usually through the efforts of parental organizations. Vocational training for these students, therefore, was often concerned with preparing them for these semiprotected work experiences.

   The prevocational and vocational programs that were designed for higher functioning disabled students enrolled in public special education programs were developed to reflect the needs of the economy and the job requirements of the Industrial Age. Therefore, students were provided with training for specific jobs, jobs in which they were expected to spend their entire employment careers. The emphasis of these programs was the development of specific work-related skills and abilities for one type of job. This basic approach to training for disabled people has, for the most part, continued to the present time. Employability of disabled people did not, therefore, change dramatically after World War II except that students received vocational instruction in simulated work environments, such as those found within vocational and technical centers. Even so, the ability to function on an actual job was still based on the same principles as in the previous period — their ability to perform the particular work task, to interact appropriately with other employees and the employer, and the ability to manifest appropriate work attitudes. One of the primary detriments to the employment of many moderately mentally or physically disabled student graduates was, and still is, their inability to drive a car. If someone who could not drive did not have access either to mass transportation or to a carpool, they were, and usually are, precluded from employment regardless of their skills. Thus, many disabled individuals in suburban and rural areas were and still are precluded from employment due to an inability to get to and from work. Also, if a prosthetic tool was needed to perform the task, it was perceived to be the responsibility of the employee to provide the tool. This, unfortunately, is still an important employment issue for many handicapped individuals, such as the blind, deaf, and physically disabled; all too often not being able to obtain the appropriate prosthetic device precludes them from employment. Although this situation is improving today, it tends to be only in large corporations and with jobs connected with the federal and certain state and local governments.[1]

## VOCATIONAL SPECIAL EDUCATION PROGRAMS TODAY

   Programs which have been termed career education have been in existence for a number of years; however, they have, for the most part, been rather unsuccessful in achieving what should be their ultimate objective — graduating students who are flexible employees and lifelong learners.

---

[1]The authors would like to express their thanks to Dr. Alonzo E. Hannaford of Western Michigan University for lending his expertise on the topics of career and vocational education for disabled people and for assisting the authors in developing the rest of this chapter.

They tend to reflect the product-oriented philosophy of today's vocational training programs and are, therefore, primarily structured to meet the employment needs of the Industrial Age. These programs, unfortunately, are continuing to focus their primary attention on preparing students for employment in a specific job area. These programs, therefore, are terminal in nature and philosophy in that they are not directed towards the lifelong needs of the students but are principally concerned with post-graduation job placement. True employment careers are developmental in nature with the employee learning new skills, retraining, advancing within a company when feasible, and often requiring reeducation for an entirely new career. These developmental realities will become more pronounced in the rapidly changing economy of the 21st century with its advanced electronic technologies, instantaneous communication systems, and the exponential growth of information. Most of today's career education programs still ignore these essential factors.

The current orientation and objectives of prevocational and vocational education programs for disabled students, for the most part, reflect a similar philosophy. Today's programs continue to focus primarily on preparing students for a specific job or a specific field of employment. The vocational preparation courses of study in most special education vocational programs often fall within rather restricted areas of employment, stressing a limited range of jobs involving manual skills. Some of the most popular offerings in these programs include horticulture and floral arrangement, food service worker, child care worker, maintenance worker, nonelectrical assembly line worker, shipping clerk, delivery service worker (a course of study usually offered in urban areas where public transportation is available), health or child care assistant, and clerical assistant. There are, of course, variations of and additions to these special occupational education courses of study that reflect geographical needs or special regional economic opportunities.

In other words, we are primarily preparing students for specific jobs that exist today and, in some instances, for areas of employment that no longer exist. For example, the authors are reminded of the numerous occasions we visited special and regular education vocational programs and were told that these programs were preparing students for computer and high technology careers. When we visited the training center, the instruction being provided to students was key punch operations for the entry of data into computers. Unfortunately, key punch entry disappeared as the primary form of computer data entry more than a decade ago. The machines the students were working on were more than fifteen years old and, in most cases, replacement parts could no longer be found. These students were being trained for an obsolete vocational field simply because this was the computer equipment the vocational training center had at its disposal and because these were the machines with which the instructors were familiar. Unfortunately, these students were receiving training for skills that were obsolete. Of course, perhaps, they could find a job in a swiss cheese factory where they could punch holes in the cheese. This example may sound farfetched, but in reality many jobs for which disabled individuals are being trained have about as much applicability.

Another difficulty encountered with today's vocational training programs for disabled students is just that — they are only vocational training programs, and as such, they begin too late in students' educational careers to appropriately and comprehensively prepare them for entry into adult society as productive and self-sufficient citizens. The vast majority of these programs begin at the secondary school age level with most starting at the high school level, providing a two- to four-year course of study. The two-year program is the most common form used when students are being prepared for a specific job and when they require intensive training in a specific series of skills. These programs are usually provided during the student's last two years of school, the equivalent of the junior and senior years of high school, and are thought of as a transition from school to the world of work. Many are half-day programs so that the pupil can attend academic classes for part of the day and spend the remainder of the day at an occupational education center for vocational training or at on-the-job training. Ideally, the academic program will provide support for the vocational program so that the basic academic skill requirements of the vocational preparation program will be reinforced through the instructional materials used in the academic classes. Unfortunately, all too often these vocational and academic programs are kept totally separate due to a lack of articulation between the vocational and academic instructors, and the student is faced with dual basic requirements, which are sometimes in conflict. This has become more and more the norm as states have increasingly instituted basic skill exit requirements for both disabled and nondisabled students.

Many special education occupational programs provide students with a prevocational career exploration program for one to two years immediately prior to the formal two-year vocational education program. These career exploration programs provide students with a structured sequence of experiences covering a variety of occupational options, which will become available to them in the two-year vocational training program. Thus, students are able to try each occupational area at the vocational training center for a period of two to three months on a half-day basis. During the period when a student participates in a career exploration unit in a specific vocational area, such as food preparation, he or she is evaluated by the vocational education staff as to whether the student would be successful in that field. These programs thus allow the special occupational education staff to evaluate student potential and skill level in a reality-simulated training situation, rather than in the more typical classroom or testing situations. This experience also allows the student to evaluate firsthand whether or not he or she enjoys this type of work and whether the actual requirements of the job are what the pupil had thought them to be. When students go through vocational options in a predetermined sequence, they generally go from the least complex in terms of skill requirements to the most complex. Should students particularly like a specific occupational training area and should the evaluation indicate that this appears to be an appropriate area of vocational training, then they are generally allowed to stay in that area for an additional mini-unit or to return to that unit after they have sampled all of the other occupational options. Career exploration programs in the year(s) immediately prior to the formal vocational training program provide students with reality testing about the actual requirements of a particular occupation and about their ability to appropriately perform the requirements of that job.

Following these career exploration experiences, students often enter a work study program. In these programs, high school age students attend school on a part-day basis and spend the remainder of the day in an actual work situation. They receive academic credit as well as payment by the employer for the work-study part of their secondary school program. A work-study teacher or counselor monitors the students in the work situation and provides assistance to the employer and supervisors who deal with them in the work situation. These instructors are typically responsible for recruiting the employers who participate in these programs and, therefore, have a close relationship with the local business community. Students participating in these programs meet with their work-study teacher on a scheduled basis in order to receive instruction and guidance about the skills required by the successful employee and about basic economic functional skills, such as budgeting.

Work-study vocational preparation programs provide the disabled student with a true reality-testing situation regarding careers. Students learn specific employment skills in a real-work situation through on-the-job training. They are forced to compare their skills to other workers who have been successful and valued employees. Of equal importance is the fact that these students learn the interpersonal communication, and job responsibility skills and attitudes that are required in order to be a successful employee. Often the work-study coordinator must be available to counsel these students in these areas and to help employers understand the students' abilities and deficits and how to approach remediation on the job. Students also learn the cause-and-effect reality that pay is directly related to employee production. Further, the student who successfully completes a work-study program and has been viewed as a valuable and skilled employee will often be offered full-time employment upon graduation.

On the other hand, work-study programs as the sole vocational preparation option for disabled students are seldom successful. The most successful programs are those that provide students with a two-year regular or special vocational education training program prior to a work-study experience at the secondary level and that are based on a career education program that starts when the student enters school at an early age. When these two forms of vocational education are combined into a secondary school sequence, the students are provided with specific employment skill training prior to a supervised work experience, and therefore, they are able to gain the prerequisite job skills in a relatively sheltered environment prior to applying these skills in a real-work environment. Since, under the provisions of PL 94-142, disabled students are entitled to attend school until graduation or their twenty-first year, these programs can extend over at least a five-year sequence of vocational education, beyond the two years of vocational education and one or more years of work-study. This approach provides disabled students with a comprehensive vocational program of study while also providing them with adequate time for academic preparation to exit school and for mastering the necessary skills of functional daily living in an increasingly complex world.

Another difficulty with work-study programs is in locating cooperative employers to participate in the program. Employers must be supportive of the program, must be sensitive to the needs of disabled students, and must not be merely looking for a source of cheap labor. In certain communities, employment opportunities for disabled students are of a temporary, part-time, or seasonal nature. Often, another difficulty is the student's inability to find transportation to the work-study employment site. Most school districts providing these types of programs do not provide transportation to participating students. Therefore, the work-study site must be either near the school, near the student's home, near public transportation (if it exists), or else someone must provide transportation. An alternative, of course, is to delay the work-study program until a time when the student secures a driver's license, if this is possible or feasible.

Another factor detrimental to vocational programs is a general lack of knowledge on the part of educators about technology and about the dynamics of the Information Age. As previously mentioned, education as an institution tends to be reactionary, responding primarily to current pressures, crises, and concerns. It has also manifested this reactionary policy in the fact that educators tend constantly to "rediscover the wheel"; that is, they always return to the old way of doing things. Other than the innovative use of computers and other related technologies, we would be hard pressed to point to any really new curricular developments in the past twenty years.

Today's vocational education programs, therefore, tend to be overly preoccupied with academic instruction and student achievement. Further, the measurement of academic success is too often concerned with the memorization and mastery of subject matter and with test-taking performance skills. Problem-solving, decision-making, and critical thinking skills have tended to receive less emphasis in these programs even though these skills are of the utmost importance to achieving functional success as an adult. Although academic preparation is very important for all students and especially for those with deficient skills and abilities, it is not the only factor that will determine the functional success of these pupils as independent adults in society. Artificial intelligence and the advanced computer systems of the 21st century will be able to provide individual assistance to disabled people in the performance of many functional skills that are based upon the knowledge of academic facts. Today's computer systems and the projected advanced technology systems of the 21st century can assist these individuals in making decisions and in solving problems, but they cannot now, and never will, be able to "think" for them. These systems are no more than obedient electronic slaves. They cannot think for themselves and must always be given directions by their human operator. Therefore, it is essential that today's career education programs begin to strike a balance between academic preparation and the mastery of thinking and problem solving.

Success is measured by the number of students who are successfully placed into employment upon graduation or upon the completion of their special education programs. Although this may at first appear to be a laudatory program objective and a realistic measurement of program success, it is an extremely limiting and static approach to the realities of the employment situation today and represents a misleading measurement of program success. In most instances, special vocational education graduates are monitored for no more than two years after their placement on a job, if at all. Employment histories and unemployment statistics have indicated that many disabled graduates of these product-oriented programs have generally been able to maintain themselves in an employment situation successfully for the first year or so. Those who experience failure in the first year generally do so because they do not have the appropriate interpersonal and communication skills and positive employee attitudes. However, it is after the disabled graduate of the product-oriented vocational training program has been in a job successfully for a few years that they begin to experience trouble, and many of them are unable to continue to maintain themselves as successful employees. This is primarily due to the fact that they are unable to change as the business and industry in which they are employed changes.

Since the current product-oriented vocational training programs are now focused on preparing students for specific jobs, they are, in fact, predestining many disabled graduates to the ultimate fate of technical displacement. Regardless of his or her area of employment, the average worker today can expect to have to retrain a number of times during an employment career. Product-oriented training programs tend to ignore this reality and the fact that it is necessary to train today's students to be flexible workers. Educating and vocationally training students only for today's jobs in a world whose economy and job market is rapidly changing is unrealistic and shortsighted. The ultimate product of vocational training programs for disabled students must be to graduate individuals who have mastered the process of being flexible workers, who can and will be lifelong learners. It is only this type of graduate who can hope to compete and maintain successful employment today and, more importantly, in the changing world of the Information Age.

Public education as an institution has, however, historically been slow to change, particularly in its curricula. One reason is that the scope, sequence, and content of most instructional programs have been determined, not by educators, but by textbook publishers. Schools use books as the primary resource to teach children, and they buy them from major textbook publishers. Publishers must design textbooks with a national appeal and cannot easily react to the needs of specific states or regions of the country. Further, it takes many years for a publisher to create a new textbook series, so the major publishers find it difficult to react quickly to changes in society and to new curricular needs. They must wait until the trend is firmly established before they produce major textbook revisions or new subject offerings. This explains why, when new course offerings are designed or major revisions in the content of an existing course are made, it is usually because of the initiative of individual teachers, the schools, or the school systems where the course content and instructional materials are internally developed. The only major exception to this trend is the computer software industry in which instructional offerings can be updated and new programs of study designed more rapidly in order to respond to new educational needs.

Another part of the reason for educators' reluctance to react to change is pressures on them from within the school system and from outside the system. Parents and the general community have forced schools to add new programs of instruction for topics that had previously been the responsibility of the family, the community, and religious institutions. The more schools are forced to add new curricular areas by their constituencies, the less time educators have to add new areas to the curriculum. The basic skill levels reported in "The Nation at Risk," on the other hand, pressure schools into returning to teaching basic skills. As society has become more complex and as the demography of society has changed, the demands upon the school have increased causing additional pressures. Factors such as the movement away from the extended family, increased family mobility, the increasing number of single parent families, and the growth in the number of families in which both parents work, have forced schools to become social service agencies. For example, they feed breakfast to students, provide after-school programs because of the number of "latch-key" children (children who have no one at home at the end of the school day because both parents work), and they provide basic health services. Further, the schools constituency has shifted so that the majority of the voters in a local tax area are individuals with no children in public schools, a factor which reflects the demographic shift in which the older segment of the population represents a large portion of the population. All of these factors, including the educational system's conservative predisposition as well as many more too numerous to cite here, have contributed to making educational institutions slow to enact the necessary changes.

Although school systems have been slow to recognize the need to change the curriculum, legislation has served to stimulate changes in the special education process. For example, the enactment of PL 94-142 resulted in some rather significant changes in the vocational preparation options for disabled students enrolled in public and private education programs. Prior to this law, most special education students were limited to special occupational education programs for vocational preparation. With the institution of the "least restrictive environment" concept, "regular" vocational education programs were opened up to special education students who could meet the intellectual, motor, and attitudinal requirements of the course of study and of the potential areas of employment. This was an important development in the annals of occupational education programs for disabled students. The ability of certain special education students to participate in regular vocational education programs also had another important impact on their vocational preparation. Disabled graduates often find themselves in employment situations that include nondisabled as well as other disabled workers. In order to properly prepare them for such a work situation, it is advantageous and important for them to participate in vocational training programs with nonhandicapped students. All too often, however, although graduates have the employment skills necessary to perform a specific job, they have not mastered the interpersonal and communication skills required to work cooperatively with nondisabled peers, supervisors, and employers. The opportunity to receive vocational training with nondisabled students does much to foster the development of these necessary employment skills which heretofore has not been a possibility for many individuals with significant disabilities.

The participation of disabled students in regular vocational education programs has a number of other positive effects on the vocational preparation of these students, effects which enhance employability and the capability to maintain jobs. Many disabled adolescents, like their nondisabled peers, have unrealistic views of job requirements and of their potential as adults. Disabled individuals often do not have the opportunities to change these attitudes because of limited opportunities for reality testing. Usually these students' views have been significantly molded by their experiences in school, with their peers, in the general community, and with their parents. Since many disabled students enter special education programs only after they have failed in school and been identified as "different," they have often developed poor self-concepts; they have learned the "failure syndrome." These feelings are frequently reinforced throughout their educational careers because they often compare their abilities and achievements to other siblings and peers; and because their family, teachers, and peers are often making comparisons. As many of these pupils begin to think about their future as employed adults, they tend to discount their abilities and focus on their deficits. When this happens, they often tend to approach career education with the attitude that they cannot compete with their nondisabled peers and, therefore, seek to enter "safe" vocational preparation programs, initially selecting occupational preparation in fields that require skills far below their actual ability levels. Participation in regular vocational education programs provides them with opportunities to match themselves against students outside of special education and to see themselves more realistically as future competitive employees. Frequently, these experiences assist them in heightening their expectations and career goals and in making more successful career decisions. They are, therefore, coming to grips with the realities of their abilities and deficits as potential employees because of their participation in regular vocational education programs.

Participation in regular vocational education programs has also served as reality testing for another group of disabled students, those with unrealistically high career aspirations. An individual's reaction to academic failure can cause them to unrealistically view their abilities as being far above their actual skill levels just as it can cause others to degrade their abilties. Sometimes these unrealistically high ability and future employment expectations have been fostered by parents, parents who have not been able to come to grips with the realities of their child's disability. When these students participate in regular vocational education programs, they are forced to come to grips with their actual abilities and, therefore, to make more realistic career decisions. Further, the parents are often able to better accept their children's capabilities and deficits when their disabled child participates in such a program. We are reminded of a moderately intellectually and neurologically impaired secondary student whose only career aspiration was to become a brain surgeon. Both of his parents were physicians and his older siblings had gone on to study and to enter the medical profession. The parents, although medical professionals, had been unable to come to grips with their son's disabling condition and his actual skill level and, therefore, did little at home to dissuade him from this unrealistic career goal. The young man participated in the career exploration and regular vocational education program provided by his school district for disabled pupils and discovered that he had particular mechanical skills equal to and superior to those of other students in the program. This experience led him to accept his limitations and abilities, and he went on to enter a two-year vocational education training program at a local post-secondary technical school. He found employment upon completion of this program and has remained with the same firm for a number of years. He entered the career development program provided by his employer and has successfully risen within the company.

Others whose expectations are too high require reality testing because of whatever influence glorifies professions — as in the situation of the mentally disabled student who has his or her heart set on becoming a professional pilot. Rather than verbally attempting to dissuade the student, it is sometimes better to provide a situation in which the student determines that career is not what he or she really wanted. One way of doing this, which has been successful, is to provide the books that are necessary for the student to understand in order to successfully enter that career. Using the pilot example, the student might be given a few flight training manuals to digest. Often, the student will return the books and decide on a more realistic career to pursue. This way, the student makes the decision and "saves face" because it is a "controlled failure" situation. These are just two examples of how participation in appropriate vocational education programs by disabled students can assist them in developing more realistic views of themselves as workers and in selecting more realistic careers.

What is really needed in order to prepare today's disabled students for employment in the economy of the Information Age, however, is career education. Vocational preparation is just one component of a total career education program, but only one component. All too often, today's vocational programs for disabled students are concerned with specific skill training and job placement rather than with career development. A total career development program should extend throughout a student's entire educational experience and should permeate all instructional areas of study. If we in the field of special education truly desire to prepare students to be lifelong learners, then we must provide them with career education throughout their educational experience.

Even when there is career education at all levels of public education, which is rare, there tends to be lack of coordination and articulation between the program levels or phases. Each level of instruction is taught as a unique unit having little to do with what occurred at the previous level and not necessarily leading into the content of the next level of instruction. This, of course, results in a lack of continuity in the total program and gives students a fragmented view of career education and of their future. Further, this results in a lack of coordination between short and long term program goals. In a fragmented structure, both the students and the teacher fail to see the ultimate objectives of the program as a whole and, therefore, often fail to see the true purpose of their unit as it relates to the total program.

This lack of coordination between levels or phases of instruction in most of today's career education programs also results in a lack of appropriate task analysis using a developmental model of career development. Since each instructional step in the various levels or phases tend to function as self-contained units, it is extremely difficult, if not impossible, for many of today's career education programs to function within the framework of a true developmental model. Yet, for a career education program for disabled students to be effective, it must be structured to reflect the developmental progress of the pupils throughout their educational programs of study. This lack of a developmental model also reflects the fact that most of these programs are operated on an Industrial Age mentality and, therefore, have only one objective — preparing and training students for a specific job. Success in the adult world and in employment encompasses many more competencies than job performance skills in a specific area of employment. Factors such as attitudes, personal philosophy, citizenship, interpersonal communication skills, feelings of self-worth, respect for others, decision-making and problem-solving skills, and many other elements are important and crucial causative agents in preparing a disabled student to be a happy, successful, and employed adult member of society both today and in the future. Career education is considerably more than vocational preparation for a specific job or area of employment, and most of today's programs have not yet accepted this reality and revised their programs of study to appropriately reflect this truth. As a result, these programs are not preparing today's disabled students for the society and the economic world of their future, the Information Age. Rather they are continuing to prepare them for the world of their parents and teachers.

Some changes in the career education curriculum must occur. The changes that must occur are not radical; however, they are significant. Career education must not be a separate curriculum area to be introduced into the programs of study of today's special education students. Nor should it be a subject area primarily directed toward secondary pupils through vocational preparation programs. A true and effective career education program for disabled students must be a central component of their total special education experience. It is a developmental and future-directed course of study that extends throughout the pupils' educational careers and throughout their lives and, as such, must be integrated into all subject areas at all instructional levels. Career program educators must also be cognizant of the fact that the students enrolled in school today will live most of their lives in the 21st century. Therefore, the focus of these programs is on preparing today's disabled students for their future life. Career education is one of the most important, if not the most important, curricular concept in the field of special education because it has as its ultimate objective the preparation of disabled students to become self-sufficient, independent, and contributing members of society — the ultimate objective of special education. Career education, therefore, encompasses much more than academic and vocational preparation; it is concerned with the development of the whole person to achieve his or her maximum potential as productive and self-content adult members of society.

Career education incorporates instruction in the academic subject areas, such as the basic skills, science, social studies, art and music, physical education, and vocational preparation; however, career education is concerned with more than isolated instruction in the areas of academics and fine arts because a successful and self-content person is much more than the sum of the facts that he or she knows. As a result, a comprehensive career education program focuses equal attention on the development of skills such as socializatioin, communication, personal work habits, positive self-concept, realistic acceptance of one's strengths and weaknesses, value clarification, logic and reasoning, problem solving, and decision making in the individual disabled student. Career education, therefore, encompasses all curricular areas of special education and extends throughout the individual's entire school experience. Further, individuals do not stop learning once they leave school and, therefore, career education is also concerned with preparing students to be lifelong learners. This comprehensive career education program may sound similar to some that are already in existence, and it is. The differences, however, lie in an attitude of continual learning — concentrating on learning and survival skills while teaching subject areas (instead of teaching these areas in isolation) and then using the latest in technology as tools for instruction, prosthetics, and compensation.

A comprehensive career and vocational education curriculum for disabled students should encompass five interrelated phases, or levels, arranged in a developmental sequence: career awareness, career exploration, prevocational education, vocational education, and vocational reeducation. Of these five phases, the last, vocational reeducation, is a rather recent addition to the curricular sequence of career education programs. Approximately every five years, a large number of jobs will significantly change or disappear, and the frequency of these events will increase in the 21st century due to the exponential growth of advanced electronic technologies. As these jobs change or disappear, a significant part of the work force will have to be retrained and reeducated in order to stay employed. The workers of the future will, therefore, have to be flexible and lifelong learners in order to maintain employment in the economy of the Information Age. Companies are now working cooperatively with schools, colleges, and universities in order to retrain workers whose jobs have become radically different or have totally disappeared. Futurists project that this cooperation between education and the private sector will increase in the coming decades, and vocationally directed adult education programs will become an essential element of educational course offerings. The increase in the percentage of the total population over age 65 is another factor contributing to the need for continuing education and vocational retraining programs in the coming decade. Career education will have to include this segment of the population in order for the society as a whole to remain economically viable in the job market. It will also have to incorporate instruction for these aging individuals in the use of compensatory and prosthetic equipment because of the dysfunctions associated with the aging process. Vocational reeducation, therefore, has been added to the scope and sequence of the career education curriculum in order to reflect the current trends in the economy, the changes in employment skills, and the projections regarding the employee proficiencies that will be required in the Information Age. All of these factors will lead to an increased need for special education expertise in order to design and assist in the implementation of individual career education plans for disabled people at all ages and at all impairment levels.

Although it is essential that today's disabled students receive instruction on and about the use of electronic technologies, in particular the computer, there is a problem for special educators in locating appropriate educational software for lower functioning students. Most of the directions contained in the programs are too complex for these pupils, and the reading levels of the software products are too high for them. As a result, teachers are forced to create career education software through the use of authoring language systems, to employ other instructional materials in order to present the instructional content, or to modify the instructional use of these materials. Whenever educational computer software and other technologies are used in career education programs for disabled students, however, they must meet the same criteria as all other educational materials used with these pupils. They must be selected to meet the specific instructional needs of the educator, to match his or her personal approach to the teaching process, and must be selected to meet the needs of an individual student.

A comprehensive career and vocational education program for disabled students must be based upon close cooperation between education and the private sector. Business and industry will be the ultimate employers of these pupils and, therefore, must be included as equal partners by schools in the establishment of common goals regarding the education, training, and retraining of the disabled student. To design a career education program without the active, cooperative, and continual involvement of the private sector, is to create an unrealistic program. It must be remembered that not all of the goals of a career education program are universal. An effective program must also reflect the local and regional economy and job market and, therefore, the active participation of the private sector is crucial to the development of a total program of instruction. Educators cannot know the specific needs of business and industry regarding the skills and attitudes that they expect and require of their employees, both new employees and those currently employed who require retraining. Further, it is only through such cooperative planning that the private sector can develop a better understanding of and sensitivity to disabled individuals.

It must be stressed that this cooperative planning should not be static or a one-time accomplishment. Rather, it must be continual and flexible in order to institute continual change into the program and meet the continual changes in society and in the job market. The master career education plan must be farsighted enough to project ten or more years into the future using holistic planning, and yet it must contain segments or phases into the foreseeable future (one or more school years). In order to accomplish this type of plan, an evaluation model, such as Michael Provus' Discrepancy Evaluation Model (Provus, 1971), should be included in the plan so that the goals and the accomplishments can be periodically compared. When a discrepancy is discovered, changes can be made either in what is occuring or in the long-range goals. Further, the goals must be continually evaluated in order to determine appropriate changes based on the changing needs of the world of work. In order to accomplish this flexible or fluid type of master plan, the cooperative effort between business, industry, and education must evolve into a partnership in which their common goals are identified so that each determines how its segment can best contribute to the meeting of those goals. For example, in addition to assisting education in setting the specific goals of career education programs, business and industry will serve as work-study training sites for students, and their employees will serve as instructors. The private sector will also provide instructional equipment and materials to schools to be used in the vocational programs for students and in the reeducation programs for its displaced workers. The experience of business and industry with operating in a cost-effective manner will also provide assistance to administrators in managing schools and school systems in an era of dwindling educational fiscal resources.

### Carl D. Perkins Vocational Education Act — PL 98-524

The federal government has become acutely interested in the apparent failure of many of today's vocational education programs in effectively providing training for special needs populations, and as a result, Congress enacted PL 98-524, the Carl D. Perkins Vocational Education Act. This act provides funding to states, municipalities, and school districts. Through its funding and grant provisions, the act also provides direction to these agencies regarding the establishment of programs for special needs populations and signals the interest of the federal government and of the general public in improving the vocational opportunities of these groups. PL 98-524 is divided into five sections: Title I-Assistance to States, Title II-Basic State Grants, Title III-Special Programs, Title VI-National Programs, and Title V-General Provisions.

The stated purpose of PL 98-524 is to provide assistance to states in order to improve the quality of education and, in particular, career and vocational education to special needs groups. The act defines special needs groups to include the disadvantaged, handicapped, incarcerated, adults requiring training and reeducation, single parents and homemakers, and the limited English proficient. The purpose of the act, therefore, is to provide assistance to states in assuring access for these special needs groups to the work force of the general economy. The act is also designed to assist men and women in entering nontraditional occupations.

The Carl D. Perkins Vocational Education Act (PL 98-524) signals education that Congress and the Department of Education recognize the need for quality education programs for special needs groups in order to promote economic growth and to improve productivity. Further, this act is a recognition of the fact that these vocational preparation programs must meet the needs of the workforce in an era of rapid economic change. Therefore, PL 98-524 provides assistance to states to develop, expand, improve, and modernize their vocational education programs for special needs groups, a population which by definition includes disabled people. Further, the act provides assistance to states to provide supportive services, special training programs, career guidance, counseling, and placement services to special needs populations. It is, therefore, one of the most comprehensive and realistic vocational education laws to be passed by the Congress.

PL 98-524 also recognizes the need for close cooperation between the public and private sectors, between education, business, and industry, as a prerequisite for the development of quality vocational education programs for these special needs groups. It also recognizes the fact that economically depressed areas often have the least fiscal resources to implement the types of quality vocational education training and retraining programs required to prepare individuals in the special needs groups for employment both today and in the future. As a result, the act provides special assistance to these economically depressed areas. This act, therefore, is future directed and is seeking to support the development of vocational training programs by states that will meet the employment needs of the general economy not only today but, more important, in the future.

PL 98-524 further recognizes the need for the workers of today and in the future to have a good foundation in the basic academic skills; and therefore, it provides for the improvement of instructional programs in the basic skills and related academic subject areas. It also seeks to coordinate academic instruction directly with the career and vocational education training programs. Further, the act recognizes the current and future impact of technology upon the economy and the employment market. Therefore, it provides aid to encourage the application of technology in the general academic instructional areas and in the vocational training programs for the identified special needs groups.

The Carl D. Perkins Vocational Education Act additionally seeks to break the cycle of fiscal dependency by many members of the identified special needs groups by providing for the improvement of consumer education and homemaking skills.

## SCOPE AND SEQUENCE OF A CAREER EDUCATIONAL PROGRAM FOR DISABLED PEOPLE

A comprehensive career education program for disabled students, as indicated, should include five developmentally sequential phases, or levels. These phases are: career awareness, career exploration, pre-vocational education, vocational education, and vocational reeducation (Hannaford & Taber, 1986). A comprehensive career education program for today's disabled students must be future oriented and must reflect the skills and attitudes that will be required for them to function in the society and economy of their future, the 21st century. The ultimate objective of such a program is to prepare today's disabled students to become self-sufficient, independent, and contributing adult members of society both now and in the future world of the Information Age.

### Phase I — Career Awareness

The career awareness phase of the career education program for disabled people begins at the preschool level and extends through the elementary school level of the special education instructional sequence. Since most mildy and some moderately impaired children are not identified until they fail in regular education programs, most students participating in formal special education preschool programs tend to fall into the moderate to severely disabled range. However, whether or not a child participates in a formal preschool program, the primary source of information and instruction for the preschool child should be the family and, in particular, the parent(s). Parents and other family members provide disabled children with concrete examples of and practical experiences with the concept of work, with the variety of employment opportunities available in society, and with the proper attitudes and interpersonal skills required to be a successful worker. Formal preschool programs can supplement and support the career awareness experiences the child receives at home; however, these programs and subsequent special education intervention can never supplant the influence of the family on the career attitudes and aspirations of the child. The greatest disservice that parents can do their special education preschool and school age children is to isolate them, limit their experiences and exposure to the world, and treat them as disabled. Children who have been treated this way in the home start the career education process already predisposed to focus on their disabilities. This focus on what they think they cannot do severely limits their career aspirations and their willingness to explore realistic vocational options. Therefore, it is vital that a close link be established between the home and the school early in this phase and that it continue throughout all phases or until such time as the parents are no longer the custodial agents for the disabled individual. This link serves three major purposes: first, to provide students with role models; second, to train parents to be better role models; and third, to provide educators with more knowledge about the parents' areas of work and their subsequent attitudes — information necessary if they are to realistically and successfully approach students within the career education curriculum.

The principle component of the career awareness phase of the total career education program is experience. Given the developmental level of children at the preschool and elementary school age and the manner in which they learn best, it is essential that the experiences provided them be as practical as possible for them to absorb the concepts that are crucial to this phase. Formal school programs, therefore, must include specifically planned trips that expose students to the variety of jobs available in the general community and to the requirements and responsibilities of these jobs. Another essential component of the instructional program at this level is to have workers who represent the variety of employment areas in the community visit the classroom in order to discuss their jobs. Obviously, parents are a very important resource for objective information about jobs and also for subjective information about such areas as work attitude and appropriate job-related behaviors. Although audiovisual aids can provide students with information about a variety of careers, they do not provide the vital practical experiences furnished by field trips and classroom guests. Therefore, these audiovisual instructional materials should be primarily employed as pre- or post-visitation instructional exercises.

The primary objective of the career awareness phase is to draw the students' attention to the variety of jobs available in the general community and, therefore, to those jobs potentially available to them. Career awareness is also directed toward educating pupils about the job requirements and responsibilities of these various areas of employment. It is important that special educators directly correlate these job requirements to other subject areas and to the total academic preparation necessary for someone to enter these fields. If the disabled child who wanted to become a brain surgeon had received this type of instruction at the elementary school level, he would probably have realized that his goal was impractical and unrealistic, and he might have revised his career aspirations much earlier. As a result, he would have been much more understanding about his abilities and interests, would have been more accepting of his disabilities, and probably would have gained more from his entire special education experience, especially if the parents had been involved early in his career education experience. It is also highly probable that he would have performed better academically and would have learned more of the content and the concepts that were presented to him.

One of the most essential concepts introduced at the career awareness phase is that there is "dignity in all work." This phase and the concept it represents remains a central element at all levels of the entire career education course of study; however, it is essential that this important concept be introduced early in the developmental sequence. Students must be helped to understnd that all work is important and provides a service to society as a whole. This is an important concept for all pupils to learn and accept, and it is particularly significant for disabled students. The intellectual, physical, or emotional disabilities of many special education students could prevent them from securing the types of employment that their parent(s) achieved and that may be available to their siblings and nondisabled peers. Unless they accept the concept of the dignity of all work, they may be unwilling to enter the type of vocational program most suited to their abilities. Further, even if they enter such a program and secure employment in that area, they may be dissatisfied with their job and, therefore, may remain frustrated and malcontent throughout their employment careers.

### Phase II — Career Exploration

The career exploration phase begins at the later elementary school years and extends through the middle or junior high school years. The primary emphasis of this phase is on more direct identification of the variety of occupations available in the general community and of the responsibilities and preparation required by these potential areas of employment. As with the career awareness phase, practical experiences through field trips and visits to the classroom by individuals representing a variety of occupations is an important element of the career exploration phase. It is extremely important that both field trips and the classroom visits include workders who represent the variety of employment options available in the general community. Merely to focus on "professional" and "white collar" jobs is to provide students with an unrealistic view of the world of work. It prejudices them about the multitude of employment options available to them and often contributes to the development of unrealistic occupational aspirations.

The career exploration phase is the beginning of potential occupational area selection by students. The content presented to students is concerned with the definite study of various occupations. Pupils are specifically made aware of the variety of employment fields available today and of those that will be viable job alternatives in the future. This includes discussions about the type, purpose, and specific requirements of these employment options. Students are also provided with assistance in recognizing the advantages and disadvantages of these various potential jobs on an individual basis and in group instructional activities. Career exploration is an essential step in developing a true understanding of the realities of the world of work, and as a result, academic information and instruction is tied closely to this occupational exploration program of study.

One of the objectives of the career exploration phase is to assist disabled students in developing realistic employment aspirations. As they begin to explore the requirements, advantages, and disadvantages of various occupations, they begin to match these factors against their own particular interests, abilities, and disabilities. It is only through such reality testing of employment options that disabled students can make appropriate occupational selections at the prevocational and vocational phases of the career education program and thus receive the vocational training that is specifically appropriate to their unique needs and abilities. There are a number of ways in which this early reality testing can occur, and the closer the experiences are to "reality," the more effective they will be. Wherever resources permit, the student should actually experience the job. In other words, allow students to be with a person who is actually carrying out duties so that students learn firsthand about job responsibilities and requirements. They will also learn appropriate behaviors and can identify the need to learn specifics within various academic subjects.

Another method of providing reality testing is to organize the classroom environment so as to provide mini-society that includes a bank, a store, and other places found in the community. For example, "It's Your Future" (Zeran Corp., Redmond, WA) is a comprehensive curricular package designed to create real life experiences. In any such setting, students not only carry out vocational tasks but also learn acceptable behaviors and other basic independent living survival skills. Thus, the career exploration phase provides for the direct preparation of students for entrance into the prevocational level of the career education program.

### Phase III — Prevocational Education

The prevocational education phase is an extension of the career exploration level of the program and begins at the middle or junior high school level. It generally extends into the high school level or until the time that a disabled student enters the formal vocational education phase. During the prevocational phase, evaluation of career characteristics continues in a more intensive manner than previously, and specific exploration of various vocations begins. Thus, students at this level match their personal characteristics, abilities, and interests far more realistically to the requirements of selected careers, and the reality testing that occurred in the previous phase becomes far more personal, precise, and extensive. Students at the prevocational phase experience a decision-making level of career matching and review just prior to their selection of a vocational education area of training. Therefore, the academic instruction presented to students is strictly correlated with the vocational education program and incorporates the skills and attitudes that have been addressed throughout all phases of the career education curriculum. For example, if the occupation selected requires a high school diploma, and the state in which the student resides mandates high school competency testing in order for a student to gain such a diploma, the academic instruction will focus on preparing the student for these examinations. Other academic instruction will be directed toward assisting the pupil in gaining the skills required by the occupation(s) that have been selected.

One of the most effective computer programs to provide pupils with advanced career exploration resources is the *Guidance Information System (GIS)*, produced by the Time Share Division of the Houghton Mifflin Company. *GIS* is an interactive computer system that provides extensive information about occupations, the armed service, two-year and four-year colleges and universities, and graduate school programs. The occupational component of the program provides extensive information about such things as the job's ability and vocational training requirements, academic preparation requirements, national and regional employment opportunities in the field, and salary range. All of the information contained in the *GIS* system is current, and the entire data base is updated semiannually.

Students using this system are able to individualize the computer search by giving the system specific variables that are important to them. For example, a student could indicate that he or she wanted a job that required manual mechanical skills, that required only a high school diploma, that paid a starting salary of $20,000, and that was located in the Southwest. Once these and other selected variables were entered into the system, the computer would provide the pupil with a listing of all of the occupations meeting the student's stated requirements, if such a job existed. The pupil could review this information with teacher or parents and request further information about other occupations. The computer system would then provide the complete listing of the selected occupational area(s), including information about all of the variables from which the student could originally have made selections.

The *Guidance Information System* is not specifically designed for use by disabled people, although many elements contained in its software data base relate specifically to them. For example, the listing of two- and four-year post-secondary programs provides the user with information about whether the school selected has special service programs for disabled students and about the specific disabilities for which the school is equipped to provide special assistance. *GIS* is used extensively by high school guidance programs, vocational rehabilitation programs, and unemployment placement agencies, and it has also proven to be an extremely effective career exploration tool for use with disabled students.

All disabled students enrolled in middle or junior high school special education programs in the Commack, NY school district used the *Guidance Information System* as an integral part of their occupational exploration program. Not only did these students learn important concepts about the dynamics of an interactive computer system and how to conduct an information search, they received personally selected information about occupations they were considering as career goals. Students received individual assistance in using the system and in entering their selected variables from the special education teachers, teacher assistants, and volunteers. These individuals also provided assistance in reading the instructions and the information about occupations, if such assistance was required.

Once students had received the desired information about the occupations they had selected from the *GIS* system, the teacher instituted a reality testing program with them both on an individual basis and as a part of group discussions. The academic and vocational training preparation requirements of the area of employment were explored, and the advantanges and disadvantages of the career were analysed with the student. The purpose of these activities, designed for students to "discover" the realities of their choices through study, discussion, simulation, and placement in an actual job situation, was to assist pupils in realistically assessing their abilities in relationship to the skills required to perform the specific selected job.

At no point in this process were students ever told that the occupations selected were unrealistic for them and, therefore, should be abandoned and another field selected. The intent was to teach reality testing and values clarification. Once a student had decided on a specific occupation, the academic preparation requirements for that position were integrated into the pupil's academic program of study. Generally, the disabled students initially selected the types of careers that they saw as high paying, prestigious, and reflecting the occupations represented on popular television shows. However, once an academic reality testing program was instituted, the students were forced to realistically assess their intellectual, physical, and emotional abilities in relationship to the preparation requirements of the job. If a student decided that the selected occupation was really not for them, another computer search was instituted and the instructional cycle was repeated.

Over a period of time, the handicapped students gradually become more realistic in their occupational selections and in clarifying which values and goals were really most important to them. This process of computer occupational exploration also continues through the vocational phases of the career education program. The use of this technological instructional tool provides them with the ability to test the reality of their occupational goals against their specific abilities. They become more and more discerning in their selections until they decide upon a potential area of employment that is personally realistic for them. Since the academic and related skill requirements of the selected occupations are always integrated into their total instructional program, they receive the types of preparation that will assist them in developing the prerequisite skills and abilities necessary to become successful employees. Further, the parents are encouraged to use the computer system in order to explore occupations and post-secondary education and training programs for their disabled children. This participation assists parents in becoming more realistic about their childrens' abilities and disabilities and results in their being more supportive of their children's ultimate occupational choices.

One of the most essential elements in the prevocational education phase is the development of the necessary personal and social characteristics required to be a successful employee. This is not to say that these characteristics were not important or not addressed in previous phases, but now they are identified and placed in the IEP to be specifically taught. Many handicapped graduates of vocational programs are able to learn the specific skills required to perform a job, and yet they are unsuccessful in maintaining employment. Therefore, the development of the necessary social, personal, and employee attitudes is as important as, if not ultimately more important than, the mastery of specific job performance skills. An employee who has these personal and interpersonal characteristics and who is flexible and willing to learn is often more valued by an employer than the person who has highly developed skills in a job performance area but who lacks appropriate social skills. The employee with the proper personal characteristics can be trained and reeducated on the job, whereas individuals without these characteristics frequently cannot maintain themselves successfully in the society of the workplace. Therefore, the prevocational phase provides special educators with the opportunity to insure that their pupils have developed the essential employee characteristics that will be required by employers in the Information Age, including flexibility, willingness to change and learn new skills, the use of technology as a daily living and working tool, communication, the development of lifelong learning attitudes, and appropriate behaviors for interpersonal relations.

Activities such as role-playing within simulations — through either classroom interaction or interactive videodisc technology — provide students with the opportunity to experiment in a nonthreatening environment with interpersonal and social situations that are likely to occur in the world of work. They are able to receive feedback about the appropriateness of their simualted responses from teachers and peers or from probable consequences of the computer programs. Although there is little instructional material currently available in career and occupational education on the interactive videodisc system, this electronic modality holds the potential of becoming a major instructional tool in this simulation process. Some programs are successfully using interactive video simulations related to interpersonal work situations. Many such programs have been developed either by the private sector for use with their employees or by the armed services for use in their training situations.

A final major component of the prevocational phase for disabled students is the initiation of intraschool, interschool, and other closely supervised and closely evaluated work experiences. Many successful programs provide disabled students "work" experiences within the school in situations involving the lunch room, the school store, the custodial staff, general office work or nurse clerical assistance. These experiences provide essential evaluation opportunities for the professional staff to assess the specific abilities of the students and to identify the areas that require continued instruction or remediation. Since most of these "work" experiences involve the pupil's interaction with other adults and peers, it is particularly beneficial in assessing the interpersonal skills of the disabled students. Often these "work" experiences do not provide the student with actual pay but, rather, are based upon a token economy system. This is particularly true when the age of the student precludes him or her from getting the necessary working papers to be truly employed. However, when these students do reach the appropriate age, many programs provide pay for this work experience. Providing actual pay for services rendered has proven to be highly motivational to students in developing appropriate work-related skills.

Another component of the prevocational phase for disabled students, which is included in certain school systems, is participation in a career exploration program at a vocational training site. This program is described in detail earlier in this chapter. Basically, disabled students attend these programs on a half-day basis. They are given the opportunity to explore a number of vocational alternatives in the training program, and each experience generally lasts three to four months. Participation in such a program allows the student to gain firsthand knowledge about the skills and work activities related to specific areas of potential vocational training and employment. It also provides the vocational education staff with an opportunity to evaluate firsthand the specific abilities, disabilities, and areas of remediation for each of these pupils. Further, it provides the educator with a relatively real-life work simulation situation in which to evaluate the students' interpersonal and work attitudes and skills. Information gained from these evaluations are reported back to the students' teachers so that appropraite remediation can be provided immediately in an environment where consequences can be controlled.

## Phase IV — Vocational Education

The vocational education phase of the program generally begins at the high school level, although in certain instances with specific disabled students it can begin as early as the last year(s) of their middle or junior high school experience. The point at which the handicapped student enters the vocational education phase of the program is determined individually, based on the needs and abilities of the specific pupil, although participation in this component is available to all. Further, the type of vocational preparation program is individually tailored to the unique needs of each student. Thus, a pupil who will ultimately be placed in a sheltered workshop environment may attend the special occupational education program or, more probably, attend a vocational training experience at a local sheltered workshop site on a part-day basis. Other students may attend the regular occupational education program at a vocational training site. Still others may be involved in a work-study program housed in a local business or industry.

The active cooperative involvement and planning with the private sector is crucial at this stage. Business and industry will not only assist in the establishment of goals and program participation criteria, they will also provide training sites for students as well as equipment and materials for the schools. Further, company employees will be directly involved in the vocational instruction of pupils. One of the most effective programs we have witnessed for rather limited disabled students, students who would normally be placed in a sheltered workshop environment, occurred through such an education and private sector cooperative program. These pupils were placed in a "sheltered" environment housed in a local industry. They performed specific low level sorting and packaging activities under the direct supervision of a special vocational education supervisor from the school system. The employer assisted in the delineation of the specific components that went into the performance of these tasks, and the students received instruction in the development of these skills in school. While they were on the job, they performed these tasks at their own pace and were paid for their production on a piecework basis. The primary requirement was that the work they produced be done properly; speed was not a consideration. The students participated in this vocational work-study experience on a part-day basis, with the remainder of the day spent at school. Although they worked in a segregated area, which was removed from any dangerous equipment, they had complete access to the employee cafeteria and ate their meals totally integrated with other workers. This program proved so successful that a post-graduation shelter workshop program was instituted, and later, the entire program was replicated by other employers in the community. The employer received a valued service and product from the disabled students and post-graduates. Further, the employer had only to be concerned with piecework payment, since medical insurance and other typical fringe benefits were covered by the Social Security Disability benefits the disabled participants received as an entitlement. The disabled participants, therefore, were provided with actual work in a true employment situation. Cooperative education and private sector vocational training programs have thus proven to be beneficial to all cooperating parties and to students at all disability levels. The example provided here is, admittedly, an Industrial Age example. However, it points to the importance of cooperative efforts that take into consideration community resources plus the Least Restrictive Environment (LRE) for this particular group in this particular community. This example also points to the difference between merely training for a particular job and being educated for success on a job — a program that involves all the necessary components for job success.

In general, the basic instruction of the vocational education program for disabled students is a cluster configuration with the primary emphasis on the transference of learning to the career and vocational training experiences. Therefore, the academic instruction is totally career related. As mentioned earlier, this can include academic instruction in preparation for a high school competency examination for specific pupils, if appropriate. All other academic instruction should be directed toward the support of the career and vocational education program. The cluster concept relating the academic to the vocational program is not a new concept. Previously, however, these programs have trained students for specific careers within a job-related cluster (that is, practical nursing or building trades) and were terminal in design. Modifications for the

Information Age would provide varying job experiences within a cluster and teach specific transference skills as well as identification of resources from which help or retraining could occur — not only during the cluster experience but at later times throughout the individual's life, as necessary.

The support of the career education program through the academic instruction component of a disabled student's vocational education phase is not intended to be in any way limiting. If, for example, a student's career goal is to attend a two- or four-year post-secondary program, then the academic program would be directed toward the preparation of the pupil for that program. Should a particular student be enrolled in a vocational program requiring the mastery of training manuals, then these materials would be integrated into the academic program for that individual. The instruction in understanding these manuals, however, could involve simulation, interactive video, robotic programming, and so forth, as necessary to teach the information while compensating for deficit areas. Disabled students who will be entering some form of a sheltered workshop program upon completion of their secondary school special education experience could receive academic instruction that prepared them for semi-independent living, which could include areas such as survival skills in the basic academic subjects, self-care, travel training, and interpersonal and general social behavior.

The vocational education phase is extremely flexible and highly individualized. There must be multiple entry and exit points based on the individual needs and abilities of the students. The ultimate objective is not only to provide specific vocational preparation but also to assist the student in transfering all of the information, attitudes, values, and experiences to adult society and the world of work throughout life. Therefore, intensive instruction and remediation of deficient skills in the areas of social behavior, interpersonal skills, communication, and problem solving remain important components of this phase. At the present time, the vocational preparation phase is the last opportunity for the special career education program to attempt to bring all of the various components of the program together in order to insure, as much as possible, that the existing student will become a well-adjusted, independent, and contributing member of adult society.

### Phase V — Vocational Reeducation

Vocational reeducation is the most recent addition suggested to the career education program for disabled students (Hannaford and Taber, 1986). This phase has been added because most workers today and in the future will be required to retrain a number of times in their employment careers. The vocational reeducation component was also added because many disabled graduates will require continued monitoring and assistance in order to maintain themselves in employment. Very often this type of follow-up service could be initially conducted by the school system and gradually taken over by other state agencies, such as the Office of Vocational Rehabilitation. As time goes on, however, interagency agreements should be established whereby a total flexible life plan is established for each individual, and each agency must develop cooperative roles with business and industry to provide consultation, support, and appropriate reeducation, including retraining as necessary. Interagency organizations are presently being developed for disabled preschool children. The post-school concept is merely an extension of this, which could eventually provide "womb to tomb" coordinated services for disabled people.

Therefore, an essential element of the vocational reeducation phase, regardless of the reason for its use with a specific individual, is the assessment and reassessment of that person's successes and failures. This type of assessment not only focuses on the employment success of the individual, but is also concerned with the personal characteristics, interests, and abilities of the person to function as an adult in society.

Should the individual require retraining for a new vocation, the reeducation phase provides such services either in an on-the-job situation or in a post-secondary instructional program. It does not matter whether the person enters such a program because of an employer or employee initiative or because of the individual's failure to maintain employment. The purpose of these programs is to develop the required personal, social, and performance skills needed to maintain a career through job modifications, to find new employment, or to become a better adjusted functional adult in society.

The most effective services provided to disabled individuals during this phase are " hot lines," which the person can call in order to gain information and recommendations for service. This aspect of Phase V is very important since many disabled adults do not know where to turn for assistance or do not know their legal entitlements. Often these "hot lines" are maintained by parent groups or disabled advocacy groups. In the future, they may, and should, become part of the extended education system.

It can be anticipated that the reeducation phase of career education will become a most important component of the career education program for disabled people in the future. As our society moves more deeply into the Information Age, the need for reeducation and retraining will become greater and more frequent. Disabled individuals will, therefore, have to be lifelong learners and the career reeducation programs will serve as the vehicles for providing this necessary educational and vocational training service. Career education must not be a terminal program, one which ends when disabled individuals complete their secondary schooling and enter society as adults. It is a program that must be available for individuals of any age and be available throughout each individual's life.

## Summary

■ Formal vocational training programs for disabled people are a fairly recent development. Originally, these programs were segregated and were directed toward preparation for low-level skill areas of employment.

■ The enactment of PL 94-142, with its emphasis on the least restrictive environment concept, legally opened regular vocational education programs to the mildly and moderately impaired.

■ A major difficulty with the current design of vocational education programs is that they begin too late and the content is concrete, whereas the long-term career needs of disabled individuals are process oriented and rapidly changing.

■ The successful future of vocational education programs for the disabled depends upon the development of close cooperation between the private sector and the educational system. Only business and industry can provide educators with necessary information about specific current and future skills of successful workers. The private sector can also help to develop successful training programs and provide necessary funds, as well as needed on-the-job training. In return the product of education, students of any age, will be better prepared for the available job market.

■ Career education should be integrated into all subject areas and all instructional levels.

■ Career education should be a lifelong experience.

# CHAPTER 8

# Teaching the Disabled Student to Use Electronic Technologies as Leisure and Recreational Alternatives

A lthough technological linguistics, problem solving, compensation and prosthetic applications, and career education are extremely important elements in the design of a total special education program, there is one additional component which must be considered and integrated into such a program. Man does not live by work alone; therefore, the concept of using electronic technologies as leisure and recreational alternatives must also be included in a comprehensive preparation program. If our special education programs are truly intended to prepare today's students to function in the 21st century, we must provide instruction that will offer them fulfilling and meaningful alternatives with which to fill their leisure hours.

All human beings require the opportunity to refresh and "reanimate" themselves after laborious activity, whether physical, intellectual, or emotional in nature. Without such respites, both alone and with other individuals, people quickly "burn out." It does not matter what type of activity the individual selects, physical, interpersonal, or intellectual, as long as the person has the opportunity to renew and refresh. Although each individual ultimately develops a highly personal repertoire of fulfilling leisure alternatives, the ability to recreate and relax is a learned activity, one which reflects the attitudes and habits of society and the traditional practices of the family. Often, the types of leisure activities initially selected by an individual are those learned from the family; however, as the person grows, develops, and is exposed to new friends and experiences, these alternatives are frequently expanded to include activities that transcend the family structure.

All of us require private, often quiet, time as a part of our leisure activities in order to reflect and refresh ourselves. Nevertheless, man as social animals most often seeks out others with whom to share recreational activities of mutual interest. These interpersonal leisure activities are extremely important to us and serve as major elements in our recreational experiences. Activities such as family gatherings, sports, parties, community and religious gatherings, and involvement with special interest clubs are all designed to provide us with fulfilling and acceptable interpersonal leisure activities.

The appropriate and personally fulfilling use of leisure time has been a particular problem for a great many disabled individuals. Many employed, independent adults remain social isolates because they were never taught how to recreate alone, and they never developed the social skills necessary to interact appropriately with their peers. Moreover, intellectual, physical, or emotional disabilities have often precluded many of them from participating in a large number of the recreational opportunities taken for granted by their nondisabled peers.

Historically, the more severely and overtly disabled people were frequently isolated from the general population because of society's reaction to them. This situation has not dramatically changed today, and many disabled individuals continue to be isolated, particularly from leisure activities. One all too common example of this can be seen in shopping centers and malls. Numerous sociologists have noted how these sites have increasingly become recreational and cultural settings for the general population; however, the movement of an overtly disabled individual through such a setting, no matter how uncrowded it is, often results in what can best be described as "the parting of the Red Sea." People move away from the disabled child or adult almost as if they were afraid they might "catch" the disorder. They isolate the individual and, in so doing, point up the person's differences. Most people are not trying to be cruel; they are simply reacting. Nevertheless, this is an extremely uncomfortable experience for all concerned, one which is particularly negative for the disabled person who is being told that he or she is not welcome. Such reactions teach disabled people that this setting is not really an appropriate leisure site for them.

Granted, individuals with certain types of disabilities must be precluded from some activities because of danger and because insurance carriers will not underwrite the activity if they participate; however, this is rare. Most public and private leisure activities are available to everyone. It is the reaction of other individuals to their participation that, in fact, deters many disabled people. Leisure activities are intended to refresh and renew, but this purpose is defeated by discomfort so that disabled individuals soon quit such social activities in favor of other recreational alternatives.

Transportation is another major difficulty. Even when disabled adults have developed the necessary interests and social skills to be accepted by a group, they very often find themselves unable to get to the activity. A general lack of public transportation in many parts of the country requires that the person be able to drive a car. Free transportation is provided when the individual is in school; however, similar forms of transportation are not available to the disabled adult. Therefore, many disabled adults, if they cannot receive transportation assistance from a relative, friend, or private agency, cannot participate in many of the interpersonal leisure activities available to others.

Play is one of the primary ways in which children learn about the pleasures of interpersonal recreation. The play experiences that many disabled children encounter as they grow up, however, often contribute to the restriction of their leisure alternatives, both as children and as adults. Their physical, emotional, and intellectual deficits frequently preclude them from enjoying the variety of play experiences afforded their nondisabled peers. We have all heard children who are starting a game say something like, "You take him this time, we had him last time." The participation of a disabled child in a community play situation is often viewed as a liability by the other children. This peer pressure and our society's focus on competition force the disabled child to seek out other, often younger, children with whom they can compete. Even then, the prejudices and attitudes of parents in the community can often be prohibitive, as when a disabled child reaches puberty and parents no longer want that child playing with their younger children. Further, consistent play with younger children deprives these disabled children of age appropriate role models from whom they can learn the required social skills of play and interpersonal recreation. When they do have the opportunity to join peers in leisure time activities, they frequently find they cannot participate because their behaviors are inappropriate to the situation.

The difficulty that many disabled children encounter in play situations tends to restrict their understanding of this aspect of interpersonal recreation. Being excluded from play robs the disabled children of the opportunity to learn game rules and experience peer cooperation. Further, the simple fact that they do not know the rules also limits their ability to enjoy the activity as observers.

Another common factor contributing to the leisure and recreational problems of many disabled individuals stems from the family itself. All too often, family members, in particular parents, will focus on the disabilities of the child. As a result, they overprotect the child, thereby limiting the child's exposure to and participation in the variety of leisure alternatives available. Unless children receive such exposure, they will be unable to make appropriate recreational choices later in life. Unfortunately, for too many disabled children, television is their primary leisure activity. Television must not be the primary recreational experience. Although enjoyable when used in moderation, it is a passive activity, one which is primarily done alone. Without participatory activities, the behaviors learned will be those of television role models, which may or may not demonstrate realistic or acceptable behaviors — even if the role model is appropriate, without practice involving natural consequences, the learning to modify behavior based upon others' reactions cannot occur.

In conclusion, interpersonal play requires a knowledge of the social behaviors required to be an accepted member of the group and participate in the activity. The restricted or nonexistent play experiences of disabled children prevent them from learning the interpersonal social skills that are necessary to participate in these and related types of activities, not only as children but also as adults.

The focus on disability further reinforces the child's attitude that he or she cannot do things in general, which often results in an unwillingness to try anything new. On the other hand, if the handicapped child is included in family recreational activities from an early age and to the greatest possible degree, then the horizons of that child are expanded and he or she is better prepared to enjoy leisure alternatives as an adult. A focus by the family on what the child can accomplish will teach the disabled child to be willing to try new things and will, therefore, better prepare them to take advantage of the new leisure alternatives the future holds. In other words, the attitude should be that some people are "differently-abled," not disabled.

One of the areas affected most dramatically by new technological advances is that of recreation. We can expect that this trend will continue and that these technological systems will become increasingly important leisure tools in the 21st century. If, however, a person has had restricted leisure experiences as a child and has developed an uneasiness about trying something new, then there is a high probability that that individual will not gain the full recreational benefits these new technologies hold.

Our educational system as a whole has also contributed to the leisure problems of disabled people, problems which become more pronounced and crucial as these individuals become adults. This is true not only in regular education programs, where mainstreaming occurs, but it is also true in the fields of special education and rehabilitation. Our basic practice has been to isolate the disabled child in order to provide a maximum level of educational, related service, and rehabilitation intervention. Although our programs are usually highly effective in achieving progress in academic areas, we have tended to ignore the entire area of recreation and the appropriate use of leisure time, despite the fact that this area of development is crucial to the preparation of a complete person. Although we do not formally teach recreation to non-disabled students, our school programs do need to encourage disabled students to engage in a wide variety of activities which are available through clubs and sports. Such activities can assist these children in developing the necessary knowledge and interpersonal skills necessary to enjoy their leisure time both today and in the future. In most instances, these opportunities are provided through after-school activities and are not part of the normal course offerings. Disabled children not only need to be included in these activities, but need specific behavioral objectives in their Individual Educational Plans to address the development of these all-important social skills.

Although PL 94-142 allows disabled children access to all aspects of the educational program provided by school systems, only some mildly disabled students have truly been able to participate in and benefit from these after-school activities. The vast majority of disabled school-aged children do not participate in these programs with their nondisabled peers because of a lack of competitive ability, a lack of opportunity, or the fact that they have not developed the required interpersonal and social skills required by the activity. Students attending special schools, of course, have little or no opportunity to participate in programs of this type with nondisabled peers. Further, the fact that most of these programs are offered after school prevents the participation by many disabled children, because many of them receive special transportation and do not have the opportunity to attend after school programs unless they can be transported by a family member or a neighbor.

Special educators and parental support groups have attempted to duplicate for disabled students some of the after-school activities that are available to the general school population. Although these programs do provide some essential recreational experiences, they are somewhat limited in their effectiveness as training programs to prepare students to use their adult leisure time in a personally fulfilling manner. Participation in special education programs is commonly limited to disabled individuals. Although students do learn some social and interpersonal skills, these experiences do not really assist them in transferring social skills to recreational activities with their nondisabled peers. Interpersonal recreation alternatives for adults are generally not overtly segregated into separate programs for the disabled and the nondisabled. Although there are some excellent leisure activity programs run by private agencies, in most instances, the disabled adult must be able to participate in programs available to the general public, and this requires them to have developed the necessary interpersonal and social skills that are a prerequisite for successful participation.

## LEISURE TIME TODAY

Recreation for most disabled children and adults today is problem oriented, centered around the individual's disability. Society tends to stress what individuals cannot accomplish rather than what they can. People are often categorized on such overt characteristics as "fat," "slow," "not one of us," and so forth, all of which are perceived as negative. People are also often rejected because of their lack of accepted social skills in a specific situation. All too often, it is not the specific functional abilities of the individual that gain acceptance by a recreational group, but the ability to interact socially with the members of the group. People are not asked to join a social club or activity because of the physical or mental abilities they do or do not possess. They are asked to join because they reflect the mores, social skills, and concerns of the group as a whole. Many disabled individuals cannot cope with these variables. On the other hand, the general public is beginning to understand the needs that disabled individuals have for recreational activities. For example, some ski clubs now accept blind skiers. Because of Section 504 and other legislation, public places have been developed with access alternatives for physically disabled people. With this access is coming visibility; with visibility, more acceptance of disabled individuals is beginning to occur — acceptance of "different ability."

Disabled individuals can now call and talk to someone else on a social basis through telephone dating; people can engage in board games, such as chess, by electronic mail; and people sharing the same disability are socializing at conventions for those in wheelchairs, dances for deaf individuals, and so on.

The key for success in employing technology to address the leisure time issue is twofold: (1) increasing visibility of disabled individuals in the Least Restrictive Environment (LRE), and (2) providing youngsters with appropriate social skills for acceptance during visibility by providing appropriate role models and carefully sequenced instruction to meet social skill objectives in the Individual Education Plan (IEP).

### The Computer as a Recreational Tool

Computers and related electronic technologies offer important recreational alternatives for disabled individuals. They are the only truly interactive electronic recreational media. They can be used by an individual alone and, more importantly, can be used with other people, either in an interpersonal social situation or through interactive telephone or cable television systems. It is, therefore, important that handicapped students receive instruction in and opportunities to use these technologies in their special education programs. A major curricular objective for use of the computer as a recreational tool would be:

> To develop the student's ability to use the computer and computer adaptive devices as leisure and "sports" activities, as communication tools, and as research for self-improvement.

There are three emerging applications of computer and related electronic technologies that can provide meaningful recreation, communication, and self-improvement for people with disabilities. First is the developing industry of computer games. The number of computer game devices and software available for both school instruction applications and for home recreational use has skyrocketed in recent years. These devices are relatively inexpensive, easy to operate, and can be connected to the variety of prosthetic interface and control devices, described in Chapter 6. The software for these systems has been designed so that the user can compete against him or herself, against the compu-ter, or against others. Most of these products are multisensory and rely more on graphics and sound than on print. Many of these software systems are intellectually stimulating and require the use of problem solving and other higher order thinking skills. Many of the products are designed so that they increase in difficulty and complexity and, therefore, can remain a challege for years. Other versions of computer games are conducted through network systems and user groups, permitting the disabled user to interact with others through the use of telecommunication systems and home computers. These network systems allow disabled users to take their turn playing at their own pace by posting responses on the network bulletin board for other members to respond. Probably the most important aspect of computer games is that they can be stimulating, interactive, personally responsive to the user, and fun.

Computer game simulations can also permit the disabled individual who lacks the motor, emotional, or social skills to physically engage in competitive sports, the opportunity to experience the "play" of tennis, golf, football, basketball, skiing, boxing, soccer, and other team and individual sports. The use of these sports simulations not only allow the user to experience the fun of playing a sport, but they assist the user in developing a better understanding of the rules and intricacies of these sports, knowledge that increases their appreciation for viewing professional and amateur sports either in person or on television. More important, these vicarious experiences can assist in the development of certain of the personal characteristics considered important by society; for example, competitiveness, assertiveness, and "stick-to-itiveness."

These experiences also have the capability of increasing skills and developing such abilities as memory, eye-hand coordination, and reasoning. Further, they can assist the phyiscally disabled individual in a physically therapeutic situation if programmed to require the user to use increasingly more physical exertion to play the game. Comprehensive interscholastic programs designed for students to reach specific IEP goals have already been conducted for physically limited students through the use of these types of sports simulations. The intensity with which these students approached their computer-simulated sports was as great as that of students who participated in the regular interscholastic and intramural activities conducted by the athletic department. These types of activities can also be experienced in the home, as evidenced by the newly emerging interactive computer-linked video industry, which has begun to offer a variety of multisensory interactive games and simulations for the home recreation market. The development of commercially produced computer programs for the home market has been and continues to be expanding rapidly. Therefore, disabled users can anticipate continued growth in the variety of new and rather inexpensive software in the future.

A second major use of computers and related electronic technologies as recreational alternatives concerns the use of the computer interactively linked via telephone, cable television, or satellite. The use of these interactive systems also permits the disabled user to communicate with friends and to participate in group activities and special interest groups, through their home computer terminal, the number of which has been increasing dramatically over the past few years. The use of special input and output adaptive devices permits most disabled individuals to enter these networks, form friendships, communicate, and participate in group activities. Since the user is in complete control of the communication process, disabled individuals can participate at their own pace and through their preferred style of communication. Further, since the user is not visible to the other members of the group, societal reactions to many disabilities are negated; thus allowing disabled and nondisabled people to compete as equals. Further, this type of electronic communication has been used increasingly in the treatment of individuals with phobic conditions, such as those individuals who feel that they cannot leave their homes or participate in social activities. The use of these systems permits them to participate and communicate with others in a risk-free environment and can often be used to assist in the process of increasing their contacts with varying environments. Thus, physical limitations can be overcome, travel limitations can be negated, and personal risk taking is minimized when these devices are used by disabled people as recreational communication alternatives.

A third major use of computer and related electronic technologies as a recreational alternative concerns the use of the home computer terminal interactively linked to a telecommunication system for study, reading, research, and other forms of self-improvement. The number and variety of data bases that can be accessed via computer continues to grow as we enter the Information Age. The disabled user can enter these systems from their home terminal in order to research a topic of interest or to gain other types of information. More and more colleges and universities are offering home study programs that often combine the use of television, videodisc systems, and home computer terminals. Many of these offerings are self-improvement courses through continuing education departments, although a number of colleges offer entire degree programs through the use of these on-line university systems. These systems can overcome the physical, emotional, or sensory limitations of the disabled user and allow them to use these interactive computer-based research, study, and self-improvement systems to be lifelong learners and to gain information previously denied them.

## ELECTRONIC RECREATION IN THE FUTURE

Most futurists predict that advanced technology systems will become central components of recreation in the 21st century. One reason for this forecast is the change in demography, which will result in the majority of the population being composed of aging citizens. The other major reason is the predicted impact of the home Net Console as the primary communication, work, information-processing, and recreational system used by most citizens. Further, the projection that there will be a far greater variety of more sophisticated and personally interactive adaptive interface devices implies that disabled people will be able to access these systems with greater ease.

The development of the interactive multisensory home Net Console system will probably be a most significant improvement in recreational alternatives for disabled people in the coming decades. The fact that these systems will be connected to the worldwide grid implies that the home Net Console user will have access to an almost unlimited variety of recreational options. Therefore, the cultural, recreational, self-improvement, instructional, and sporting events of the entire world will be available to the disabled individual at home. Further, the almost instantaneous communication capabilities of these systems will permit users to expand their network of electronic friends and special interest groups. In addition, these systems are predicted to incorporate advanced computer systems, interactive television, interactive videodisc systems, and advanced telecommunication systems with audio, visual, and motoric capabilities. Such interactive and multisensory elements of the home Net Console system will permit disabled users to have both input and output that is more closely matched to their personal sensory needs. Recreational communication, self-improvement, and games will, therefore, be enhanced and personalized.

The development of artificial intelligence systems in the 21st century will also have a significant impact on the electronic recreational alternatives of the disabled individual. These systems will learn the user's needs and recreational preferences. They will be able to personally assist the disabled user in making decisions about the type and form of electronic recreation desired. These systems will be able to communicate with individuals in their personal inner language system and will act as input and output translation devices for them. Communication, information processing, self-improvement, games, simulation, and access to world events will be personally translated. The projected artificial intelligence systems of the Information Age will also be important because of their ability to learn from the user and to modify both input and output. Different modifications can be made for different types of programs based on user response. Therefore, all of the recreational options on the Net Console will be available to the disabled user and will be able to be personally modified to the functional level and disability needs of the user.

Artificially intelligent systems will further assist the user in accessing the world grid and in asking the correct questions of this vast data network in order to receive the desired recreational options. These expert systems are projected to be developed for recreational purposes in the coming decades, particularly for games and simulation experiences. These expert systems will also provide individual assistance in activities such as planning a vacation and in making travel itineraries. Disabled users, therefore, will be able to obtain much needed advice and assistance in planning for life experiences and will be able to personally modify computer programs to address a variety of recreational alternatives.

It is projected that the size of the data base available through the world grid will be vast by the 21st century, probably containing all recorded history in a multisensory format that would include sound, speech, graphics, pictures, and film. Access to libraries and their holdings will also be available through the grid's data base. Projections indicate that increasing numbers of colleges and other training institutions will offer their educational and self-improvement services through the world grid network. When one considers the implications of the artificial intelligence components and the multisensory data base access capabilities of this system, one can readily envision the variety of new recreational options that will become available to disabled people in their homes in the not-too-distant future.

The electronic recreational alternatives for disabled individuals in the 21st century hold great promise and will be greatly expanded over those available today. Their options will be vast and their selections will be individually modified to meet personal needs and abilities. Through the home Net Console, users will have the world and its vast recreational alternatives brought to them in an interactive, multisensory, and interpersonal format. As the world shrinks in the Information Age due to instantaneous communication and the world grid, the electronic recreational alternatives will develop and expand to meet the imagination and creativity of 21st century citizens.

## Summary

■ Access to a wide variety of recreational alternatives has been a major problem for disabled individuals, and all too often these problems are the direct result of society's reaction to the handicaps themselves.

■ Overprotection of disabled individuals also has contributed to their lack of recreational alternatives and experiences.

■ Lack of recreational alternatives often results in lack of development of appropriate interpersonal skills.

■ Computers and related electronic technologies provide a variety of stimulating experiences for handicapped people. Computer games are stimulating, can be intellectually challenging, can assist in developing appropriate social behaviors, and are fun.

■ Interactive computer systems are a positive recreational alternative since they require the user to become actively involved.

■ Computers can also bring disabled users closer to the rest of world, through telecommunication systems which can provide access to research, study, and self-improvement programs.

■ The future of computer technology will greatly expand the world of handicapped people. However, in order to make full use of such alternatives as they continue to develop, it is important for these students to receive instruction now in the recreational uses of electronic technology.

# CHAPTER 9

# Future Perspectives

**F** uturists do not work with a crystal ball, and some of their predictions may not occur within the projected time frame or even at all. Nevertheless, the trends that will structure life in the future are apparent today and must be considered as we plan instructional programs to prepare our handicapped students for life in the world of the future.

The current applications of computers and related electronic technologies with handicapped people have had dramatic impact on both their educational achievement and their daily functioning abilities. These applications in the fields of special education and rehabilitation have shown that the proper use of these technologies holds the potential of taking limitations out of many handicapping conditions by acting as compensatory and prosthetic devices, improving the functional abilities and potential of handicapped students. Electronic technology systems have already proven themselves to be important normalization agents for many handicapped individuals, especially as they are being used increasingly as tools of daily living.

The advanced technology and communication systems currently being planned and designed hold even greater potential to act as normalization agents and tools of daily living for disabled people. The Net Console, advanced computer systems, artificial intelligence, interactive worldwide communication networks, and robotics are some of the basic electronic technological tools with which our current population of handicapped students will have to deal in the 21st century. Each of these advanced technologies holds the potential to dramatically improve their lives and functional abilities. These technologies can assist them in areas such as daily living, employment, communication, and recreation;

however, if we in special education do not immediately begin to design technological literacy programs for today's handicapped students, they will not be prepared to use these advanced technologies as prosthetic and compensatory tools of daily living, and they will be more disabled in the Information Age.

It would appear that we in education, including special education, seem to move in a cyclical manner, returning to old trends and practices in ten to fifteen year cycles. For example, in the last fifty years, the field of special education has been moving between the two extremes of self-contained and intergrated placement settings. Most recently PL 94-142 and subsequent legislation have started the cycle toward integrated programs with an emphasis on "the least restrictive environment" and the concept of mainstreaming. It must be remembered that many mild and moderately disabled students in public education programs thirty years ago were integrated into regular education simply because they had not been identified as disabled; they were merely the "slow learners." Currently we are experiencing the beginnings of a cyclical swing back to more self-contained programs for disabled students with the pressure for this coming from the federal and state levels, from the local level, from regular education, and often from the general public. If this does occur, and if education continues to move in cycles, we in special education will probably "discover" integrated programs again about the turn of the century, and then once again "rediscover" the concept of mainstreaming sometime during the first quarter of the 21st century. Fortunately, technology will modify the direction of special education programs causing the classroom of the future to be vastly different from what we have today. Our total education system will change becoming competency based, coordinating business and industry with education, and requiring lifelong curricula.

Because of the probable changes in societal requirements for living and working, we in special education cannot afford to think cyclically or reactionarily about current and future applications of electronic technology for the disabled individual. We must be farsighted and constantly keep in mind the reality that our disabled students of today will live most of their lives in a radically more complex world.

The historical reactionary pattern of education and its resistance to change has contributed to its lack of knowledge about current and planned electronic technologies and about the future impact of the Information Age. Of all the business and social institutions, education has been one of the last to adopt technology both as a management technique and as an instructional tool. School administrators are responsible for the management of funds and personnel equivalent in size to many companies in the private sector. There are many similarities between the annual operational budgets of moderately sized school districts and moderately sized businesses. Business and industry have already adopted computer technology and it is rare that their managers and supervisors do not use this technology as a daily management and communication tool. How many school administrators have a computer on their desks? How many would know how to use them effectively, employing some of the basic management software tools such as word processing, data base management, and electronic spreadsheets? Yet these individuals are the ones in a school system who recommend program changes; course requirements; and purchases of equipment including instructional materials. Is it any wonder that technology has not been enthusiastically adopted by the educational community?

The lack of knowledge about technology and the Information Age cannot and should not be laid wholly at the feet of educational administrators, whether they be middle- or upper-level management. These individuals react to the pressure and concerns of their school boards, people who are elected and who represent the general community. Although the purchase of computers has risen dramatically in the past few years, the level of use of this technology in schools cannot in any manner be said to be anywhere near what is needed to prepare students for the future. Members of the community may use electronic technology as daily tools of business, but they tend to be concerned primarily with the rigors of daily life, appearing to have little time or inclination to attend to the future. For most people, planning for the future is planning for retirement. Since the general community has not, for the most part, been terribly concerned with the future impact of technology or with the Information Age, there has been little pressure on the reactionary educational community to learn about or to plan for these eventualities.

Not only are the overall educational institutions, in general, reactionary, but so are many of their employees. Many individuals in the profession are using the same teaching techniques by which they were educated, modified only by what they learned in college and in the first few years of professional employment. Change in instructional practices come principally through teacher-involved curriculum development projects and through teacher training programs, areas which, in most educational budgets, are woefully underfunded or totally excluded. Further, tenure laws and union contracts often preclude the mandatory attendance of teachers at such training programs unless the attendees receive salary payment or release time, a factor which often makes the institution of such programs fiscally prohibitive. It is, therefore, not surprising that many teachers, other than those in the secondary subject areas of science, mathematics, and business education, have, for the most part, been resistant to learning about technology or about the impact of the Information Age upon their students. They are simply reflecting the reactionary attitudes of their employers.

One possible exception to this trend may be in the field of special education. This segment of the educational community has been somewhat receptive to the use of technology because of being traditionally concerned with the future and with the tools that assist their students. In many school districts, programs involving computers and computer literacy began in special education long before they were instituted in general education programs. In others, unfortunately, special education gets the "hand-me-downs," the computers that have been replaced by newer models. The interest in technology is often present, in special education, at any rate, because of the philosophy of special education. It is a field that has as its ultimate objective the preparation of its students to achieve to their maximum potential and to achieve the greatest possible degree of independence as adults. Past history, along with assessed needs and diagnostic and abilities information, are used to develop individual student programs for the future. The entire concept of the Individual Education Plan (IEP) is that of planning for future achievement. It seems reasonable, therefore, that special educators should take advantage of technology to help them reach the goals set up for their students and to help them monitor students' progress. Probably the greatest push to use technology for the handicapped in the schools has come from parents, who have accepted the importance of the potential of these technologies and have lobbied for their inclusion in their children's instructional programs.

Despite the general acceptance of and interest in technology, however, special education has suffered from a lack of information about it, partly because of reactionary attitudes in the education community, and partly because there has not been much interest by futurists in the potential impact of the Information Age and its technologies upon special needs groups.

This book is only a first step in the development of a future-oriented curriculum for all disabled children. Holistic planning by all individuals concerned with special education will be required to develop such a comprehensive program. We hope that you, the readers of this book, will expand upon the concepts presented here and will continue to develop creative curricula that use the benefits of technology to enhance your students' potential, thereby helping to prepare them for their future world. If this occurs, the 21st century will witness vast and miraculous improvements in the lives of disabled individuals.

# References

Abbott, W. (1982). Beating unemployment through education. In L. Jennings and S. Cornish (eds.), *Education and the future* (pp. 25–30). Bethesda, MD: World Future Society.

Albus, J. S. (1983). Robots in the workplace. In E. Cornish (ed.), *Careers tomorrow* (pp. 50–55). Bethesda, MD: World Future Society.

Baran, P. (1973). Thirty services that two-way television can provide. In E. Cornish (ed.), *Communications tomorrow* (pp. 151–158). Bethesda, MD: World Future Society.

Barnes, R. E. (1982). An educator looks back from 1996. In L. Jennings and S. Cornish (eds.), *Education and the future* (pp. 15–18). Bethesda, MD: World Future Society.

Best, F. (1978). Recycling people: Work-sharing through flexible life scheduling. In E. Cornish (ed.), *1999: The world of tomorrow* (pp. 122–133). Bethesda, MD: World Future Society.

Cain Jr., E. J. (1985a). *The potential of advanced technology: Conference on computers for the handicapped.* Baltimore, MD: The Johns Hopkins University.

Cain Jr., E. J. (1985b). *The present is the only prologue — technology for the information economy* (convention presentation). Minneapolis, MN: Closing the Gap.

Cetron, M. (1985). *Schools of the future.* New York, NY: McGraw-Hill Book Company.

Cetron, M., and O'Toole, T. (1982). Careers with a future. In E. Cornish (ed.), *Careers tomorrow* (pp. 10–18). Bethesda, MD: World Future Society.

Cleveland, H. (1982). Information as a resource. In E. Cornish (ed.). *Careers tomorrow* (pp. 126–131). Bethesda, MD: World Future Society.

Coates, J. F. (1982). Populations and education: How demographic trends will shape the U.S. In L. Jennings and S. Cornish (eds.), *Education and the future* (pp. 9–14). Bethesda, MD: World Future Society.

Coates, V. T. (1983). The potential impact of robotics. In E. Cornish (ed.), *Careers tomorrow* (pp. 45–49). Bethesda, MD: World Future Society.

Cornish, B. M. (1983). The smart machines: Implications for society of tomorrow. In E. Cornish (ed.), *Careers tomorrow* (pp. 36–44). Bethesda, MD: World Future Society.

Dillon, B., and Wright, R. (1982). Educational predictions: Past, present and future. In L. Jennings and S. Cornish (eds.), *Education and the future* (pp. 102–110). Bethesda, MD: World Future Society.

Dunn, S. L. (1980). The case of the vanishing colleges. In L. Jennings and S. Cornish (eds.), *Education and the future* (pp. 50–57). Bethesda, MD: World Future Society.

Edwards, K. (1983). The electronic newspaper. In E. Cornish (ed.), *Communications tomorrow* (pp. 54–59). Bethesda, MD: World Future Society.

First annual conference on the employment of the disabled. (1987). Miami, FL: University of Miami, Continuing Education.

Freeman, M., and Mulkowsky, G. P. (1982). Advanced interactive technology: Robots in the home and classroom. In L. Jennings and S. Cornish (eds.), *Education and the future* (pp. 41–45). Bethesda, MD: World Future Society.

Friedman, D. (1985). A fantasy: Educational computing in 2010. *Electronic Education, 4*(7), 10–11, 33.

Fuller, G. (1987). Confessions of a desktop junkie. *PC/SIG Magazine, 2*(2), 16–17.

Gannon, J. (1980). *Deaf heritage* (p. 372). Indianapolis, IN: National Association for the Deaf.

Hagen, D. (1984). *Microcomputer resource book for special education.* Reston, VA: Reston Publishing Company.

Haigh, R. W., Gerbner, G., and Byrne, R. B. (eds.). (1981). *Communications in the twenty-first century.* New York, NY: John Wiley and Sons.

Hald, A. P. (1981). Toward the information-rich society. In E. Cornish (ed.), *Communications tomorrow* (pp. 9–12). Bethesda, MD: World Future Society.

Hamrin, R. D. (1981). The information economy. In E. Cornish (ed.), *Communications tomorrow* (pp. 66–71). Bethesda, MD: World Future Society.

Hannaford, A. E., and Taber, F. M. (1986). Career education for the handicapped in the information age (unpublished article). Kalamazoo, MI: Western Michigan University, Special Education Department.

Higgins, M. (1986). The future of personal robots. *The Futurist, 20*(3), 43–46.

Jaffe, D. L. (1987). *New research promoting independence for disabled individuals.* First Annual Conference on the Employment of the Disabled. Miami, FL: University of Miami, Continuing Education.

Jennings, L. (1979). The human side of tomorrow's communications. In E. Cornish (ed.), *Communications tomorrow* (pp. 37–42). Bethesda, MD: World Future Society.

Jones, M. V. (1973). How cable television may change our lives. In E. Cornish (ed.), *Communications tomorrow* (pp. 147–150). Bethesda, MD: World Future Society.

Judd, D. H. (1983). Programming: An experience in creating a useful program or an experience in computer control. *Educational Computer, 3*(2), 20–21.

Koehn, H. E. (1986). Techtrends interview. *TechTrends, 31*(2), 27–31.

Kornbluh, M. (1982). The electronic office: How it will change the way you work. In E. Cornish (ed.), *Careers tomorrow* (pp. 59–64). Bethesda, MD: World Future Society.

Larick, Jr., K. T., and Fischer, J. (1986). Classrooms of the future. *The Futurist, 20*(3), 21–22.

Lesse, S. (1978). The preventive psychiatry of the future. In E. Cornish (ed.), *1999: The world of tomorrow* (pp. 75–80). Bethesda, MD: World Future Society.

Lindsey, J. D. (ed.). (1987). *Computers and exceptional individuals.* Columbus, OH: Merrill Publishing Company.

Madian, J. (1986). New flexibility in curriculum development through word processing. *Educational Leadership, 43*(6), 22–23.

Mankin, D., Bikson, T. K., and Gutek, B. (1982). The office of the future prison or paradise? In E. Cornish (ed.), *Careers tomorrow* (pp. 77–80). Bethesda, MD: World Future Society.

Martino, J. P. (1979). Telecommunications in the year 2000. In E. Cornish (ed.), *Communications tomorrow* (pp. 30–36). Bethesda, MD: World Future Society.

Medicine in the post-physician era. (1978). In E. Cornish (ed.), *1999: The world of tomorrow* (pp. 81–84). Bethesda, MD: World Future Society.

Michels, D. L. (1982). Bringing the future into your office. In E. Cornish (ed.), *Careers tomorrow* (pp. 72–76). Bethesda, MD: World Future Society.

Middleton, T. Personal communication. Menlo Park, CA: Science Research International.

Molitor, G. T. T. (1981). The path to post-industrial growth. In E. Cornish (ed.), *Communications tomorrow* (pp. 84–88). Bethesda, MD: World Future Society.

Munroe, J. R. (1981). Up with the new — and the old. In R. W. Haigh, G. Gerbner, and R. B. Byrne (eds.), *Communications in the twenty-first century* (pp. 35–42). New York, NY: John Wiley and Sons.

National Commission on Excellence in Education. (1983). *A nation at risk: The imperative for educational reform.* Washington, DC: U.S. Department of Education.

Northwest Regional Lab Telecommunications Conference. (October 1985). Seattle, WA: Northwest Regional Lab.

O'Toole, J. (1983). How to forecast your own working future. In E. Cornish (ed.), *Careers tomorrow* (pp. 19–25). Bethesda, MD: World Future Society.

Philbin, G. (1986). Robotics: Tomorrow's technology here today. *Market Monitor,* Feb., 1–4. Fairfax, VA: International Communications Industry Association.

Provus, M. M. (1971). *Discrepancy evaluation for educational program improvement and assessment.* Berkeley, CA: B. McCutchan Publishing Corporation.

Publish or perish. (1987). *PC/SIG Magazine, 2*(2), 21–22.

Reinhold, F. (1986). Houston's schools ride the third wave. *Electronic Learning, 5*(8), 25–28.

Response to Mortimer Adler's proposal. (1984). *Journal of Education, 36*(2), 70–78.

Schiffman, G., and Tobin, D. (1987). Software center workshop (The Multisensory Language Authoring System (MAC) presentation). San Antonio, TX: ACLD Convention.

Schramm, J. (1985). *Time share division*. Boston, MA: Houghton-Mifflin Corporation.

Shane, H. G., and Tabler, M. B. (1981). *Educating a new millennium*. Bloomington, IN: Phi Delta Kappa Educational Foundation.

Shaw, S. J. (1986). New satellites provide links to remote terminals. *Interpreter, 19*(11), 37–44.

Skarnulis, L. (1982). Is there an electronic byline in your future? In E. Cornish (ed.), *Careers tomorrow* (pp. 82–88). Bethesda, MD: World Future Society.

Strom, R. (1982). Education for a leisure society. In L. Jennings and E. Cornish (eds.), *Education and the future* (pp. 19–23). Bethesda, MD: World Future Society.

Stunkel, E. L. (1979). Let's abolish retirement. In E. Cornish (ed.), *Careers tomorrow* (pp. 147–149). Bethesda, MD: World Future Society.

Sturdivant, P. (1983). School, business partnerships may be an answer. *Electronic Education, 5*(8), 25–28.

Taber, F. (1982). *Microcomputers in special education: Selection and decision making process*. Reston, VA: Council for Exceptional Children.

Technology task force might shape your future. (1985). *TechTrends, 30*(2), 3–5. Washington, DC: United States Commission on Excellence in Education (LA217-V49 1983).

Turoff, M. (1975). The future of computer conferencing. In E. Cornish (ed.), *Communications tomorrow* (pp. 131–140). Bethesda, MD: World Future Society.

Tyderman, J. (1982). Videotex: Ushering in the electronic household. In E. Cornish (ed.), *Habitats tomorrow* (pp. 16–23). Bethesda, MD: World Future Society.

Vail, H. (1980). The home computer terminal: Transforming the household of tomorrow. In E. Cornish (ed.), *Communications tomorrow* (pp. 13–19). Bethesda, MD: World Future Society.

Vallee, J., Johansen, R., and Spangler, K. (1975). The computer conference: An altered state of communication. In E. Cornish (ed.), *Communications tomorrow* (pp. 125–130). Bethesda, MD: World Future Society.

Weil, R. (ed.). (1982). *The Omni future almanac*. New York, NY: Omni Publications International, Ltd. (Crown Publishers, Inc.).

Williams, L. P. (1982). Inventing the future. *Creative Computing, 8*(12), 167–174.

Zimmer, J. W. (1985). Choices '85: A national conference on computers and the disabled. Saskatoon, Canada: Saskatoon Association for Rehabilitation Centres.

# Index